Operational Risk Management

Founded in 1807, JohnWiley & Sons is the oldest independent publishing company in the United States. With offices in North America, Europe, Australia and Asia, Wiley is globally committed to developing and marketing print and electronic products and services for our customers' professional and personal knowledge and understanding.

The Wiley Finance series contains books written specifically for finance and investment professionals as well as sophisticated individual investors and their financial advisors. Book topics range from portfolio management to e-commerce, risk management, financial engineering, valuation and financial instrument analysis, as well as much more.

For a list of available titles, visit our Web site at www.WileyFinance.com.

Operational Risk Management

Best Practices in the Financial Services Industry

ARIANE CHAPELLE

WILEY

Library of Congress Cataloging-in-Publication Data is Available:

ISBN 978-1-119-54904-8 (hardback); ISBN 978-1-119-54906-2 (ePDF); ISBN 978-1-11954907-9 (epub)

Cover Design: Wiley
Cover Image: © zodebala / E+ / Getty Images

Set in 10/12pt TimesLTStd by SPi Global, Chennai, India

Printed in Great Britain by TJ International Ltd, Padstow, Cornwall, UK

10 9 8 7 6 5 4 3

To the students, course delegates, clients and peers who made this book possible.

To my husband Robert Lang and our children Victoria, Talitha and Tristan, whose loving support made this book equally as possible.

To my parents and sister for teaching me from early on the virtues both of caution and of daring in life.

Contents

About the Author

ARIANE CHAPELLE, PhD, is Associate Professor (Honorary Reader) at University College London for the course 'Operational Risk Measurement for Financial Institutions' and is a Fellow of the Institute of Operational Risk and a trainer for the Professional Risk Managers' International Association (PRMIA), for whom she designed the Certificate of Learning and Practice in Advanced Operational Risk Management. She is a former holder of the Chair of International Finance at the University of Brussels. She has been active in operational risk management since 2000 and is a former head of operational risk management at ING Group and Lloyds Banking Group. Dr. Chapelle runs her own training and consulting practice in risk management. Her clients include Tier 1 financial organisations and international financial institutions.

Foreword

It is both a pleasure and an honor to write the foreword of Ariane Chapelle's *Operational Risk Management* textbook.

Ariane is one of the world's leading teachers, thinkers and writers about operational risk. The combination of her professional experience as a practitioner in the financial services industry, her role as an advisor to regulators, her deep and growing knowledge of the multilateral financial institutions and her working relationship with professional risk associations (like PRMIA) gives her a unique perspective over the evolution of operational risk management practices, a breadth of recognition across the universe of risk professionals, and a depth of authority which make this textbook a "must read" at all levels of both regulated and unregulated financial institutions.

As we are fond of saying at the World Bank, there are no spectators in risk. Everybody has an essential role to play – and while financial or market risk remain the domain of expertise of a specialized few, operational risk is inherent to the working lives (not to mention personal lives) of everybody across the enterprise, whether public or private, financial or non-financial, regulated or unregulated. Operational risk is now integral not only to problem fixing but also to product design and implementation, to the deployment of human capital across the globe and across business lines, and most importantly to risk governance and decision-making at the C-suite level.

In the same way that we deal with risk as part of our everyday life, operational risk forms an integral part of the everyday life of any enterprise which relies on people, processes, systems, and engages with both clients and contractors – be it a commercial bank, a manufacturing company, a utility, a medical facility, a university or an airline. So, as we think about the similarities between operational risk management in the financial sector and what is simply called risk management in the real sector of the economy, I believe that Ariane's textbook will resonate with risk practitioners across a broad and rapidly expanding universe. Indeed, while commercial banks must be concerned about satisfying their regulators' requirements, operational risk as a discipline has moved beyond a purely defensive posture and is being recognized as an important contributor to value creation at the strategic level. Good operational risk practices are essential not only to the good health and sustainability but also to the growth and long-term profitability of the enterprise.

One of the themes which underlie many of my conversations with Ariane is the accelerating pace and growing impact of operational risk events and consequently the rising interest of audit committees, boards and rating agencies. In truth, while catastrophic financial risk events can be debilitating, the attention of regulators since the global financial crisis and the continued dedication of leadership teams across the financial services industry seem to have resulted in a reduction in the frequency and severity of such events. Operational risk events, however, have the potential to become what some practitioners refer to colloquially as "game over" events. They have already resulted in significant financial losses in recent years and while there is a need to continuously review and strengthen operational risk practices across operations, treasury, financial reporting, loan disbursement, AML/CFT, procurement, vendor risk management, IT, cybersecurity, HR and budget functions (just to name a few), an enterprise is only as strong as its risk culture. In other words, the goal should be to build a strong learning culture where talent, time and energy are focused not only on responding to expected risk events and reducing exposure in well-known and well-understood risk domains but also on learning from unexpected risk events in emerging risk domains. This require the creation of "safe spaces" for problem solving and the preservation of open bandwidth to recognize and analyze new threats. It also requires wisdom and humility, as the leadership team must ensure that the authority to respond is clearly vested at the most appropriate level of expertise and responsibility within the enterprise.

Finally, Ariane, like me, is an avid reader of psychology, cognitive science and behavioral economics. She is known by the many people she has worked with for systematically trying to draw from the latest research and scientific insights regarding human behavior and decision-making in complex systems with a view toward reducing the frequency and severity of risk events. Readers will therefore undoubtedly appreciate the fact that her book and the application of her insights and recommendations can help them, their colleagues, the members of their teams and maybe their bosses have a positive impact on the enterprise as they strive to improve their batting average in making small, daily, marginal decisions as well as big strategic ones. Ultimately, mastering operational risk is about making the enterprise more resilient, better fit for purpose and more successful in creating value for all its constituents.

Amédée Prouvost
Director, Operational Risk
The World Bank

Preface

This book presents in 20 chapters everything I know in operational risk. Everything I have learnt since becoming involved in operational risk management in 2001 and from my previous experience as an internal auditor. Everything I retained from hearing, reading, observing, teaching, researching and consulting in risk is distilled in this book, to present the most current overview of practices of operational risk management in the financial services industry. You will see many case studies and other examples that highlight the good, the best or sometimes the poor practices in non-financial risk management. The book presents some of the more mature developments in risk management, like managing risks interdependencies and adopting a single framework. Finally, I like to insist on the benefits of positive risk management, where lessons are learnt from successes and positive outliers just as much as from failures, and where risk management is used as an enabler of performance rather than the avoidance of downside.

The book is the result of two fortuitous events as well as 17 years of work in the discipline. The first event was a tragedy in 2001 that left open the rather new function of operational risk management for ING South West Europe. I applied for the job and was appointed. I am extremely grateful to Jean-Pierre Straet, then General Risk Manager, and Tamar Joulia, General Credit Risk Manager, for releasing me (part-time) from my credit risk responsibilities so I could become Head of Operational Risk. Working alone, I dedicated half my time to ORM, with a scope of five business units totaling 11,000 employees – one reason why I've never been a huge advocate of heavy central risk management functions.

Inevitably, my one-woman team increased to a few people. I was incredibly fortunate to take my first steps in operational risks at ING, headed from the Netherlands by Huib ter Haar, with support from Peter Schermers on the modeling side. From the very beginning of ORM, the bank had decided to go for AMA (advanced measurement approach) accreditation and, along with 11 other visionary banks, founded the ORX organization to help financial businesses measure and manage operational risk.

I must thank Philippe Meunier, who took over from me when I left ING in 2003 to take a chair at the University of Brussels (ULB). We still happily catch up today to discuss operational risk modeling and KRIs. I must also thank Camille Villeroy, who helped to continue the ORM initiative after I left, as well as many other ING colleagues and friends too numerous to mention. I thank them all for their friendship and the knowledge they imparted.

Next came the years of full-time academic teaching and research at the ULB in Finance and Corporate Governance, with colleagues Ariane Szafarz, Andre Farber, Hugues Pirotte, Mathias Schmit and my brilliant assistants Celine Vaessen, Benjamin Lorent, Laurent Gheeraert, now lecturers. I thank them all, as well as my many other friends, colleagues and students at the ULB for those wonderful years. With Yves Crama, Georges Hubner and Jean-Philippe Peters at the University of Liege, and with the support of the National Bank of Belgium, we published an article and a book on AMA modeling using real data. I thank them here for their invaluable input.

My first important business partner was the Belgian consulting firm Risk Dynamics (now part of the McKinsey group). In partnership with Risk Dynamics, I delivered my first ORM training program, participated in the overhaul of an ORM framework at an AMA bank and helped to introduce the scenario quantification methods. I thank the founders of Risk Dynamics, Dominique and Olivier Bourrat, and also Marie-Paule Laurent, Marc Taymans, Thierry Pauwels, Olga Reznikova and many others for the shared moments and innovative work.

Euromoney Plc was the first private training firm to trust me in delivering executive courses for its audience. Twelve years on, I am happy to say that they still do. I thank Martin Harris and everyone else that I've worked with at Euromoney for their continuous trust and support. It was on the strength of my work with Risk Dynamics and Euromoney that I launched what later became Chapelle Consulting (www.chapelleconsulting.com).

I've gained many clients over the years and have run hundreds of courses for thousands of people worldwide, either by myself or with the help of associates and guest speakers. I thank particularly David Lannoy, Jimi Hinchliffe, Bertrand Hassani and Evan Sekeris for being such faithful friends and colleagues. Risk.net, now Infopro-Digital, has been a long-term partner, organizing and promoting my courses on both sides of the Atlantic. Special thanks to Helen McGuire, my course organizer, and to Alexander Campbell, for giving me a column in *Operational Risk* magazine and later at risk.net. Equally, thanks to Tom Osborn, my supportive article editor, and to all the many people at InfoPro Digital with whom I work regularly.

For more than a decade I have worked closely with a wide range of businesses. They include banks, insurance companies, settlement agencics, trading houses, international financial institutions, universities, training companies, regulatory bodies and even hospitals and governmental agencies. I am very grateful for the trust they have placed in me and would gladly recognize them here but for the need for confidentiality. Thank you for sharing your practices, ideas and visions, and for embracing operational risk management. This book would not have been possible without you.

Besides, I have always kept my lifelong attachment to academia. After almost 20 years with the University of Brussels, University College London (UCL) in 2013 offered me the post of Honorary Reader for the course "Operational Risk Measurement for the Financial Services" in the department of Computer Science. The course is now in its sixth year and I'm delighted to see some of my former students following successful careers in operational risk. I'm indebted to Donald Lawrence, who introduced me to UCL, to Tomaso Aste, for appointing me as part of the university's prestigious faculty, and to Gareth Peters, for his brilliant collaboration in research and teaching. I thank UCL for its kind support and am honored to be part of the UCL community.

A separate category of appreciation goes to Amédée Prouvost, Director of Operational Risk at the World Bank, for agreeing to write the foreword and for doing it in such laudatory terms. Amédée's vision of operational risk and of learning made us immediate friends and work partners. Together with his ORM team at the World Bank – Riaz Ahmed, Kyalo Kibua, Jeronimo Perrotta, Jacinta Da'Silva – we piloted, in June 2018, the first PRMIA Certificate of Learning and Practice of Advanced ORM, certifying 33 risk champions at the end of the course. Many thanks to the World Bank team and all the course participants for this successful pilot.

For this project, as for many, PRMIA has been a fantastic business partner, innovative and responsive. My special gratitude goes to Mary Rehm and Ashley Squier for their skill and dedication in sourcing and organizing courses, webinars and certifications all over the world. A big thank you to PRMIA for its continuous support and for endorsing this book.

The second unexpected event at the origin of this book is recent. Scott Porter, director of Global Market Insights (GMI), had frequently asked me to write a book about operational risk. I had always declined because of other commitments – but Scott was persistent and I eventually agreed, despite what it meant in studious evenings and weekends, hours of redaction on planes and trains, and days of concentration in the silence of the library of the Institute of Directors. I thank him for that – without his insistence, this book would probably not have seen the light. However, the real catalyst was that GMI ceased all operations after I had delivered the manuscript. The rights returned to me and I was left with a 50,000-word manuscript and no immediate route for publication. This unexpected event let me experience first hand the benefits of crisis management and necessary resilience. After a short period of intense contacts, happily, Wiley & Sons stepped in, picking up the project, and together we decided to even enlarge the scope, adding a fifth part. The result is undoubtedly better than it would have been without Wiley's intervention.

I'm immensely grateful to Gemma Valler, the commissioning editor, for believing in the book, to Elisha Benjamin, the project editor, for the formatting and seeking all permissions so quickly, and to Caroline Vincent, for overseeing the production and keeping deadlines tight. I'm equally grateful to Gladys Ganaden for her help with the graphics, as well as the entire production and sales team at Wiley.

Importantly, this book would not have been the same without the fantastic editing work of my English editor, Sean Martin. He conscientiously reviewed every chapter, every line and every word of the manuscript, cover to cover, before submission to publishers. He corrected the French in my English, simplified sentences and even fact-checked me at times. I thank him for his tremendous work.

My final and heartfelt thanks go to my family: my father, for teaching me prudence and the capacity to see and avoid danger; my mother and my sister, for showing me optimism and boldness, its virtues and its perils; my daughter Victoria, for the incredible adult she became, both daring and astute, embracing a life of altruism and testing right now the limits of our risk appetite with her international projects; my husband Robert Lang, for his unwavering love and support, for our deep conversations on risk and management, allowing me to witness how CEOs think and act, and for bringing excellent risk management practice in the companies he runs so successfully.

No acknowledgment would be complete without thanking our youngest children, Tristan and Talitha, for being so wonderful and patient, so clever and joyful. And of course thanks to the kind people who help to look after them while we travel worldwide for our work. I hope that the passion, hard work and dedication that our children witness will help them thrive in whatever they choose to do later in life. Finally, I have a promise to keep: my next book will be for children . . .

–Ariane Chapelle

Introduction

WHAT IS RISK?

From locking our front door to planning for retirement, risk management is an intimate part of our everyday life. We continually identify, mitigate or even acquire risks, often without thinking about it as risk management practice. Yet it is. For all of us, risk means what can go wrong in our lives, and managing risk is how we protect ourselves.

For academics, risk is the uncertainty of an outcome for which you know the distribution of probability (like the throw of a dice), while uncertainty refers to unknown probabilities of occurrence. In this book we will use the ISO definition of risk: the effect of uncertainty on objectives. This definition is particularly suitable for organizations as it highlights the importance of aligning risk management with strategy and business objectives.

Risk doesn't exist in isolation: it needs to be defined and mapped in relation to objectives. A key risk is one that might negatively impact a key objective. Risks or uncertainties that cannot affect a firm's objectives are irrelevant. Mapping risks to objectives is an effective way to encourage risk management discussions in the boardroom and at every level of a company's operations. We understand risks here as uncertainties that have the potential to impact negatively the achievement of objectives. While we will recognize, throughout the book and in particular in Part 2, the benefits and even the returns of taking operational risks, we focus on the downside of risks and the need for risk management rather than the possibility of unexpected gains. In our daily lives, risk generally refers to the eventuality of losses or of accidents rather than unexpected wealth or achievement. In life, we often take risks to acquire wealth or fame; but in the context of this book, risk refers to a downside, not an upside.

The scope of the book is operational risks for the financial industry, as defined by the Basel Committee: "The risk of loss resulting from inadequate or failed internal processes, people and systems or from external events" (2002). The regulatory definition of operational risk covers seven types of risk that relate loosely to fraud, security and error risk:

1. Internal fraud (frauds and unauthorized activities by employees).
2. External fraud (hold-ups, thefts, system hacking, etc.).

3. Employment practices and workplace safety (contract termination, disputes with employees, etc.).
4. Clients, products and business practices (client misinformation, complaints and discounts due to errors, products misspecification, etc.).
5. Damage to physical assets.
6. Business disruption and system failures (IT breakdown, etc.).
7. Execution, delivery and process management (processing error, information transfer, data coding, etc.).

A simpler way to understand operational risk is to refer to the original, unofficial definition used in banking: "Operational risk is everything that is not credit and market (risk)." Another general definition of operational risk is a "non-financial risk," i.e., any risk type that is not purely financial, such as credit, market or liquidity risk in banking and an underwriting risk in insurance. Indeed, "operational risk management" in the financial industry is just "risk management" in other industries. Even though this book is specifically targeted at financial companies, their consultants and their regulators, risk managers from other industries, such as the police, healthcare or charities, might find it useful as well.

Scope and Motivation of this Book

This book presents and reviews the most current operational risk management practices in the financial services industry. It builds on my experience of working with, advising and observing financial services companies for nearly 20 years, since the early days of the discipline in the late 1990s. Any risk manager new to the discipline, whether in banking, insurance, consulting or regulatory bodies, will find that the book provides a useful overview of the current methods and good practices applied in financial companies. The last chapter in each part of this book has advanced tools and techniques developed by the most mature firms in operational risk management. Experienced operational risk managers can use these resources to strengthen and consolidate their knowledge.

RISK MANAGEMENT FRAMEWORKS

A risk management framework is a representation of actions, techniques or tools deployed to manage the risks of an entity. There are numerous frameworks published by different professional organizations. Among the best known are ISO (International Organization for Standardization) and COSO (Committee of Sponsoring Organizations). In 2009, ISO published the international standard for risk management: ISO 31000, revised in February 2018 to place "a greater focus on creating value as the key driver of risk management and (. . .) being customized to the organization and consideration of human and cultural factors".[1] An evolution aligned with COSO's previous review of its well-known "cube" framework for enterprise risk management, entitled "Aligning risk with strategy and performance," opened for comments in June 2016 and was finalized in September 2017. COSO places the mission, vision and risk culture in concentric circles at the center of the framework and details 23 tools and actions for performing enterprise risk management that enhance strategic performance.[2] Both the COSO and ISO frameworks apply to financial as well as non-financial organizations.

Regardless of their shape or form, many risk management frameworks boil down to four main activities: risk identification, risk assessment, risk mitigation and risk monitoring. The first four parts of this book correspond to these activities; the fifth part is dedicated to some specific types of operational risks that rank high on many firms' risk registers. When using the term "risk management," I refer to all these four actions. The following subsections review three alternative representations of risks found in different risk management frameworks across the industry:

Sequence: cause – event – impact

Actions: identification – assessment – mitigation – monitoring

Techniques: the tools used for each risk management action

Risk Management Sequence

A familiar representation of risk, mostly in non-financial industries, is the sequence of cause – event – impact and its corollary definition: risk of (impact), due to (event), caused by (cause). This risk structure is more common in the energy and technology sectors, but some financial companies have adopted it. Figure I.1 presents the sequence of risk management, from the exposure to risks and their causes to the financial and non-financial impacts of events when a risk materializes. It highlights the importance of assessing the size of the risk exposure, and its causes, before introducing the preventive controls. The exposure to a risk, whether in the form of assets at stake, number of employees involved or number of transactions per period of time, has been rather neglected by the financial sector during risk assessment. I will get back to this point in Part 1. Similarly, for a long time many firms have largely neglected incident management and corrective controls and have dedicated most of their risk management attention to the prevention of incidents, on the basis that prevention is better than cure. This resulted in several of them being thrown off guard when a crisis struck. Nowadays, in the midst of cyber threats and political upheavals, our increasingly volatile and unpredictable business environment has shifted much of the focus toward early intervention, incident management and crisis response, presented in Chapter 20.

---

[1]"Risk management", ISO 31000, February 2018.
[2]"Enterprise risk management – integrating with strategy and performance," COSO, 2017.

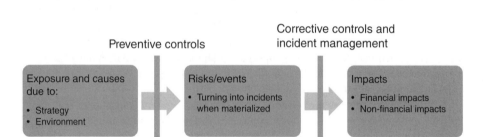

FIGURE I.1 Risk management sequence

The elements of a sequential framework are as follows. Each element will be detailed in a subsequent chapter.

Causes

Exposure: the surface at risk. It ranges from the distance driven in a car (exposure to accidents) to the number of employees with access to high-value transfers in banks (exposure to internal fraud). The only way to eliminate the risk is to remove the exposure, but that will eliminate the business as well. This is a strategic choice linked to risk appetite and will be covered in Chapter 6.

Environment: this refers both to external and internal environments, which are controllable only to a certain extent. For example, externally, a firm can choose where to expand its business, but it cannot choose the business conditions in its home country. Internal business environment refers to the organizational features of the firm, such as effective straight-through processing, competent staff and inspiring leaders, which will typically generate far fewer operational risks than disorganized businesses with disjointed processes and a culture of fear. Risk culture will be discussed in Chapter 12.

Strategy: the most controllable part of risk causes. A firm may decide to expand overseas, launch a new line of business, replace manual processes by automation, and outsource its call centers or its payment systems. Every major decision will affect the risk profile of the firm and its exposure to operational risk. Strategy, along with the operating environment, is the major driver of exposure to operational risk.

Events

Risks turn into "events" or "incidents" when they become a reality rather than a possibility. An event is the materialization of a risk. For example, a collision with another vehicle is one materialization of the risk of a car accident, but not the only one. The detailed analysis of past incidents helps greatly with future prevention. Risk analysis and mitigation are covered in Part 3.

Impacts

Consequences of incidents are not always immediately financial, but there is inevitably a financial impact at some point. Reputational damage, customer loss, regulatory breach and disruption of service, all typically described as non-financial impacts in operational risk assessments, eventually result in financial losses. The taxonomy of impacts, risks and causes is covered in Chapter 2.

Risk management

Preventive controls: besides process design and sensible organization of tasks, internal controls, both preventive and detective, are the main methods for risk reduction. Chapter 9 presents the main types of controls and activities.

Corrective controls and incident management: prevention is not the only risk mitigation; once an incident occurs, early intervention and contingency planning are critical to reduce impacts. Obvious examples are fire detectors and accessible fire extinguishers; data backups and redundancy measures are also typical corrective controls. While none of them helps to prevent accidents, they are particularly effective at reducing the damage when an accident occurs. The importance of incident management is covered in Chapters 9 and 10.

Risk Management Actions

Put simply, risk management covers four essential actions: identification, assessment, mitigation and monitoring (Figure I.2). Identification is the first step; the various

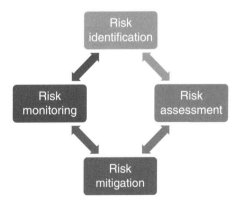

FIGURE I.2   The four fundamental actions of risk management

aspects, tools and techniques for risk identification are detailed in Part 1. Next is risk assessment, which involves evaluating the extent of each risk, its probability and possible impacts, because it is crucial to prioritize risk mitigating actions, internal controls and reduction of exposure. Assessment of operational risk is critical but still in its infancy in the financial industry compared with credit, market or actuarial risk. Even so, some progress has been made and will be explored in Part 2. Mitigation includes the body of directive, preventive, detective, corrective controls, contingency planning and incident management, which will be reviewed in Part 3. The reporting, monitoring and communication of risks, whether in the form of alerts, key risk indicators, or top risk reports, are discussed in the fourth part of the book.

Risk Management Tools

Some representations of risk management frameworks focus on actions, while others focus on tools and techniques. We have yet to see a picture of a framework for financial firms[3] that combines actions with tools and techniques. Figure I.3 fills this gap. It matches each technique with its corresponding risk management activity. We believe it is valuable for firms to develop a holistic and precise picture of their risk management practices: one that clarifies the relationship between actions, tools and techniques. Figure 3 offers a synthetic or composite view of most risk management actions and methods, to be tailored by each firm based on its own practices.

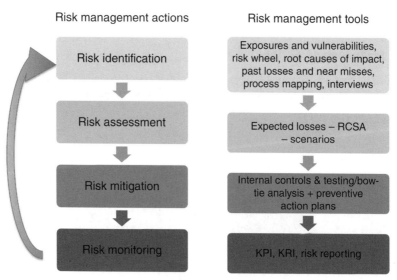

FIGURE I.3   Risk management actions and corresponding tools

---

[3]The new COSO framework for enterprise risk management tends to present both.

One

Risk Identification

"Forewarned is forearmed."

## CHAPTER 1

Risk Identification Tools

TOP-DOWN AND BOTTOM-UP RISK IDENTIFICATION

The most dangerous risks are those we ignore, as they can lead to nasty surprises. Before organizing risks in a register, it is important to identify the risks that are specific to your own business, not just those based on an external list, and then assess, mitigate and monitor them.

Risk identification in an organization should take place both top-down, at senior management level, looking at the large exposures and threats to the business, and bottom-up, at business process level, looking at local or specific vulnerabilities or inefficiencies. These procedures are different but complementary, and both are vital because it is not sufficient to have one without the other. My favorite analogy for top-down and bottom-up risk management is the crow's nest versus the engine room of a boat, both of which are necessary for a complete view of an organization (see Figure 1.1).

Top-down risk analysis should be performed between one and four times a year, depending on the growth and development of the business and the level of associated risks. The aim is to identify key organizational risks, the major business threats that could jeopardize strategic objectives. Top-down risk identification sessions will typically include senior risk owners, members of the executive committee and heads of business lines. Sessions are best organized as brainstorming workshops with supporting techniques and tools, such as review of exposures and vulnerabilities, risk wheel, and causal analysis of potential impacts and expected revenues. These are explained in the next sections. Top-down risk identification exercises are similar to scenario generation, which is the first phase of scenario analysis. For small to medium-sized firms, I recommend conducting these meetings with both risk identification and scenario generation in mind in order to save time. The results can then be used as inputs to both the risk and control self-assessment (RCSA) exercises and scenario analysis. The links between RCSA and scenario analysis will be explained in Part 2.

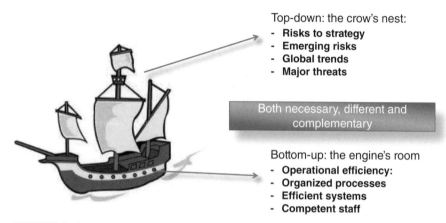

Top-down: the crow's nest:
- **Risks to strategy**
- **Emerging risks**
- **Global trends**
- **Major threats**

Both necessary, different and complementary

Bottom-up: the engine's room
- **Operational efficiency:**
- **Organized processes**
- **Efficient systems**
- **Competent staff**

FIGURE 1.1   Top-down and bottom-up risk management: the boat analogy

---

CASE STUDY: FTSE 100 INSURANCE COMPANY – TOP-DOWN RISK IDENTIFICATION

A large insurer in the UK calls its top-down risk analysis TDRA. It was set up by the chief risk officer (CRO) several years ago and provides a quarterly platform for the executive committee to review principal risks and emerging threats to the business, and to implement any required changes to the firm's risk profile. The insurer calls bottom-up risk identification RCSA, which focuses on the business process level and is the abbreviation for the more classic risk and control self-assessment technique.

Top-down risk analysis is one of the most efficient ways to identify important threats to a business. However, bottom-up risk analysis is still more common in the industry. Bottom-up risk identification is the only type of risk identification in many firms, especially among firms new to the discipline, where the practice is the least mature. In such firms, risk and control self-assessments are carried out as a first step to risk management, at a granular level. If the scope of the bottom-up risk identification exercise is too restricted, too granular, the output will be a disparate collection of small risks, such as manual errors and process risks, which are not always of much value to senior management. In the same way that we might fail to see a beach because we are too busy observing the grains of sand, we may miss the big picture when it comes to risks and their interactions because identification takes place at a level that is too low in the organization. The most common bottom-up risk identification techniques are process mapping and interviews, which we explore in this chapter.

CASE STUDY: TRADING FIRM – COMPLEMENTING TOP-DOWN AND BOTTOM-UP RISKS

Reconciling top-down and bottom-up risks is a goal for many firms and consultants. However, I don't believe it is a useful or even correct approach. Rather than *reconciling*, I would recommend *informing* one type of identification with the other, and *adding* the results of both exercises to obtain a comprehensive view of the operational risks in an organization. This is what we did during an ICAAP (Internal Capital Adequacy Assessment Process) in a trading group in the UK. After performing two risk identification workshops with top management, we compared the results with the findings of the bottom-up risk identification and assessment process. The findings were similar for some risks, but there were also some differences. The sum of both results provided the firm with its first risk universe, which was subsequently organized in a risk register and properly assessed.

EXPOSURE AND VULNERABILITIES

Risk exposure is inherent in every business and relates to key clients, principal distribution channels, central systems, primary sources of revenue and main regulatory authorities. In particular, large company projects and critical third parties are among the typical large exposures for a business. Operational risks related to projects and to outsourcing practices are an increasing focus in operational risk management, and rightly so. Large exposures to certain activities or counterparties aggravate the impact of possible incidents should a failure materialize for one of those activities. We will revisit exposure in Part 4, when we review the key risk indicators (KRIs) of impacts.

Vulnerabilities are the weakest links in an organization. They include inadequate or outdated products and processes, systems overdue for maintenance and testing, pockets of resistance to risk management and remote businesses left unmonitored. Large exposure typically relates to high impact/low probability risks, whereas vulnerabilities relate to higher frequency or more likely risks, hopefully with low impacts, but not necessarily. If vulnerabilities relate to large exposures, you have a heightened threat to the business. Examples of exposures and vulnerabilities are displayed in Figure 1.2.

There are two significant benefits to the risk identification method of exposure and vulnerabilities: it's business-driven and it's specific. Discussing exposures and vulnerabilities with line managers doesn't require risk management jargon. It's a natural process, grounded in the business, which everyone can relate to. The second advantage, shared by the other brainstorming techniques in this chapter, is that it is tailored to a given organization, a given business. In other words, it is individual and specific, which is a characteristic of operational risk. When identifying risks, you may be tempted to

Exposures	Vulnerabilities
• Key distribution channels • Main clients • Main suppliers and third parties • Critical systems • Regulatory exposure • Main drivers of revenues, drivers of value • Brand value • ...	• Weakest links • Fragile systems • Revenue channels at risk • Systems or processes not integrated • Parts of the business resistant to risk management • Small, unmonitored operations or people • Unmaintained systems • BCP due for testing or updates • ...

FIGURE 1.2   Exposures and vulnerabilities as a risk identification tool

use ready-made lists from industry bodies or from the Basel Committee. These lists are useful, but only as an ex-post check, to ensure that the exercise has not missed some significant threat. If used as a starting point, they may miss what makes a business particularly exposed or vulnerable to certain types of event.

THE RISK WHEEL

Popularized by the Institute of Risk Management (IRM) in London, the risk wheel is a classic support tool to spark creativity and imagination during risk identification brain-storming sessions. There are many versions of the risk wheel. The wheel in Figure 1.3 is a modified version of the one from the IRM training course 'Fundamentals of Risk Management', which I have delivered many times over the years. It usually applies to enterprise risk identification in non-financial sectors, but experience has shown that risk managers in the financial industry find it useful to debate themes that are not necessarily considered in financial organizations, such as risks from natural events, supply chains or political and social events. However, these themes are now increasingly considered by the financial sector when looking at outsourcing risk and anticipating business disruption due to extreme weather events, terrorist attacks or social unrest. Between Brexit and the election of Donald Trump, political risks and instability have climbed up the agendas of risk managers across financial services.

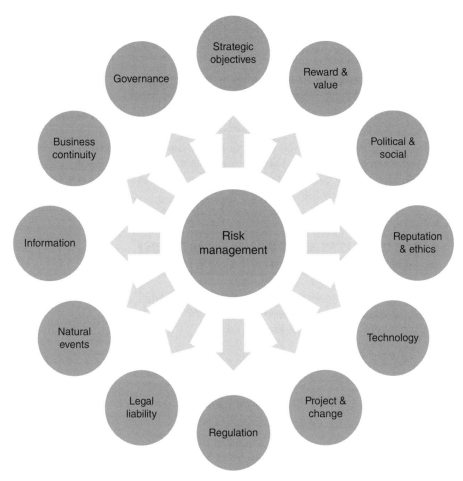

FIGURE 1.3   The risk wheel

By presenting risks – or risk sources – in a circular way, the risk wheel encourages managers to make connections between risk types, highlighting possible chains of causes and effects. The following are examples:

Reward and value → Personal effectiveness → Project and change → Technology → Business continuity → Reputation
  Natural events → Supply chain → Business continuity → Reputation

Such causal relationships, even when approximate, help to prioritize risk mitigation. Chapter 4 presents the concept of risk connectivity and illustrates the value for risk management and mitigation. The evolution of risk lists into risk networks is one of the foreseeable advances in operational risk management.

THE ROOT CAUSES OF DAMAGES AND REVENUES

Apart from incident analysis, the "five whys" and other root cause analysis techniques can also be used to reflect on risks to the business. The starting point can either be an impact to avoid or a revenue source to preserve. By answering successive questions about "why" an accident might happen – or revenues might be affected – managers can build a focused picture of both the threats to the business and the conditions for success, as the case study illustrates.

CASE STUDY: LEASING COMPANY – ROOT CAUSE OF DAMAGES AS RISK IDENTIFICATION TOOL

During a training session on risk identification, a participant from a business line of a leasing company was puzzled by the content and felt unable to start identifying the risks to her business. I asked:

"What is the worst thing that can happen to you?"

" A damage to our reputation," she replied.

"What can cause a damage to your reputation?"

"If the product is faulty, or the price is not right, or the customer service is poor."

"And what could cause those things to happen?"

"If the quality control fails, or there has been a mistake in the pricing of our goods, or if the call center has not been trained properly, or if the broker is fraudulent or disengaged."

"And why would that happen?"

etc.

We had this conversation without mentioning the word "risk." She completely understood the method and was able to start the risk identification of her business, without any established list, because it was rooted in her reality and circumstances.

PROCESS MAPPING

Process mapping is probably the most common risk and control identification approach, bottom-up. It is well developed in information technology, operations and project management, and can also be applied less formally, or at a higher level (e.g., process mapping does not need to be as detailed in other areas compared with IT and operations in any other area). It is useful to establish the tasks performed and to map the different controls with the risks they intend to mitigate. Or it may be easier and more practical to start by observing the controls and inferring which risks they are supposed to address. This exercise should highlight the possible under- or over-control of some risks compared with others.

It may be difficult to decide the appropriate level of analysis. If too granular, the process mapping will be excessively time-consuming and likely to raise only minor issues; if too high-level, it will not be revealing enough. A process description at level 2 or level 3 is usually the right balance, where each step is a significant action and individual key controls are described with their related risks. Figure 1.4 illustrates the principles of process mapping.

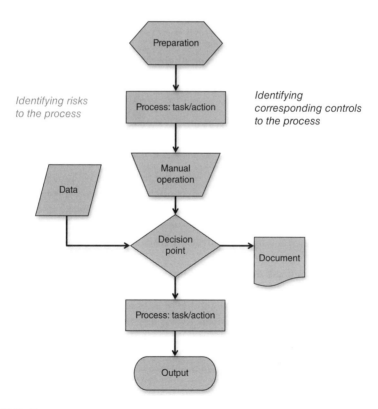

FIGURE 1.4   Common symbols and flows in process mapping

INTERVIEWS OF KEY STAFF

"Ears on the floor are better than any report."

When I was an internal auditor, my boss, who had more than 30 years of experience in the bank, was a great believer in observation and in "auditing with your feet." That means collecting information from the ground up, walking around the office, talking to people, encouraging and overhearing conversations. Similarly, the chief risk officer of a large UK bank once said that the Friday afternoons she used to spend in retail branches provided more valuable information than any credit risk report she ever read.

There is a lesson here for all of us and in particular for operational risk managers: risk-manage with your feet; take the pulse of the business by walking around, talking to people, listening and observing. No risk report is likely to beat first-hand experience.

Two types of employees stand out when it comes to risk interviews. One group is the most experienced employees, who have been with the business since it started and are the living memories of what happened, used to happen, and why things operate the way they do. The other group comprises recent hires, especially those who come from a different firm and culture – and most of all, a different industry. Many things may surprise them about their new company, compared with their previous experiences, and the contrast in practices, good or bad, is a rich source of information about the strengths and weaknesses of a business. Some CROs have distilled these observations into a so-called "amazement report" to highlight the experience of new employees in their first six weeks with the organization, before habit tames their surprise.

WHAT ALREADY HAPPENED: INTERNAL LOSSES, EXTERNAL LOSSES AND NEAR MISSES

Past losses, or "lagging indicators," are often the first things we review in most institutions. While the past is at best an imperfect guide to the future, it is natural for us to look at what has happened when trying to predict what might happen. We all do it. In relatively stable environments, the past may be a reasonable predictor of the future. To refine the approach, we should distinguish between internal losses, external losses and near misses.

Internal losses indicate the concentrations of operational risk in a firm. In banks, these losses typically affect back offices, with financial market activities first, retail next and then the IT department. The number of transactions and the size of the money flows are natural operational risk drivers, especially for incidents related to processing errors, business malpractice and fraud. If repeated internal losses do not represent a systematic failure in internal controls but simply the level at which a business is exposed to operational risk, then those internal losses should probably be budgeted and accounted for through pricing. If they do come as a surprise, then they may constitute new information regarding risks.

External losses, for risk management in mature organizations, are a systematic benchmark that helps risk identification and assessment. A common good practice in such organizations is to monitor all large incidents communicated by peers and after each one ask objectively: "Could this incident happen to us?" If "yes" and the existing risk controls for that type of incident are deemed inadequate, appropriate mitigation measures must be taken. Although good practice, the review is limited by the reliability of information filtering through from external incidents and their causes.

Near misses are incidents that could have occurred but did not because of sheer luck or fortuitous intervention outside the normal controls. An example of a near miss is leaving a smartphone visible in a car overnight without it being stolen, or forgetting to pay for parking and not receiving a fine (especially in London). In the business context, it could mean mistyping a transaction amount with too many zeros and having it returned because you also made a mistake in the bank account number. Even though most firms claim to record near misses, only the more mature ones actually collect a reliable number of near misses. Those firms typically have a no-blame culture, where teammates feel comfortable admitting mistakes without fearing consequences. It is too easy to sweep things under the carpet when nothing goes wrong in the end, but near misses often provide the most valuable lessons about risk management. We will return to this in Chapter 14 on risk information.

## CHAPTER 2

Scenario Identification Process

Scenario analysis (SA) is one of the four pillars of the advanced measurement approach (AMA) for operational risk to calculate regulatory capital. It is also a pillar of good risk management, as well as internal capital assessment, regardless of whether the institution performs capital modeling for operational risk. Scenario analysis is accurately defined as "the assessment and management of the exposure to high severity, low frequency events on the firm." It includes management as well as measurement. It focuses on the extremes and is not limited to financial impact.

Scenario analysis identification and assessment is a natural extension of the risk identification exercise. In fact, most of the top-down risk identification tools presented in the previous chapter can be used for scenario identification as well. This chapter focuses on the first two steps of the scenario analysis process. The different methods for scenario assessment and quantification are covered in Chapter 7.

Scenario analysis typically includes the following steps:

1. Preparation and governance.
2. Generation and selection.
3. Assessment.
4. Validation.
5. Incorporation into management.
6. Scenario aggregation.
7. Incorporation into capital.

SCENARIO PREPARATION AND GOVERNANCE

One of the main challenges in scenario analysis is the consistency of approach and the mitigation of behavioral biases. It is, however, a strong regulatory requirement that scenario analysis should lead to repeatable results, both quantitative and qualitative. The regulator demands that firms minimize subjectivity and biases as far as possible when conducting scenario identification and assessment. To do this, assumptions must be based on empirical evidence, the rationale behind each scenario must be explained, and the assumptions and process for generating scenario analysis must be rigorously documented.

SA preparation and planning is normally the role of the risk function, unless the business has taken full control of the SA process. The general documentation of the organization and methodology is usually the role of the risk function. The business lines own the documentation relating to the workshops, the experts involved and the results of the various meetings.

The preparation phase includes defining the scope and objectives of the exercise, identifying the relevant participants, organizing meetings and setting schedules. Participants are business managers (generally, the more senior, the better) and risk owners (HR, IT, Compliance, etc.). Representatives of the risk functions are there mostly to facilitate meetings and to document the process and the content of the meetings, if the second line is actively involved.

The preparation phase also involves compiling a "preparation pack" of documents that will help later with the selection and assessment of scenarios. You may choose to withhold the documents from the participants during the generation phase, in order to keep the brainstorming sessions as free from influence and as creative as possible. However, the more common practice is to distribute documents before the first meetings (and they are not always read anyway). Preparation documents include:

- External loss data
- Internal loss data, large past incidents and near misses
- RCSA results
- Key risk indicator scores
- Audit issues and other issue logs, if any
- Concentrated exposures, known vulnerabilities (if reported differently than KRIs)
- Any other relevant documents for risk and exposure assessment

The participants in SA workshops and brainstorming sessions should be senior managers within the different corporate functions and as a consequence should have significant experience and understanding of the risks in their area. Ideally, they should be knowledgable about operational risks and be open-minded thinkers. The involvement of additional external experts is recommended (although uncommon), particularly to mitigate behavioral biases. A frequent bias is myopia: the over-estimation of recent events. Another widespread bias is the excessive focus on scenarios driven by external causes. Interestingly, the majority of scenarios considered by financial institutions are substantial losses caused by external events (terror attacks, pandemics, weather, outsourcing, cyber crime, etc.). However, in reality, most large losses experienced by the financial industry are due to internal causes, such as rogue trading, LIBOR rigging, mis-selling, embargo breaches, data losses and internal fraud.

SCENARIO GENERATION AND SELECTION

Brainstorming is a creative technique where groups generate a large number of ideas to solve a problem. There are four main rules in brainstorming, which tend to foster group creativity and reduce social pressures.

1. **Focus on quantity first:** the underlying idea is that quantity breeds quality. The selection will be done at a later stage.
2. **No criticism:** the participants and facilitator are asked to suspend all judgment to create a supportive atmosphere where everyone feels free to express their ideas, however unusual or seemingly eccentric.
3. **Unusual ideas are welcome:** unconventional and unusual ideas may lead to important scenarios that no one has considered.
4. **Combine and improve ideas:** blending suggestions may create fresh insights and scenarios. The facilitator has an important role to play by encouraging new ideas and combining existing ones. Free association and discovery help to generate useful ideas.

SA workgroup facilitators are ORM professionals. Their task is to initiate the discussions at each step of the process, to coordinate the debates and to reach the best consensus based on the input of every member.

It is helpful to start the meeting with simple warm-up questions that engage the participants and encourage reflection. For example:

- What's the biggest operational incident that you've experienced in recent years?
- How bad was it and why?
- If you've avoided a large loss, how did you do it? What could have gone wrong otherwise?

These questions will help participants to think about past frights or disruptions and potential large losses, before focusing on specific scenarios. Next, the facilitator introduces scenario analysis and asks the participants for their ideas, encouraging everybody to speak (see case study). The participants explore each scenario idea, to refine the quality. When no more ideas are expressed, the facilitator categorizes the ideas according to the type of risk or the type of consequence and encourages discussion. Additional ideas may be generated. The initial output should contain at least 20–30 scenarios, and the participants are expected to produce around 15 scenarios after the selection. Small firms may produce fewer, while large international organizations may generate more.

An important drawback of risk identification is that the findings are strongly biased by what happened in the past, when in fact the biggest risks may be those that have never materialized and most people have not seen coming. Therefore, screening any new elements in a business will lead to more revealing and rigorous scenarios that embrace, amongst other things, changes to products, technology, business processes, management structure, lines of business, third parties and software.

A comprehensive picture of risks is more likely if everyone in the group has a chance to speak. Inevitably, strong personalities will dominate the debate, but it is useful to draw out the views of the more reticent participants, who often have great insights, and the group facilitator must encourage them to speak up. Generally, scenario analysis meetings should not last more than three hours on the same day, as productivity and creativity will decline the longer the meeting goes on. To maintain focus, phones should be switched off and other external distractions avoided. Arrange meetings in the morning, when people are fresh, or in the second part of the afternoon, as attention levels are generally low immediately after lunch.

CASE STUDY: FTSE 100 INSURANCE COMPANY – SCENARIO GENERATION PHASE

A large international insurer based in the UK asked the regulator to approve its internal modeling approach (IMA) of operational risk, which was essentially based on the quantification of scenarios. After years of preparation and hundreds of pages of documentation, the insurer received approval in 2014. During this long and demanding process, I was in charge of the brainstorming workshops to identify the scenarios to model.

We ran six groups from six different significant business entities. Each workshop session had senior managers from the business lines. These were reflection meetings, without slideshows or set agendas and with as little external interference as possible. We politely discouraged participants from using their phones and checking emails.

At the start of the meeting each participant was asked to write down two or three worries, recent near misses or other past incidents that they felt could still threaten the business. By starting with written contributions from everyone, all the participants were immediately involved and engaged in the meeting. This avoided the all-too-common occurrence where the most opinionated and outgoing individuals set the agenda and frame the debate.

Once the participants had taken time to reflect and then write down their thoughts, they were asked to share their ideas on risk one at a time. This provided a wealth of information on losses, current and emerging threats, and the overall business environment, which could be developed into scenarios. The same approach was used for each business unit in turn.

The resulting scenarios are usually organized either by business units, risk types or risk owners, depending on the institution. All of this is fine, particularly if it fits well into the structure of the firm. However, you should not confuse the organization of scenarios with their comprehensiveness. A common flaw in many immature organizations is analyzing just one scenario for each risk type, often simply matching the seven risk categories identified by Basel II. I recommend moving away from this rigid framework, as risks and exposure rarely fall neatly one into each box. In some businesses, there will be many disruption scenarios, while internal fraud remains negligible; and in others, compliance scenarios (for clients, products and business practices) may dominate, while scenarios for damage to physical assets are very limited.

The generation phase may produce a long list of scenarios, possibly too unstructured to be presented for assessment. Scenario selection is an intermediary phase where some scenarios are consolidated and others eliminated or added, in order to obtain a list relevant enough to be fully assessed. Examples of consolidated scenarios are those relating to the same internal impact but different external causes, such as damage to physical assets; indeed, building damage due to extreme weather events, political unrest or terrorist attacks has the same effect on the firm and can be seen as the same event with various possible causes. Scenarios that quickly appear as negligible in impact can be excluded during the selection phase, in order to spare time for bigger scenarios during the assessment phase. Tail risks scenarios can be eliminated if the risk owner can convincingly demonstrate that the maximum loss is moderate enough to be absorbed by normal operating margin and without significant disruption to the business. For instance, if the HR director credibly demonstrates that all the key people in the firm are identified, have a back-up or substitute worker and a succession plan in place, the "key man risk" scenario is likely to drop out of the list before the assessment phase.

Some scenarios may generate a great deal of debate and strong opinions, but the required levels of knowledge do not always back the views expressed. Cyberattacks and information security are prime examples of operational risk topics where misinformation, or incomplete knowledge, is dangerous. This underlines the importance of involving true experts in the scenario assessment phase when necessary.

In some particular cases, scenarios relate to risks that have already materialized and firms have made provisions but the settlement loss is uncertain. This is typically the case in litigation. These are more risk events than scenarios in the strict sense, although the uncertainty of outcome may be large enough to be considered as a scenario. An example is BNP Paribas' record fine of $8.9 billion in 2015 for sanctions violations: the fine was expected, but the amount was much larger than the firm had provisioned initially.

Comparisons with other internal and external evidence can also help with selecting more scenarios from the initial list generated. For this, support documents detailing similar events in peer firms, examples of past internal incidents and near misses, key risk indicators and organizational changes are useful.

Finally, a firm may find it useful to compare its generated scenarios with an industry list of scenarios, to check whether it has missed anything relevant. The Operational Risk Consortium (ORIC) and the Operational Riskdata eXchange

Association (ORX) are examples of industry bodies that provide ready-made scenario lists to their members. However, I would recommend doing this check only *after* the scenario generation exercise, not before, so it won't influence or bias the generation process. You should avoid a practice still widespread in the industry whereby all scenarios are evaluated in a benchmark list and those that don't appear to apply are excluded. This method makes the dangerous assumption that the benchmark list (from an industry body, a consultant, or last year's list) is the full risk universe, whereas it can only be representative of risks at a given time. I know a sizeable financial institution that used this type of benchmarking, but its largest exposure scenario was not on the list. Thankfully, the missing scenario did not materialize and the financial institution has now revised its scenario identification process.

CHAPTER **3**

Risk Definition and Taxonomy

DEFINING RISKS

Defining a risk is less straightforward than you may think. The following examples illustrate some of the common inaccuracies that occur in risk identification exercises.

Technology is not a risk; it's a resource. All firms rely on technology, and risks linked to technology are best defined as potential incidents and accidents due to failures, such as systems interruption, model error, wrong pricing calculation, overcapacity and application crashes.

Manual processing is also not a risk; it's a cause or a risk driver. It increases the probability of another risk occurring, such as input errors and omissions. Risks due to manual processing may include errors in the valuation of funds, errors in accounting records, omitting to send reports to clients, etc.

Compliance and regulatory change is a priority for every regulated financial entity. It's an obligation and a constraint, but once again, not a risk in itself. Rather, it brings risks such as compliance breach, mostly through oversight due to the sheer number and complexity of regulations that must be followed. However, it can also be deliberate, perhaps temporarily when adjusting to new regulatory requirements.

Inadequate supervision or insufficient training are also commonly cited as risk factors, but they are not risks per se; they are control failures. The answer to a control failure is simple: fix the control. Or add a secondary control. If that sounds all too familiar, you are not alone. I know a very large financial institution whose entire risk categorization is expressed as failed controls. Although not an industry leader in operational risk management, it is nonetheless a household name, which shows that no business is immune from weaknesses. Inadequate supervision can lead to the risk of internal fraud, errors and omissions, and sub-standard productivity resulting in customer dissatisfaction or loss.

Risks should be defined as much as possible as negative events, uncertainties, incidents or accidents. They should be specific and concrete. *"What could go wrong?"* is a simple, jargon-free question that can help to define risks. The more specific you are, the easier it will be to assess risks and to find the relevant mitigating actions. Later on, you will categorize information into different levels of detail in a similar way to the Basel categories in Table 3.1.

19

TABLE 3.1 Examples of defined risks – Basel categories Levels 1, 2 and 3

Event-type category (Level 1)	Definition	Categories (level 2)	Activity examples (level 3)
Internal fraud	Losses due to acts of a type intended to defraud, misappropriate property or circumvent regulations, the law or company policy, excluding diversity/discrimination events, which involve at least one internal party.	Unauthorised Activity	Transactions not reported (intentional) Trans type unauthorised (w/monetary loss) Mismarking of position (intentional)
		Theft and Fraud	Fraud/credit fraud/worthless deposits Theft/extortion/embezzlement/robbery Misappropriation of assets Malicious destruction of assets Forgery Check kiting Smuggling Account takeover/impersonation/etc. Tax non-compliance/evasion (wilful) Bribes/kickbacks Insider trading (not on firm's account)
External fraud	Losses due to acts of a type intended to defraud, misappropriate property or circumvent the law, by a third party	Theft and Fraud	Theft/Robbery Forgery Check kiting
		Systems Security	Hacking damage Theft of information (w/monetary loss)
Employment practices and workplace safety	Losses arising from acts inconsistent with employment, health or safety laws or agreements, from payment of personal injury claims, or from diversity/discrimination events	Employee Relations	Compensation, benefit, termination issues Organised labour activity
		Safe Environment	General liability (slip and fall, etc.) Employee health & safety rules events Workers compensation
		Diversity & Discrimination	All discrimination types

Clients' products & business practices	Losses arising from an unintentional or negligent failure to meet a professional obligation to specific clients (including fiduciary and suitability requirements), or from the nature or design of a product.	Suitability, Disclosure & Fiduciary	Fiduciary breaches/guideline violations Suitability/disclosure issues (KYC, etc.) Retail consumer disclosure violations Breach of privacy Aggressive sales Account churning Misuse of confidential information Lender Liability
		Improper Business or Market Practices	Antitrust Improper trade/market practices Market manipulation Insider trading (on firm's account) Unlicensed activity Money laundering
		Product Flaws	Product defects (unauthorised, etc.) Model errors
		Selection, Sponsorship & Exposure	Failure to investigate client per guidelines Exceeding client exposure limits
		Advisory Activities	Disputes over performance of advisory activities
Damage to physical assets	Losses arising from loss or damage to physical assets from natural disaster or other events.	Disasters and other events	Natural disaster losses Human losses from external sources (terrorism, vandalism)

(Continued)

TABLE 3.1 *(Continued)*

Event-type category (Level 1)	Definition	Categories (level 2)	Activity examples (level 3)
Business disruption and system failures	Losses arising from disruption of business or system failures	Systems	Hardware Software Telecommunications Utility outage/disruptions
Execution, delivery and process management	Losses from failed transaction processing or process management, from relations with trade counterparties and vendors	Transaction Capture, Execution & Maintenance	Miscommunication Data entry, maintenance or loading error Missed deadline or responsibility Model/system misoperation Accounting error/entity attribution error Other task misperformance Delivery failure Collateral management failure Reference Data Maintenance
		Monitoring and Reporting	Failed mandatory reporting obligation Inaccurate external report (loss incurred)
		Customer Intake and Documentation	Client permissions/disclaimers missing Legal documents missing/incomplete
		Customer/Client Account Management	Unapproved access given to accounts Incorrect client records (loss incurred) Negligent loss or damage of client assets
		Trade Counterparties	Non-client counterparty misperformance Misc. non-client counterparty disputes
		Vendors & Suppliers	Outsourcing Vendor disputes

Source: Bis.org – Operational risk loss data collection exercise, 2002.

Level 1 is the highest-level category, level 2 is a detailed version of level 1 and level 3 provides even more detail. The Basel Committee recognizes only two levels of regulatory categories, with level 3 reserved for examples and illustrations. We support that view. The number of risks to assess, manage and report needs to be kept at a reasonable level. Too much detail is detrimental to the quality of information and is difficult to review. It drains effort and resources without corresponding benefits.

While firms are required to map risk categories to the Basel categories, the classification doesn't have to define a firm's risk taxonomy these days. This simple taxonomy might have been effective some ten years ago, but it is no longer a good idea. The Basel classification was drafted almost 20 years ago, in the late 1990s, and does not fully reflect current risk exposures across the financial sector. Technology advances have completely transformed the financial services industry since Basel 2 was drafted, and mass digitization has led to a huge increase in cybercrime. Business transformation and wider international operations have multiplied the risks of outsourcing, of project and change management, and of information management. Finally, the 2008 financial crisis underlined the need for better regulation, with a particular focus on business practices, now renamed "conduct," and on anti-money laundering (AML) controls, enforceability of international sanctions and prevention of tax-evasion mechanisms. In light of these global developments, new risk categories have emerged that are insufficiently represented in the Basel classification's seven risk categories, especially for internationally active institutions.

RISK MANAGEMENT TAXONOMY

The distinction between cause, risk and impact is a recurrent puzzle in almost every firm. Risk management taxonomy is an important step toward solving this puzzle. A dictionary definition of taxonomy is a "scheme of classification." In risk management, it means not only categorizing risks but also recording the causes, impacts and controls as a MECE system: Mutually Exclusive and Collectively Exhaustive. Figure 3.1 shows the structure and components of a risk management taxonomy.

The Basel definition of operational risk is a valuable starting point for categorizing causes, risks and impacts: "The risk of loss resulting from inadequate or failed internal processes, people and systems or from external events" (bis.org).

First is the risk of loss. In the late 1990s, the Basel Committee considered financial losses only. Reputation damage was added as a type of non-financial loss, and by the early part of this century, every institution I met was including the risk of reputation damage as part of its operational risk management. Since the financial crisis of 2008, the vast majority of firms have included the impacts of operational risks on regulatory compliance and on customers. Thus, there are now four commonly used categories for the impacts of operational risks: financial loss, reputation damage, regulatory non-compliance and customer detriment. For firms where continuity of services

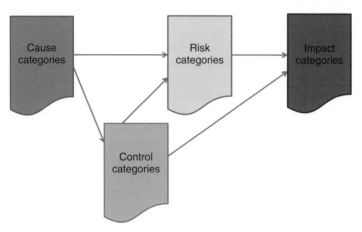

FIGURE 3.1   Risk management taxonomy

is particularly important, such as online financial services or trading platforms, service disruption is another common category of impact.

Usually, negative impacts are simply defined by one word: *Finance, Reputation, Compliance, Customer*. Personally, I prefer more precise definitions to avoid confusion or misunderstandings. These categories of impacts are very common among many firms and stay at a level 1 definition. In most of the firms I observed, there are no further subdivisions to these categories of impacts. However, there will be subdivisions in levels of intensity as part of the risk assessments, presented in Chapter 6.

Now let's consider the causes. Basel defines operational risk as *due to* failed or inadequate people, processes, systems or external events: PPSE. These four initials are quite useful to explain the nature and drivers of operational risk to everyone in an organization. Many firms have adopted some form of categories of causes for operational risks, and normally these four. The categories do not always progress to level 2. This is regrettable because a finer categorization provides useful insights into the causes of incidents and also helps to select leading key risk indicators, as detailed in Chapter 14. Table 3.2 provides some examples of cause categories at level 1 and level 2.

So far we have defined the impacts and the causes. Next, categorizing internal controls should be easy enough, since the practice of internal controls is well-developed and the internal audit discipline has provided quite a lot of structure in the field. Chapter 10 focuses on risk mitigation through internal controls. The four main categories of control are defined as:

- **Preventive:** the aim is to reduce the likelihood of risks materializing by mitigating their possible causes.

TABLE 3.2 Examples of cause
categories – level 1 and level 2

Level 1	Level 2
People	Resources/Capacity
	Competence
	Engagement
	Experience
Process	Manual complexity
	Documentation
	Multiple input
	Automation
Systems	Availability
	Bug
	Capacity
	Performance
	Obsolescence
External events	Socio-political changes
	Regulatory
	Stakeholder interference
	Natural events
	Third party

- **Detective:** this takes place during the event or soon after, with early detection helping to reduce impact. There is a preventive element if detection also identifies the cause of an incident.
- **Corrective:** this reduces impacts caused by incidents. Damage is repaired or loss is compensated for by using backup and redundancies.
- **Directive:** this comprises guidelines and procedures that structure the mode of operations to reduce risks.

We now have three fixed points in our risk taxonomy: *impacts*, *causes* and *controls*. By agreement, everything else constitutes a risk, so that you have, de facto, a MECE risk management taxonomy, as illustrated in Figure 3.2. I have assisted several firms in defining their risk taxonomy. An example of one of these projects is presented in the case study. An abstract of some firms' risk list categories is provided in Table 3.3. The next chapter will explore a more advanced way of presenting risks, not with a list but as a network. Some firms have started adopting risk networks and the practice is on the rise.

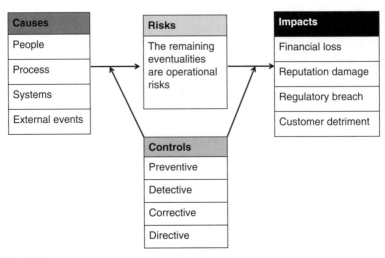

FIGURE 3.2   Mutually exclusive collectively comprehensive taxonomy

TABLE 3.3   Examples of risk categories – level 1 and level 2

	Risk categories		
Code L1	Risk level 1	Code L2	Risk level 2
5	Operations risk	5.1	Unavailability/disruption of services Delivery
		5.3	Capacity gap (leading to underperformance)
		5.4	Maintenance incident (change management)
		5.5	Operational support errors (slips and mistakes)
		5.6	Customer support errors (slips and mistakes)
		5.7	Reporting inaccuracy
		5.10	Damage to building and facilities
		5.11	Supplier failures (utilities or others)
6	Information security risk	6.1	Accidental data corruption (integrity)
		6.2	Confidentiality breach
		6.3	Cyber threats (external)
		6.4	Malicious act (internal)
		6.5	Accidental data loss

CASE STUDY: MARKET INFRASTRUCTURE COMPANY – BUILDING A RISK TAXONOMY

When I first arrived in this company, the risk register was a 27-page Excel spreadsheet, printed in a small font. This is what a lack of standardized risk categories leads to. There was no agreement on the risk types, and all risk identification and assessments were performed on an ad hoc basis. Many lines in this very long register expressed similar risks in slightly different ways. And many risk identification and assessment exercises were carried out in various departments and in various projects, without anyone taking the time to order the results into fixed categories. This company needed a risk taxonomy badly.

The level 1 risk categories turned out to be easy to establish and to tie in with an existing governance structure. A handful of committees took charge of different risk types, around which it was sensible to build the main risk categories.

The definition of risk categories at level 2 required a few more iterations. The first version was drafted by the enterprise risk management department and was based on the knowledge of the business and on the existing risk register. Each risk category was then presented to each risk owner or specialist department for review and comments. The comments were collated and refined until we reached a consensus. The exercises took about four weeks.

## CHAPTER 4

Risk Connectivity and Risk Networks

The trouble with risk lists and risk registers is that all the risks appear independent of each other. However, in the same way that causes lead to risks and then to impacts, risks are interrelated and interdependent. The segmentation described in the last chapter between causes, risks and impacts is purely for convenience. The distinction between people, processes, systems and external events is a way to order the causes of operational risks, in keeping with the Basel definition. Similarly, for convenience, the impacts of operational risks are defined as financial loss, reputation damage, compliance breach, customer detriment and sometimes disruption of services. But risks transcend categories, and it is a mistake to assume they behave independently. In reality, everything is connected, which is why so many firms are confused when it comes to defining causes, risks and impacts.

Risk networks are a promising and growing resource in firms with more mature operational risk management. Also known as risk connectivity and sometimes risk visualization, these networks provide risk managers with useful insights. They highlight the dependencies and other connections between different risks, and are not just tools for risk modelers and quantitative analysts.

The best-known user of risk networks is probably the World Economic Forum (WEF). Every year, in its global risk report, published on its website (weforum.org), WEF presents a network view of global risks. Diamonds represent individual risks, and they are joined by lines of different thickness that denote the strength and intensity of the connection. The more lines that connect with a diamond, the larger the diamond is to reflect the significance of that risk. In recent years, risks such as governance failures (2015) or large-scale involuntary migration (2017) have gained the most connections, while interdependence is strongest among ecology risk groups, such as extreme weather events, climate change, water and food crises.

This last example highlights one of the main benefits of a risk network representation: the identification of clusters. Risk clusters are types of risks that are linked to each other and should be considered holistically. For WEF, climate change, weather and food crises constitute a cluster, mostly triggered by climate change. Identifying a trigger risk for a group of other subsequent risks is a second important benefit of this type of approach, as it gives risk managers clear indications of where to prioritize risk management after focusing on the first trigger. The following sections illustrate these benefits by applying networks to top risks and by using case studies.

MANAGING RISKS IN CLUSTERS

Investment in risky financial assets such as shares or bonds is managed through portfolios, not independent lines. Financial theory demonstrates that in a portfolio of ten assets, the risk and return are nearly solely determined by the correlations between those assets (known as the portfolio covariance). The risk and return of each individual asset is insignificant (10% of the total in the case of a portfolio with ten assets). The same applies to a portfolio of non-financial risks; what matters are the interconnections.

Besides the modeling aspect, the interconnection between risks has important lessons for management. Even if the connections are based on intuition and business experience, which is sometimes more reliable anyway than complex or questionable data, these links allow us to apply risk management resources and mitigation efforts more efficiently. They highlight clusters or trigger risks that need attention, possibly before isolated risks. A large mining company experienced it the hard way, as illustrated in the case study.

CASE STUDY: LESSONS FOR THE FINANCIAL SECTOR FROM A MINING COMPANY

A large mining company decided to move from a risk list to a connectivity view after experiencing an incident that turned out to be far more damaging than anticipated. The risk related to that incident had been assessed as minor in the risk register and so was not strongly mitigated. What the register failed to show was that this supposedly small risk was actually connected to a number of much larger risks to the business, resulting in a cumulative impact that took everyone by surprise. Since then, the company has established a risk connectivity view, with the help of the firm Systemic Consult (see Figure 4.1).

Understandably, the company did not reveal publicly what this apparently small risk was. We can easily find equivalents in the financial sector, however – an example is obsolete human resources applications. Would you be concerned if some HR applications in your firm were not up-to-date? You should be. Application obsolescence is typically associated with performance, but it also increases vulnerability to cyberattacks. Furthermore, HR departments are natural backdoors for cybercriminals as they hold all the personal and banking information on staff. Watch for interconnections.

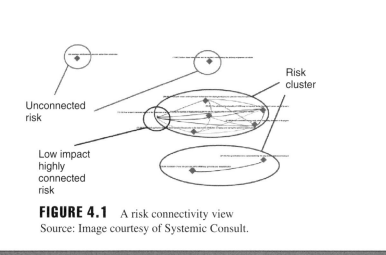

FIGURE 4.1 A risk connectivity view
Source: Image courtesy of Systemic Consult.

RISK CONNECTIVITY TO PRIORITIZE RISK MANAGEMENT ATTENTION

Risks can be represented in networks, in clusters or in cascades. The second case study in this chapter is based on a risk connectivity workshop that I held with the board of a medium-size bank in Southern Europe. Instead of listing the top risks identified by the board as the main areas for attention, we organized the risks in a cascade of causes and consequences that naturally ordered the priorities for mitigating and monitoring those risks. Just like we categorized causes, risks and impacts in the previous chapter, the risk connectivity approach can organize risks as a waterfall.

CASE STUDY: SOUTHERN EUROPEAN BANK

During an executive training session in a beautiful sunny part of Europe, my aim was to show the board members of a mid-size bank the benefits of moving away from risk lists. I used the results of a top risk identification workshop to present the risks as a cascade of causes and consequences. Inputs ranged from global strategy changes to the consequences for the operations. It resulted in something like Figure 4.2.

(Continued)

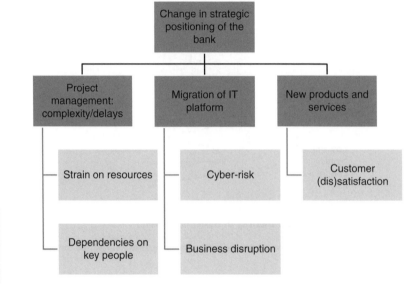

FIGURE 4.2   Risks: a cascade of causes and consequences

The board appreciated, and discussions reinforced, the intention to carefully plan and phase the business transformation to avoid project management collapse due to excessive strain on resources and to prudently manage the migration of the IT platform before making any significant changes to products and services.

RISK CONNECTIVITY APPLIED TO TOP RISK SURVEY

As a final illustration, I applied the connectivity representation to the top 10 largest operational risks for 2017, as determined by specialists surveyed for risk.net. Geopolitical risk was the most significant entry, taking fourth place. This reflected the concerns and threats felt following the Brexit referendum and the election of Donald Trump. Unsurprisingly, cyber-risk remained in pole position. When displayed in a network (Figure 4.3), this set of risks reveals some interesting points:

- Geopolitical risk possibly drives or at least exacerbates five other top risks, either directly or indirectly: organizational change, outsourcing, IT failures, cyber-risk and data security, and physical attacks. This finding highlights the necessity for firms and CROs to carefully watch their political and business environment, given

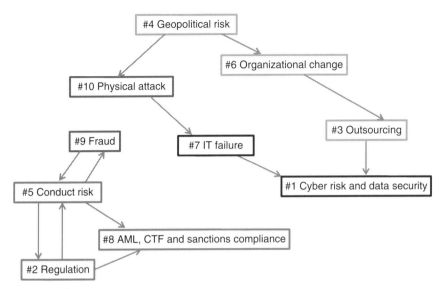

FIGURE 4.3   A network view of the top **ten operational risks for 2017**

the many repercussions this environment can have for an organization. Geopolitical risk is a serious candidate for the largest emerging risk in the G8.

- Cyber risks, the most commonly cited top risk in recent years, appear to be caused, or at least worsened, by many other top risks, as varied as physical attack, organizational change, outsourcing or fraud. This result highlights the importance of treating data protection and cybersecurity as consequences of good, or bad, holistic risk management throughout the firm.
- The network in the picture is essentially split into two poles: the geopolitical and organizational pole (top right) and the regulatory pole (bottom left). It suggests that sanctions are generated by regulatory changes and are somewhat isolated from the 'real' risks faced by organizations due to a changing world. Only internal fraud, a new top risk in the 2017 list, links the two clusters.

Figure 4.3 is based solely on my personal opinion and from my experience of working in risk management in the financial industry for 20 years. Other people might have different judgments. However, this approach underlines the benefit of representing a risk register as a network, rather than in a list, to better highlight connectivity and prioritize mitigation effectively.

Risk Assessment

"Because the reward is worth the risk."

Susan Mallery

## CHAPTER 5

Risk Appetite

CONTEXT AND OBJECTIVES

Risk appetite is the amount of risk an organization is ready to take in pursuit of its strategic objectives.

This concept of risk appetite has gradually made its way into various corporate governance codes since the 1990s.[1] Nowadays, most corporate governance codes state that the board is responsible for making sure that the monitoring and internal controls of the company are such that the firm operates within its risk appetite.

Given its implications for the board, risk appetite has attracted considerable attention since the financial crisis of 2008. This chapter presents the features and challenges in defining risk appetite for non-financial risks. It highlights the necessary tradeoff between risk and reward, and between a fast-moving organization and the cost of controls. Building on several established sources such as COSO,[2] it explains the most common recent standards regarding the structure of risk appetite, linking the different parts of a risk management framework.

"The Board is responsible for determining the nature and extent of the significant risks it is willing to take in achieving its strategic objectives (. . .) and should maintain sound risk management and internal control systems."[3] Since they are directly named as responsible for determining risks, board members generally take a keen interest in defining risk appetites. But this is easier said than done, and many firms or institutions struggle with both the concept and its practical application.

Defining a risk appetite means assessing all the possible risks facing an organization, establishing the boundaries for acceptable and unacceptable incidents, and

---

[1] The Cadbury report in 1992, the Turnbull report in 1999 and the Walker Review in 2009, to name a few.

[2] The Committee of Sponsoring Organizations of the Treadway Commission.

[3] "A Review of Corporate Governance in UK Banks and Other Financial Industry Entities," Walker report, 2009.

creating the necessary controls that these limits require. Done thoroughly, risk appetite definition may lead to difficult conversations and highlight painful truths, such as inner contradictions about what an organization officially states and what is happening in reality. Unsurprisingly, some dread the exercise. Yet, one of the key roles of the risk function is to provide conceptual and methodological assistance to define risk appetite. Once the risk appetite is defined, the risk function is responsible for monitoring risk exposure and ensuring that it is consistent with the risk appetite. It must advise on all important business decisions and challenge unacceptable risks.[4]

In addition to a reluctance to uncover inner contradictions, there is another reason why risk appetite struggles for acceptance – namely, the suggestion of "appetite." Why would you have an *appetite* for risk? Even more so for operational risks, perceived by so many as being purely downside risks? Many prefer the term "risk tolerance," or for some, "risk acceptance." Regardless of semantics, we believe it is a common, yet fundamental, flaw when financial firms fail to recognize the business revenues that can be generated by taking prudent operational risks.

REWARD: THE MISSING PIECE OF RISK APPETITE

When choosing an investment portfolio for pensions or savings, we balance the expected portfolio returns with the risk of volatility: the bigger the volatility, the larger the possible upside, bringing capital gains, but also the larger the possible downside, bringing losses. Some will choose bigger risks in the hope of larger profits, and some will feel more comfortable with less risk for correspondingly smaller returns. When considering a loan to corporates or individuals, a bank will either calibrate its interest rate with the risk of debtor default or reject the loan altogether if the perceived risk of default is beyond its tolerance. Some banks will be very conservative in their lending policy, while others will accept subprime customers and shaky businesses because the revenues that these clients bring to the bank (as long as they don't default) are significantly larger than the revenues generated from lending to solid businesses and affluent individuals. In other words, it's a calculated risk.

Credit risk and market risk have clearly defined returns in the form of credit margin and capital gains, and the tradeoff between risk and return is well understood by financial institutions. Banks never struggle to write a credit risk policy, which is another name for a risk appetite statement for credit risk, or to establish a market risk policy, which is the same thing as a risk appetite statement for market risk. So, why does it seem so difficult for operational risk? Because financial institutions thrive on taking credit risk and market risk, or underwriting risk in the case of insurance companies, but consider operational risk as an annoyance when it is small, a scary threat when it is

---

[4]Chapelle, A. and Sicsic, M. (2014) "Building an invisible framework for risk management," *Operational Risk and Regulation*, July.

large, and a regulatory burden in every case. Most financial organizations, even today, simply ignore or choose to ignore the revenues generated by operational risk.

When a risk is presented with no indication of potential returns, the rational reaction is to reduce the risk as much as possible. And this will remain so as long as risk managers keep presenting operational risk assessments to the board without highlighting the benefits of taking those risks *in pursuit of strategic objectives*. The risk appetite (for operational risk, fraud risk, regulatory risk, people risk, etc.) will be "low" or "zero" by default. However, one could argue that all the non-financial revenues of banks and insurance companies, particularly fee revenues, are the visible returns of operational risk. Industrial companies and technological companies have very little revenue from financial activities; they do not allocate credit, nor do they manage a trading room or underwrite insurance policies. All their revenues come from operational activities. Risk management is called *operational* risk management only in the financial sector, to distinguish it from credit and market risks.

I argue that operational risks have a visible return for financial firms: the fee income and, less visibly, the return from gaining new revenues with new products and new operations. By increasing the size and complexity of a business, you also increase operational risk from, among other things, processing errors, IT failures and regulatory non-compliance. So how much risk is acceptable and for which reward?

Of course, operational risk, like every risk, has downsides and indeed very large ones; these are the so-called tail risks. The vast majority of operational risk incidents are minor or negligible, but once in a while things go very wrong. The worst operational risk incidents can wipe out a firm, as happened to Barings, Arthur Andersen, MF Global and Knight Capital. Other risks are large enough to cancel more than a year's operating revenues, like the embargo fines of BNP Paribas (18 months of gross revenues lost) and the rogue trading at Société Générale (a loss of one year's operating revenues). There are also reputation risks that are embarrassing enough to stain a firm's image for a very long time, such as the LIBOR rigging scandals at Barclays and elsewhere, the tax evasion scandal at UBS and the fake client accounts at Wells Fargo.

The benefits of operational risk must always be balanced with the potential for damage or even devastation, as in the examples above. Managing risk is like heating a pan of milk: you must keep your eye on it or it will boil over. Or, to use a better analogy, it's like handling a rebellious child. It's not enough to say you won't tolerate a child's bad behavior; you must also educate the child, provide guidelines and boundaries for behavior, and apply appropriate sanctions when required. The next section details how comprehensive risk appetite structures should be tied to exposure limits, controls, KRIs and governance of the firm.

RISK APPETITE STRUCTURE

When defining risk appetite, the natural tendency is to express what we do *not* want. For instance: no major data breach, no incidents causing more than x million of losses, no regulatory breach. What many risk appetite statements fail to specify is *how* to avoid these events. You must link these statements to the corresponding risk management measures and controls, otherwise risk appetite fails in its primary objective: to guide the level of risk-taking and necessary controls within the organization.

Using a funnel analogy, Figure 5.1 expresses the various steps and actions between the strategic objectives of an organization and its tolerance for adverse events. First, the mission and strategy of the organization determine its risk exposure and therefore its inherent risks, either by choice or by constraint. For example, a European bank may choose to expand to the United States and willingly take on the operational risks generated by international growth, such as a different regulatory environment, new labor laws, and increased complexity of processes and communication. For those operating in the U.S., complying with the U.S. legal and regulatory environments is not a matter of choice: it's a given. Risk exposure and inherent risks are therefore a result both of choices and of compliance. Next, to reduce these inherent risks to a level of tolerable loss, the multiple activities of risk management need to take place: preventive controls, allocation of limits, and guidance and policies to limit residual risks (post controls) to an acceptable level for the firm. Then, if accidents happen, you need early detection and rapid reaction using agreed steps to reduce, as far as possible, the net impact of

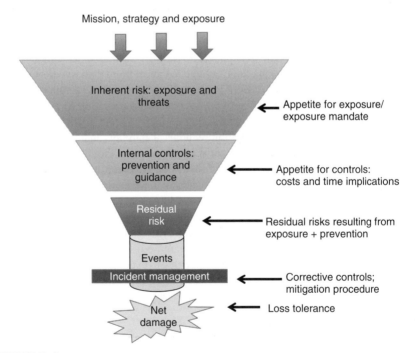

FIGURE 5.1   The risk appetite funnel

events, especially in crisis situations. From NatWest system outages to LIBOR rigging, from systems failures at British Airways to passenger mistreatment by United Airlines, and from Deepwater Horizon to the Grenfell Tower fire, effective crisis management can mean the difference between saving a reputation or seeing it destroyed. Part 3 of this book focuses on the importance of risk mitigation and controls and Chapter 20 explores the interconnections between reputation and resilience.

Turning these funnel steps into a table creates an actionable risk appetite structure – one that is being adopted by the financial organizations with a more mature approach to operational risk management. Figure 5.2 presents the five elements of a comprehensive risk appetite framework.

Risk appetite statements come first, and they are usually qualitative and organized according to risk categories, even if an overarching statement is common at the top level of the firm. Although risk categorization is the usual way of organizing risk appetite, other options are possible, depending on the firm's organizational structure. Some firms articulate their risk appetite through board subcommittees, each loosely related to risk types, which has the benefit of linking directly to the governance structure of the organization. Another example is a clearinghouse that defines its risk appetite around its three main business processes because its activities are organized around those processes, with a different level of risk appetite for each process. Some organizations may prefer to define risk appetite in relation to the main business lines because the line management structure is the dominant one and different risk appetite levels apply to different business lines.

To define their appetite level, some firms have replaced the classic "low – medium – high" by the more colorful "Averse," "Cautious," "Open" and "Seeker"/"Hungry." The latter is reserved for risk types that relate to business revenues, such as credit risk for banks, actuarial risks for insurance companies and investment risks for asset

FIGURE 5.2 Structure of actionable risk appetite

managers. Risk-taking is typically "Averse," "Minimal" or "ALARP"[5] for compliance risk, conduct and fraud, while firms will be "Cautious" for operational risk types such as human errors and system downtime (depending on nature and frequency of activity, however) that may be too costly to reduce to minimal levels.

In the COSO approach,[6] risk tolerance is the quantitative expression of risk appetite but expressing the same level of risk-taking. This is the approach I favor. However, for many firms, tolerance is the higher level of risk-taking accepted in practice, with an amber, buffer-type zone before reaching the forbidden red zone beyond risk appetite and tolerance. In these firms, risk appetite is seen more as an aspirational safety level than a realistic one. This widespread attitude, however, begs the question of the credibility of the risk appetite limits: if you give a higher tolerance, will that become the new norm? Moving goalposts, blurry limits and discrepancies between talk and action have long undermined governance and discipline. There is little room for acceptable deviations in market or credit limits, so why should there be for operational risk? Governance is a necessary condition for effective risk appetite structures, and policies and practices must define what to do and who is accountable for actions when risk limits are breached.

Most importantly, once the appetite and tolerance are stated (they are sometimes merged into one statement), the key controls, or systems of control, are documented to support and validate the statements. Documentation, such as the list of key controls for each main risk type, is particularly useful for demonstrating to internal and external stakeholders, including regulators and clients, that the organization lives up to its objectives. Next, monitoring thresholds and key indicators for control reliability, activity limits and other KRIs should provide management with the relevant information and assurance that the business operates as it should. Direct experience of incidents and near misses, compared with estimates of acceptable limits, reveals whether current actions are appropriate for the frequency and severity of adverse events under the tolerated limits. Monitoring tools and reporting are discussed in Part 4.

Table 5.1. displays examples of risk appetite and tolerance statements in firms I know or have worked with. Elements of the text have been removed to protect the firms' information without affecting understanding. Some firms prefer to merge appetite and tolerance in one statement and express the limits of risk-taking in the controls and key risks indicators. Many will express risk appetite through maximum tolerance for events. However, large banks and mature firms have moved away from that practice and instead express their risk appetite through internal controls to limit certain losses at certain probabilities of occurrence.

---

[5]ALARP: "As Low As Reasonably Practicable" – a concept commonly used in safety systems and in the military, that raises interest among risk managers in the financial industry without still fully picking up.

[6]Understanding and Communicating Risk Appetite, Rittenberg & Martens, COSO White Paper, 2012.

TABLE 5.1   Examples of risk appetite and tolerance statements

Risk appetite statement	Risk tolerance statement
Market infrastructure firm: core business process	
"[The firm] has minimum appetite for any failures occurring in the core [business] process. Systems and controls are designed to ensure that the service offering to our stakeholders continues to be the best in class."	"[The firm] has a zero tolerance for transaction failures and for any incidents affecting the effectiveness and speed of (. . .). [The firm] does not tolerate delays in (. . .) over 60 seconds, and requires immediate processing (. . .). Capacity buffer is monitored and maintained to ensure efficacy in the event of exceptional volume inflows."
Retail bank: conduct & mis-selling risk	
"The bank has no tolerance for intentional breach of conduct in its sales process. Complacency with regards to ethics or customer detriment will be immediately and severely sanctioned. Controls and reward structures are designed in such a way that a systematic breach in the sales process, impacting large numbers of customers, is extremely unlikely. However, the bank accepts that, in isolated cases, conduct breaches may occur. They need to be quickly addressed and the customer compensated."	"Isolated conduct breaches are inevitable in a large retail network employing thousands of agents. The bank accepts the risk as long as it does not involve more than 0.2% of the sales force and that the errors are corrected swiftly. Agents who forced a sale intentionally/fraudulently will be dismissed if the breach was intentional, while those who made unintentional errors will receive remedial training and special monitoring. Affected customers must be fully compensated as soon as the case is identified. Customer complaints must be answered within 24 hours and fully resolved within five working days."
International financial firm: legal & compliance risk	
"[The firm] aims to minimize its legal and compliance risks to the extent possible, in all its business operations and in all its countries of operation. Liability risk must be reduced in all relevant areas via the establishment of appropriate contracts accounting for size, standardization and strategic aspects of a contractual engagement. [The firm] does not tolerate any known deviation from the rules and regulation in place in the countries where it operates. The risk of regulatory breaches occurring due to unexpected changes in legislation is accepted, provided that these breaches are temporary and rapidly remediated."	"Legal and compliance risk in each country of operation is minimized by systematic checks on compliance with the competent authorities. Legal and compliance checks must reach 100% for all significant operations defined as [xx]. Any known deviation must be escalated within five working days and resolved within 20 working days, unless reasonable extensions of remediation delays are requested and approved."

(Continued)

TABLE 5.1   (*Continued*)

Risk appetite statement	Risk tolerance statement
Reputation risk (arising from third party)	
"[The firm] has a very low risk appetite for any reputation damage resulting from unethical or controversial behavior by its suppliers and third-party providers."	"Onboarding procedures and screening controls are set up so that no known deviations to the firm's ethical standard are occurring in the firm's third parties. Any deviation will lead to the dismissal and removal of the third party as quickly as reasonably practicable from one day up to three months. In this period, remediation programs and communication plans with relevant stakeholders will be executed."

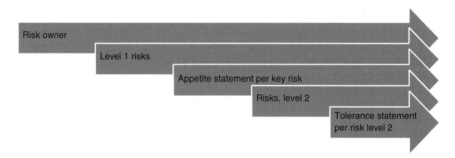

FIGURE 5.3   Risk appetite and tolerance governance structure

Often, however, tolerance levels are expressed more easily at the second level of the risk taxonomy. This is because definitions of level 2 risk are more specific and more adapted to quantitative limits and restrictions. In a number of firms, mature risk appetite structures are similar to the one described in Figure 5.3. Risk owners are designated and risk appetite statements are defined for each level 1 risk, while risk tolerances are defined at level 2 risks and tied to further risk limits and control requirements.

TOP-DOWN AND BOTTOM-UP APPROACHES TO RISK APPETITE

Risk management theory states that risk appetite must be defined top-down, beginning with the board, with risk exposure allocated to the different businesses and translated into the corresponding risk management measures at different levels of the organization. This is the approach described earlier in this chapter and the one recognized by regulators and risk institutes. It mostly applies to the businesses, divisions or risk types that so far have little in place for risk assessment and monitoring.

There is, however, a different, more pragmatic and possibly easier way to define risk appetite: namely, bottom-up. The head of operational risk in an international organization told me once: "Risk appetite is the sum of what you are doing." That's exactly right: while an organization expresses its risk appetite explicitly, its overall actions and safety measures are an implicit reflection of its attitude toward risk. In the same way, some people are naturally more risk-averse than others and their attitude to risk will be revealed in their individual behaviors. Table 5.2 illustrates some of the business requirements for certain top-down risk appetite statements.

Defining risk appetite bottom-up will create risk appetite and tolerance statements that reflect the accepted level of risk-taking in a firm, which can then be observed in its business practices and policies – assuming they are effectively applied and followed, with internal controls, thresholds, and monitoring all in place. This method is particularly useful in well controlled and risk mature environments. I recommend it to mid-size organizations (size complicates bottom-up exercises) that have generally well documented and controlled business operations but find it difficult to describe their risk appetite.

Moreover, comparing the results between a top-down risk appetite statement and bottom-up observations may reveal interesting gaps and, sometimes, wide discrepancies between what senior management say should not be tolerated, and what is really happening within the organization. When I was helping an organization's department heads to define risk appetite limits, one of the heads said: "What are intolerable incidents? Like the one that happened last week?" In organizations like these, either the board risk appetite statements need to be relaxed, or the exposures and controls need to be seriously tightened.

TABLE 5.2 Top-down and bottom-up: the reality checks of risk appetite

Top-down statements	What it should mean in practice in terms of
▪ The organization has no appetite for data breaches ▪ The board will not tolerate any violation of ethics by its personnel ▪ The institution has no appetite for physical security incidents involving its personnel	**Exposure** to the inherent risk: e.g., volume and sensitivity of data handled, number and diversity of staff members, country of operations and business environment **Controls** for that inherent risk: e.g., procedures for data handling and protection procedures, rules of hiring and firing, vetting process, staff supervision and compensation structure, physical security procedures and safeguards Additional **remedial actions** if loss event experience is larger than tolerance

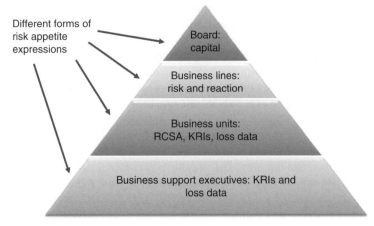

FIGURE 5.4 Alignment of the framework to the different forms of risk appetite expression

TYING RISK APPETITE WITH THE REST OF THE FRAMEWORK

Alongside qualitative statements, risk appetite has different forms of expression within the firm, as illustrated in Figure 5.4. The pyramid summarises some of the findings of an expert group on risk appetite hosted by the Financial Services Authority, the UK regulator at the time. It shows that at board level, the level of capital the firm holds, compared with the minimum regulatory requirements, reflects risk appetite. This is similar to the common concept of *sur-solvency* in insurance companies (see case study).

At business line level, risk appetite is reflected in the actions to be taken by management in the face of certain risks. Risk management tools communicate risk appetite and tolerance within businesses and divisions, and in each risk assessment unit. The risk scales or definitions of risk ratings reflect risk appetite. The colors of the risk and control self-assessment matrix (heatmap), where each combination of impact and probability corresponds to a color representing a risk above risk appetite (amber and red) or within risk appetite (yellow and green), will trigger risk mitigation actions if risk appetite is breached. This common operational risk management tool is presented in the next chapter. Firm-wide KRIs are another expression of a firm's risk appetite. Their selection and thresholds are linked to the level of accepted risk-taking by the organization. Chapter 14 details the concepts, selection and design of KRIs for operational risk. Finally, risk appetite is expressed as a tolerance level for losses. Often, the concept of loss data is extended to the more general case of operational incidents causing non-financial impacts such as business disruption, delays in execution, stakeholders' detriment and reputation damage. Monitoring the level of all these types of impact is another way to both ensure and demonstrate that the firm operates within risk appetite.

At business support level, risk appetite is expressed by bottom-up, process-based KRIs. These indicators are essential in the day-to-day monitoring of the activities. The more essential the activity, the lower the risk appetite and the more numerous and strict the operation's KRIs. These KRIs comprise the body of alerts, flags, thresholds and other monitoring and activity-tracking devices embedded in a firm's systems and processes. Finally, monitoring incident levels that have financial and non-financial impacts, in comparison with tolerated levels, will help to demonstrate whether the organization operates within risk appetite.

CASE STUDY: A FTSE 100 FIRM BOARD-LEVEL RISK APPETITE

[The firm's] available capital remains at all times xx% above its regulatory capital (green level) – it is reported as amber if it falls below that percentage and red if it falls below yy%.

[The firm] aims to protect its brand value at all times by offering the best customer services; each complaint or poor customer experience needs to be remediated fully and as soon as possible.

[The firm] does not tolerate any deviations in ethics by its personnel. All cases will be sanctioned.

Putting it all together, a perfectly consistent framework would look like Figure 5.5. There is an overarching risk appetite statement tied to the firm's strategic priorities and articulated in risk-taking and risk-mitigating actions per risk level 1 of the risk taxonomy. Tolerance levels, corresponding key performance indicators (KPIs), KRIs and control requirements relate to level 2 risk definitions in order to contain potential adverse events within the limits in the RCSA matrix (or heatmap) in terms of couple probability/impacts. The impacts are defined according to the firm's taxonomy, which is usually: financial, regulatory, customer service and reputation.

HOW MUCH IS TOO MUCH?

How can we tell if a firm takes too much risk? An obvious answer is when risk exposure, i.e. the exposure to possible losses, exceeds the firm's capacity to absorb loss. In other words, it would wipe out its capital. It's unlikely, however, that a firm, let alone

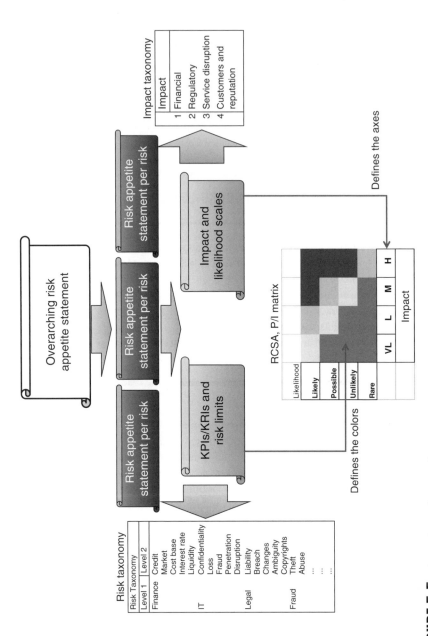

FIGURE 5.5 A consistent framework

a regulated firm such as those in financial services, would willingly take risks beyond its capacity. More common is the lack of risk identification, or rather, lack of proper risk assessment when excessive risk-taking begins. Risk assessments used in risk control and self-assessment (RCSA), scenarios and capital measures are presented in the next three chapters. In addition to failing risk assessment, denial or willful blindness[7] is probably a bigger factor in excessive risk-taking: it takes courage and resolve to face up to risks, which is why many may choose to turn a blind eye and instead hope for the best rather than take action.[8] This human weakness is exacerbated by the contradiction between the short-term objectives (and mandates) of senior management and the long-term effects of operational risks. These effects can take years to materialize, often after the previous management team has moved on, sometimes with bonuses for their apparently profitable (but risky) actions.

Overall, a firm is in danger when a risk is not assessed, when top management has no global view on risk exposure or when business priorities overwhelm risk considerations. In this respect, and anticipating the chapter on KRIs, my top four key risk indicators for operational risk in firms are:

1. Aggressive profit growth targets.
2. Under-investment in infrastructure and people.
3. Regulatory negligence.
4. Top-level wishful risk appetite statements that are not consistently tied to actual controls and limits.

---

[7]See "Willful blindness: why we ignore the obvious at our peril" by Margaret Heffernan (Simon & Schuster, 2011) for brilliant illustrations of human behavior in the face of hard prospects.
[8]"Hope ain't a tactic," Deepwater Horizon, the movie, 2016.

## CHAPTER 6

Risk and Control Self-Assessments

STRUCTURE AND OBJECTIVES OF RCSAS

As the name implies, a risk and control self-assessment exercise is a process by which a business line, an entity or a division known as the risk assessment unit (RAU) evaluates the likelihood and the impact of each significant operational risk it faces.

RCSAs are workshop-style discussions leading to the self-assessment of a unit's main inherent risks and the key controls mitigating those risks and how effective they are. This leaves the unit with only residual risks, given the current control environment. Inherent risks are usually understood as the size of risk exposure before the application of any controls. However, this theoretical definition can appear quite unrealistic to line managers, especially those in highly controlled environments such as IT or finance departments. An alternative and possibly more workable definition is *a risk that could materialize in case of multiple control failures.*

In RCSAs, risks are most often assessed in their two best-known dimensions: probability of occurrence and impact if occurring. Some organizations add the notion of "velocity," which is commonly understood as the speed at which the impacts of a risk materialize in an organization. Velocity may also mean the pace at which a risk evolves in the environment and relates to the concept of risk horizon, i.e. the timeframe in which the risk will become significant for the firm. This is particularly relevant for top-down risk analysis around emerging risks and market trends analysis around the various characteristics of the risk environment: competitive, technological, political, regulatory or criminal. Although velocity and horizon can be relevant in describing and qualifying significant risks to the firm, I believe that the additional complexity they bring to the risk assessment is worth it only for strategic, top-down risk assessment at group level and shouldn't be generalized to all risk assessment units.

There are many variants of RCSA in the industry, such as risk and control assessment (RCA) by an independent party and residual risk self-assessment (RSA). The latter hides the reliance of key controls for large risk exposures, such that risks that are inherently small and others that are small because of heavy control systems are represented the same way. Risk and control assessments are usually qualitative and judgment-based, although some firms demand evidence of control testing before controls can be rated as effective and inherent risks decreased to acceptable levels. Other firms simply rely on the business's word. Mature organizations backtest the results of risk assessment against the incident experience at the end of the period – usually a year; incidents and losses are compared to what had been assessed initially.

RCSA exercises have become a classic in the operational risk manager's toolbox and are now the principal operational risk assessment method for firms. Line managers usually perform RCSAs themselves with support from the risk function. For firms still maturing in risk management, it is advisable for risk managers to help the business run risk assessment workshops and to facilitate debates and reflections. The results of assessments must be documented and submitted to line managers for approval and sign-off. Line managers are responsible for the output and for implementing any actions as a result of the analysis.

Line managers and risk managers should expect the following from RCSA exercises:

1. Key risks exposures (inherent risks): a view of the magnitude of impacts if key controls are missing or failing.
2. An assessment of controls, both preventive and detective, reducing the risk exposures to residual levels.
3. Estimates of the expected losses, i.e. the most likely impacts and likelihood of those risks materializing in normal business conditions and under normal controls (typical case).
4. Estimates of stress shortfalls or stressed losses, i.e. a pessimistic assessment of the impact if the risk materializes in an adverse business environment and/or in case of multiple control failures; this assessment can be closer in impact to inherent risks, but with a lower likelihood (adverse case).
5. A list of further mitigating action plans for the residual risks sitting above risk appetite. This is the central outcome of an RCSA: *Should we do more?* As a risk manager in a very secure technological firm once put it: "Risk assessment is not important; what's important is what we must do."

The key value of risk and control self-assessments is to determine whether the control environment of a given unit or activity is in line with the firm's risk appetite. If the answer is yes, then the actions are simply to keep everything as is and continue monitoring the activity. If the answer is no, there is a need for further risk mitigation in the form of action plans. Risk mitigation does not necessarily mean adding controls; other options are available, such as reducing risk exposure by minimizing transaction volumes, limiting access rights, redesigning or improving existing controls and buying external insurance. Action plans should have business owners, milestones and deadlines. The plans are tracked and reported in a similar way to audit recommendations. Part 3 details the various aspects of risk mitigation.

RCSA exercises are typically performed once a year and updated, in mature firms, after each trigger event, i.e., any significant and relevant change in the firm's risk environment. Most often this will be an incident at a peer firm that changes the perspective on the risk: for example, cyberattacks, a third-party failure, rogue trading or fines for misconduct.

IMPACT AND LIKELIHOOD RATINGS AND ASSESSMENTS

RCSA is a straightforward exercise, using a simple tool. Judgment-based assessments using a heatmap are accessible to almost anyone. However, high-quality output is difficult to achieve for a number of reasons, including subjectivity of judgments, behavioral biases and the inability to compare results. The main challenge is to achieve comparable results, which means making sure that the definitions of likelihood and impacts are calibrated so that "high" risks for some are not considered "low" for others. Without comparable assessments, there is no ordering of risk and hence no proper prioritization of risk management actions.

Defining Impacts

Operational risk events are not limited to financial impacts: remediation time, customer experience, regulatory scrutiny and reputation damage are common by-products of incidents of a breakdown in processes. Most firms nowadays assess risks against four types of impact: financial, regulatory, customer and reputation. A common variant is: financial, regulatory, service delivery, customer and reputation. In the past, most impact ratings used a five-point scale, ranging from "insignificant" to "catastrophic." Today, a four-point scale is more common, with the lowest point from the earlier scale often removed. Indeed, one can question the benefit of spending time, effort and resources assessing risk with "insignificant" impacts. Furthermore, it's debatable whether there is any value at all in using RCSAs for the inevitable small risk events that are part of the cost of doing business. Repetitive and minor losses are "expected losses" and are better included in the cost base and therefore the pricing of an activity.

The impact scales in Figure 6.1 are expressed in relative terms (percentages) rather than in absolute quantities (dollar amount or number of customers impacted), as well as in qualitative terms (limited/significant). Relative definitions are slightly more complex to use, as respondents may not know how much 1% of the budget is in dollars, but they are much more adaptable to risk assessment units of different sizes.

A major point of debate in the RCSA process is indeed whether to use one risk rating scale for the whole firm or to allow for different scales. Keeping the same set of impact ranges for the whole firm will almost inevitably lead to high thresholds being irrelevant for smaller business lines and divisions, except in the smallest organizations.

Rating	Financial	Service delivery	Customers and reputation	Regulatory
Extreme	>25% of yearly budget	Critical service disruption with major impacts to internal and external stakeholders	Significant, possibly long-lasting damage to the firm's reputation and trust toward many stakeholders	Significant compliance breach leading to large fines and regulatory scrutiny
Major	>5–25% of budget	Significant interruption of service leading to crisis management mode internally and customer detriment externally	Large number of customers or stakeholders impacted, to be actively addressed during incident and through post-incident remediation	Compliance breach with or without fines, leading to lasting remediation programs with damage vis-à-vis the regulator
Moderate	>0.5–5% of budget	Noticeable interruption of service but with no significant consequence for stakeholders besides inconvenience	Small reputation impact among limited number of customers and stakeholders, short-lived and addressed during incident management	Some breach or delays in regulatory compliance necessitating immediate remediation but with no lasting impact
Low	<0.5% of yearly budget (profit or cost, depending on type of center)	No interruption of service noticeable to external party	No impact outside of internal parties	Minor administrative compliance breach not impacting the firm's reputation vis-à-vis the regulator

FIGURE 6.1 Impact scale per type

Even in mid-size financial firms, what would be a significant impact at division level might be minor at group level. Similarly, what would be a moderate impact for the group might be an extreme one for a regional office or a department.

Only a small number of firms keep a unique RCSA matrix for the whole firm. Some use just a group-level matrix, which may mean there are not enough relevant risk assessment tools for the business units. Others use a single RCSA matrix that is relevant at the process level, which brings the significant challenge of aggregating hundreds and thousands of granular risks. Unsurprisingly, good practice has evolved towards using different sets of impact scales. Generally there are two: one at group level, collecting the results of a top-down risk assessment, and one for business units. Additionally, in many firms each business unit has the freedom to use its own definitions of impact range, effectively enabling the units to develop customized tools. However, this practice creates mapping challenges when comparing results. The case study at the end of the chapter gives an example of RCSA matrices used in a mid-size insurance company using two ranges of impacts, one at firm level and one at division level. This company will be mentioned in Chapter 17 as well, when reporting on portfolio of projects.

Defining Likelihood

Likelihood scales are most commonly defined in terms of timeframes: "occurring once in x years." Although intuitive and easy to discuss, this definition can be slightly misleading as it actually means: "occurring once if the next year reproduces x times." When risk managers talk about a 1-in-10-year event, they actually mean an event with

Qualitative rating	Frequency of occurrence	Probability of occurrence % (at one-year horizon)	Definition	Guidance
High	1 year or less	>50%	Likely to occur within one year	More likely than not of happening within a year; historical evidence indicates that such event occurs once or more per year
Medium	>1–5 years	10–50%	Likely to occur in the medium term	Likely to occur at least once in a five-year horizon (e.g. strategic plan horizon)
Low	>5–20 years	2.5–10%	Unlikely to occur in normal business circumstances	A remote possibility exists for such an event to occur, less than 10% chance of occurrence within a year
Rare	>20 years	<2.5%	Should not happen, unless very rarely	Very unlikely, may occur in exceptional circumstances. Has not occurred yet in the company but the possibility should be envisaged

FIGURE 6.2   Example of likelihood scale

a 10% chance of occurring next year. It is particularly important to be aware of this distinction when assessing risks that are rapidly evolving, such as cyberattacks, technological changes or regulatory sanctions. Figure 6.2 presents an example of likelihood scales. Here again, the general practice has evolved from a 5-point scale to a 4-point scale. Workshop facilitators should ensure that all participants in the risk assessment use the same definitions, thus avoiding conflicting interpretations when qualifying the risks.

In Practice – Helping with Risk Assessment

Although simple on paper, risk assessment can prove particularly tricky in practice. The two suggestions below might help risk managers to run RCSA workshops. Figure 6.3 is an example of an overall impact scale definition – valid at firm level – aggregating the various possible impacts into a more intuitive definition, and provides parallels from recent market events to help put the assessment in perspective.

On a less serious note, but probably just as revealing, are the responses illustrated in Figure 6.4. A "low" impact would be the equivalent of a shrug of the shoulders ("Whatever . . . let's fix it and move on"). A "moderate" impact would be a major embarrassment but with no major consequence – like the time when, as a young credit risk professional, I accidently deleted hundreds of documents from the department server, destroying hours of some of my colleagues' work. I apologized profusely, IT brought in the overnight backup and things got back to normal within a few hours. Operational risk wasn't even defined in banking in those days, whereas today such an

Extreme	• Impact that could threaten the firm's survival. Exceptionally high impact that should never happen, large enough to trigger a crisis management process. • Market examples: VW pollution testing scandal, JPMC London Whale.
Major	• Doesn't threaten firm's survival, but large enough to trigger immediate top-level attention and involvement, and with long-term consequences in terms of remediation plans. • Market examples: BNPP embargo fines, HSBC AML fines.
Moderate	• Significant impact within the firm, but mostly circumvented to internal effect and limited external impact. Limited or no reputation damage toward the direct stakeholders and regulators. Will trigger internal remediation and action plans if any more than exceptional in occurrence. • Market examples: usually don't hit the press, besides passing embarrassment.
Low	• Big enough to qualify as an incident, but generally accepted as the cost of doing business. To be treated, but without putting current risk management practice into question, as long as it does not reveal a systematic weakness in controls or processes.

FIGURE 6.3   Impact scales – intuitive definitions

FIGURE 6.4   Risk assessment hint: what would be your reaction if it happens?

incident would probably require an action plan for read and write access to server files. A contemporary example would be an employee clicking on the link of a test phishing attempt while having access to highly restricted information. In contrast, a "major" event would trigger immediate alerts to senior management, while an "extreme" event would place the firm in crisis management mode.

In my experience, many risk assessments tend to overestimate impact and to underestimate likelihood. The overestimation of impact comes from the fact that assessors fail to take into account the important role of incident management in reducing net impact. Rapid reaction and effective crisis management plans can do wonders in reducing the actual impacts of material incidents. I will come back to this in Chapter 20.

COMBINING LIKELIHOOD AND IMPACT: THE HEATMAP

The probability/impact matrix, or "P/I matrix," combines two dimensions of risk and is often called the RCSA matrix or heatmap (Figure 6.5). It is, or at least should be, the most tangible expression of a firm's risk appetite. It determines the limits of risk-taking and exposure, and leads to further mitigating actions when residual risks are assessed and land on a map zone that is outside of risk appetite. The various combinations of impact and likelihood correspond to colors that denote the intensity of the risk. The colors most commonly used are red-amber-green or red-amber-yellow-green. Some firms have shades of red, black or even purple for the highest impact and likelihood combinations. Other firms have shades of green for the lowest risks. More rarely, shades of blue are used, sometimes because management is reluctant to use red; the darker the blue, the higher the risk.

Color-coded risk levels

- Green (or equivalent): risk level within risk appetite, no further actions needed besides regular monitoring to ensure activities and controls take place as intended.
- Yellow/amber: risk level still within risk tolerance but approaching excess levels: active monitoring is in progress and further mitigation is possibly required.
- Red (or equivalent): risk level beyond risk appetite and must be subject to a risk mitigation action plan.

Of course, the colors and corresponding risk appetite are fully dependent on the definition of impacts and likelihood on the axes; axes and color should be defined jointly.

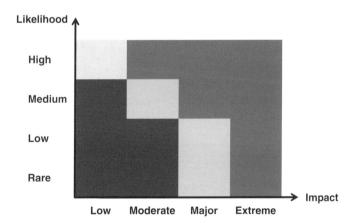

FIGURE 6.5   An operational risk heatmap

Note that only colors or qualitative ratings qualify the risks. A still widespread mistake is to multiply probability and impact to reduce risks to a single numerical quantity. Indeed, a frequent and low-impact risk (1×4) is not the same as a rare event but with extreme impact (4×1). Performing arithmetic on qualitative ratings is inaccurate and can produce misleading results.

Aggregating RCSA results can be challenging, especially when qualitative impact scales are used. This is why some firms have returned to impact scales expressed only in financial terms. Indirect potential impacts on customer experience, regulatory scrutiny and remediation costs are quantified in financial terms and added to the total impact. Part 4 of this book addresses risk-reporting challenges in more detail.

CASE STUDY – A MODERN REPRESENTATION OF RCSA

Figure 6.6 replicates the group RCSA matrix of a mid-size insurance company in Europe. Instead of using similar-size squares or rectangles we decided to represent each rating box with a size roughly proportional to its range. Almost certain events (>50%), the largest frequency, are longer than the second range of likelihood (1/2 to 1/6) and so forth. Similarly, the impact boxes are wider if the ranges of impacts are more severe. The matrix is not exactly to scale, but it gives a better representation of the magnitude of the risk exposures.

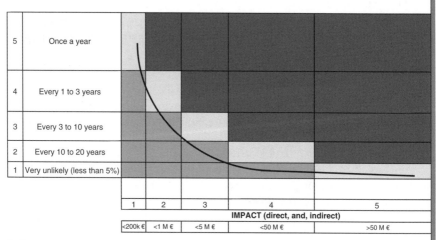

FIGURE 6.6   RCSA – a modern representation

The matrix reflects the risk appetite limits of the company; it even calls it a "risk appetite matrix." We focused on the definitions of the zones within appetite (on or below the curve line and green if using a RAG rating) and outside of appetite (above the curve line and typically red) in need of further mitigation. The "tolerated" areas (on or just above the curve line, often yellow or amber) are limited to one range per type of impact, as they represent the firm's risk tolerance thresholds, where managers have a "neutral" view and they should not be bigger than necessary. Interestingly, this zone appears to follow – closely enough – the shape of operational loss distribution. This type of RCSA matrix shows how opinion-based risk assessments are the qualitative counterpart of quantitative loss distribution modeling. It is also why P/I matrices should always be represented with the likelihood on the vertical axis and the impact on the horizontal axis. Over time, risk assessment based on forecasts should be compared with actual loss experience. In a perfect world, the distribution of loss experience would match, closely enough, the distribution of the risk assessment. However, because we don't live in a perfect world, risk assessments are not very accurate and they will not match loss experience. Even so, it is good practice, at the end of each year, to compare the assessment made with the actual realizations in order to inform the next assessment.

This matrix at group level is complemented, in the firm, by a second matrix, used for risk assessments at department level. In the departmental matrix, the likelihood ranges are unchanged, but the impact ranges are shifted by one notch, the lowest impact range being €50k–200k and the highest being €5 million and above.

LINKS WITH OTHER PARTS OF THE FRAMEWORK

A single point, a single combination of probability and impact, can hardly summarize risk assessment. Each risk can materialize at different degrees of severity and, usually, the larger the impact, the lower the likelihood and vice versa. A simple illustration is system downtime: minor interruptions of a few minutes are almost certain at a one-year horizon, while 1–2 hours are less likely and 2–4 hours shouldn't occur with more than a 5–10% likelihood (sometimes much less, depending on the type of firm and its systems). A shutdown of more than a business day is, for nearly every firm, a rare scenario with extreme impacts. For any risk, there is not one but a multitude of likelihood-impact combinations. To simplify this continuum of options, firms generally use three types of assessments:

1. Mild case of expected loss: incidents resulting from control failure or mishap in normal business conditions.

2. Stressed case: a pessimistic version of possible losses, following key control failure or multiple control failures and/or in adverse business circumstances (accounting error at year-end, system halt in peak time, etc.).

3. Worst case: lower likelihood, but loss as bad as it can get when risk materializes in its extreme version and in particularly adverse business circumstances, or in conjunction with other aggravating factors (for instance, personal data loss on high-profile individuals just after an awareness campaign or with massive social media effect).

Many large institutions assess these three versions of outcomes per risk. Those assessing only one point focus on stressed case. The least mature firms fail to give the business guidance on assessing risks, which creates confusion and disparity in the results and makes them nearly useless. One of the main challenges of RCSA exercises is to make sure that all assessors are using the same types of assessment to produce comparable results. In practice, this is difficult to achieve and requires active involvement from the risk function.

A possible alternative used by some mature institutions is to explicitly link the RCSA matrix to other elements of the risk management framework and in doing so recognize the continuum between the different severity and likelihood levels at which a risk may materialize (Figure 6.7). On the left-hand side of the matrix sit the expected losses (EL); these are the inevitable processing errors, halts and incidents that are always part of the cost of doing business. It is important to identify and quantify these losses so they can be included in pricing, but it is a waste of resources to dedicate time and effort in RCSA workshops to petty incidents. Good risk management is good management. On the right-hand side of the RCSA matrix lie the extreme but hopefully unlikely catastrophic scenarios. While large losses are not rare by nature, they are rare by occurrence because they are usually prevented from happening when the right controls are in place. Scenarios are useful for tail risks identification, crisis

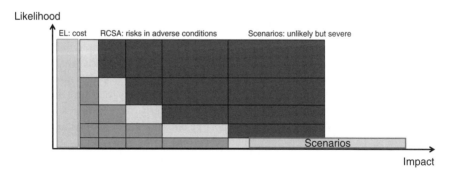

FIGURE 6.7 RCSA and risk continuum

management and continuity planning, own risk and solvency assessment (ORSA) and capital assessment. They can be run in a related exercise, consistent with the findings of the RCSAs. Scenario assessment, ORSA and capital assessment are presented in the next two chapters.

With its left and right borders defined, RCSA positions itself as the happy medium of risk assessment. Like the tale of Goldilocks, our selections are neither too mild nor too severe but sit in the middle. And when you focus on "the stuff in the middle," as a manager put it one day, with full involvement of business partners, risk conversations will deliver great business value.

## CHAPTER 7

Scenario Assessment

Chapter 3 listed the seven steps of a scenario analysis process, from preparation to incorporation into capital, and focused on the first two. This chapter reviews the next three steps: assessment, validation and management lessons. The final two steps – aggregation and incorporation into capital – will be covered in the next chapter.

Scenario assessment is probably the most challenging task in the scenario analysis process. Assessing likelihood is tricky, if not illusory in some instances. Assessing severity needs the rigorous inclusion of business data to avoid exaggerations and distortions affecting the process. Scenario assessment requires a structured and reasoned approach, rooted in the business reality. This chapter reviews different methods financial companies use to assess the likelihood of rare and extreme events impacting their businesses. These methods will be presented from the least sophisticated to the more sophisticated, after presenting the principles of severity and frequency assessment.

SEVERITY ASSESSMENT

The severity assessment of each scenario is the evaluation of the total negative impacts, direct and indirect, financial and non-financial, that the scenario would generate. Non-financial impacts, such as interruption of service, regulatory scrutiny or customer detriment, need to be assessed and converted in financial terms, to ensure a comprehensive assessment of the scenario severity. Direct losses may include money loss, compensation payment, legal expenditures, fines, replacement costs, loss of resources and write-offs. Indirect impacts may include damage to reputation, resulting in loss of customers, loss of funding or higher funding costs. The cost of remediation plans, more intensive regulatory scrutiny and lost or reduced future revenues are other possible indirect impacts of extreme events.

Total impact to assess is the impact after post-event mitigation but before considering external insurance policies. Insurance recovery is an important element of loss mitigation, but it needs to be identified separately. Additionally, insurance policies need to fit certain criteria in order to be recognized by the regulator as a substitute for regulatory capital.

Impact assessment must be linked to the business reality and to the loss drivers in order to be justifiable vis-à-vis both the regulator and management. For instance, where financial impacts are driven by customer loss, they must include, as a minimum, an estimation – or a range of estimates – of the percentage of customers who leave in relation to the range of revenue brought by customers (e.g., from 3% to 10% of customers leaving the firm, bringing revenue to the firm of between $1,500 and $5,000 per year). For a business line serving 100,000 customers, that is a financial impact ranging from $4.5 million (lowest estimate) to $50 million (highest estimate) in lost revenue. This would apply to a scenario where incidents damage the trust customers have in a firm or a product. Different customer value weightings, as well as the likelihood percentage range of customers leaving, can be introduced to these types of estimates to obtain a proper distribution range for possible impacts. This is illustrated in more detail in case studies and examples further in this chapter.

Peer comparisons from loss data provide benchmarks for severity assessment, especially for events when the loss drivers are not as straightforward as the example above, or for events when the firm has no experience of regulatory sanctions or cyber-attacks. Losses from large institutions can be scaled down to suit smaller businesses assessing the scenario. External loss databases can also provide useful benchmarks to assess the frequency – or likelihood – of scenarios.

FREQUENCY ASSESSMENT

Frequency assessment investigates the probability of each scenario happening in the coming year. The one-year horizon for the forecasts aligns the scenario analysis process with the measurement of the economic capital. Probabilities of occurrence can be expressed either in percentages (%) or in fractions (1/200, 1/400 . . .).

In workshop-based assessments, participants are asked to assess the chance of each scenario occurring over the next 12 months, with similar environments for risk conditions. The exercise is updated every year, in light of new events and new experiences, using the same one-year horizon.

Attributing probabilities to rare events is complex. Traditional sampling and past statistical observation are insufficient in this context. Additionally, human minds are not well equipped to distinguish between several low probabilities (1 in 100 can be easily confused with 1 in 500). Therefore, relying on the sole judgment of the scenario assessment workgroup participants may lead to major discrepancies between members, let alone potential large divergence from the true probability. The following subsections are dedicated to techniques to overcome some of these difficulties.

Scenario probabilities will be based, whenever possible, on external statistics and quantitative data. Different types of data can be used, depending on the nature of the scenario. For external events such as natural disasters, pandemics, earthquakes and terrorist attacks, probabilities can be derived from insurance and reinsurance tables. If they are not available, an option is to use the implicit probability in the prices of catastrophe bonds. For scenarios inspired by large events observed in external databases, the frequency assessed can be related to the frequency observed in the external database, or adjusted based on the similarity judgment method. Other scenarios are the worst-case version of the crystallization of risks assessed during the RCSA exercise (see previous chapters). The frequency assessment should then be aligned to the results produced during the RCSA exercise.

RANGE OF SCENARIO ASSESSMENT TECHNIQUES

Regulators are well aware of the difficulty of scenario assessments. Given the important role scenarios play in the measurement of capital for operational risk, it is particularly important to get quantifications as reliable and as justifiable as possible. Regulators request a high level of repeatability for the process used to generate scenario data, through consistent preparation and application of the qualitative and quantitative results. Firms are asked to reduce subjectivity and biases as much as possible in the process. This is achieved by basing assumptions on empirical evidence, explaining the rationale behind the level at which a scenario is analyzed, and maintaining good quality documents on the assumptions and process for delivering scenario assessment.

This section reviews some of the most common techniques used for scenario assessment in financial services. The practice has evolved significantly over the last few years and now offers better, more structured and reliable techniques. For a comprehensive discussion on scenario analysis and assessment techniques, see Hassani (2016).[1]

Expert Judgment

In its most unstructured version, expert-based scenario assessment is limited to interviewing subject matter experts related to the scenario in question. A typical question is: "What would be the worst impact generated by an internal (or external) fraud at a probability of 1 in 40 years? And of 1 in 100 years?" This method is quick and inexpensive. However, results are highly dependent on the selection of experts, and even with the support of preparatory documents, it does little to mitigate behavioral biases in estimation. This method was common in the industry ten years ago, but because it lacks structure and reliability, it is now increasingly less acceptable to regulators and so is fading.

---

[1]Hassani, B. (2016) *Scenario Analysis in Risk Management*, Springer.

Systematic Estimation and Mitigation of Bias

This form of expert analysis uses more structured questions and benchmarks, based on experience and similar events, to help reduce estimation biases. The following cases present examples of assessment biases and how to mitigate them in the context of scenario assessment.

Availability bias and recency bias: this occurs when recent events are perceived as more likely than earlier events. For example, pandemic scenarios proliferated after the bird flu and swine flu outbreaks of recent years; and terrorist attack scenarios were common after 2001, before disappearing from the lists of many institutions and then reappearing in late 2016, after the wave of terror attacks in Europe. To counteract recency bias, it helps to use longer time spans of data, with the length depending on the type of risk environment. Long data spans are appropriate for natural events, destruction of physical assets, pandemics, fraud and other types of stable incident. Fast-evolving risks, particularly technology-based risks such as cyberattacks, will require smaller time spans to be relevant.

Anchoring, confirmation and group polarization bias: anchoring is the tendency to focus on the first piece of information that we encounter (such as a number), anchoring it high or low and allowing it to influence other judgments. Confirmation bias is the tendency to believe anything that confirms our existing views and opinions – a psychological effect used by politicians, marketers and journalists. Group polarization bias appears when people exhibit more extreme views as a group than they would as individuals. History reveals many tragic consequences of this bias. One way of addressing these different biases is to introduce a first round of "silent estimates" amongst participants, so that the first person to comment doesn't anchor the rest of the group's assessments. Workshop participants are asked to answer questions in writing without consulting each other. The answers are then revealed and discussed. During the debate, the workshop facilitator must allow everyone to express and defend their opinion freely, without being dominated by the loudest or most opinionated person in the room. Often, a small group of subject matter experts is better than a large group of semi-informed managers, who can add noise to the estimates. The "wisdom of the crowd" is not recommended in complex topics such as scenario assessments.

Estimation biases are ingrained in human psychology and are unlikely to be completely eliminated. Being aware of our own limitations is an essential step toward mitigating bias. Specific training courses are available in expert elicitation and calibration techniques for those who want to study those questions further.[2] Overall, it is better to support judgment with as much data as is available and to use the right specialists for each scenario.

Delphi Method: Pooling Expert Judgments

The Delphi technique has been used for decades in opinion surveys. It is a relatively easy and inexpensive technique to run and is well suited to scenario assessment. The method has the following steps:

Step 1: Silently collect individual opinions: each expert writes down his/her assessment or answer to a question.

Step 2: Disclose the overall set of estimates to all participants: answers are collated and redistributed to all participants, who can then compare their answers to everyone else's.

Step 3: Participants have the option to reassess their views: each respondent is free to modify his/her answers following disclosure. If the responses have changed significantly, reassessment can be repeated until a greater convergence is reached. However, in the case of operational risk scenarios, I would not recommend forcing convergence. The variety of answers and the levels of disparity or agreement can be informative. Strong agreement, or convergence, may give some comfort about the reliability of the results, while strong disparity may indicate the need for more data and changes to the questions. If there is a single outlier in the group, you should investigate the reasons for the deviation. Perhaps this person is the only expert in the room or is a newcomer (see Figure 7.1).

Step 4: The final estimate is the average value of the responses, weighted by the lowest and highest estimates, that is:

$$\text{Final estimate} = (\text{lowest response } + (n-2) \times \text{average response})$$

$$+ \text{ highest response})/\text{number of participants (n)}$$

Fault Tree Analysis (FTA)

Fault tree analysis is a technique of deductive failure analysis developed in the 1960s. It is used predominantly in safety engineering: high-risk industries such as aerospace,

---

[2]See, for instance, Hubbard Decision Research and the calibration techniques; or for a more academic approach, SHELF, the Sheffield Elicitation Framework by Tony O'Hagan from the University of Sheffield.

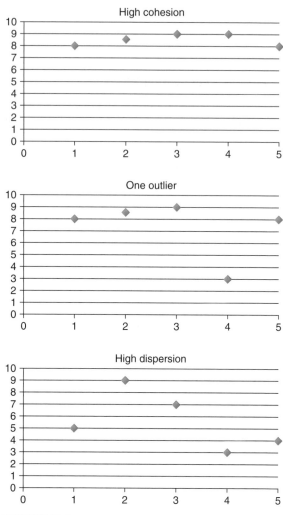

FIGURE 7.1   Delphi study – different configurations of opinions

nuclear energy and pharmaceuticals. Fault trees decompose scenarios into the various conditions (and failures) that need to take place for a disaster to happen. This method, which originally focused on safety failures and control breakdowns, is gradually making its way into the financial sector.

There are many parallels between the series of successive failures that are necessary for a plane to crash, or perhaps a gas to explode, and large accidents that occur in banks, such as internal fraud on large-value transfer ($500 million-plus), successful cyberattacks or sustained systems disruptions. In lax organizations, disasters are not unlikely, they are waiting to happen. Even used in a simplified format, fault tree analysis, in my view, is one of the most fruitful techniques for assessing likelihood of events. Most importantly, it orients debates toward controls, their number, their effectiveness and their mutual interdependence.

When events are fully independent, the probability that they will all happen simultaneously is equal to the product of their individual probabilities of occurrence. This mathematical reality is at the center of layering independent controls in high-reliability organizations (HROs). Consider three independent controls that each fail 10% of the time but are individually sufficient to prevent an incident. The likelihood of the incident happening is the same as the likelihood of the three controls failing at the same time; that is: $10\% \times 10\% \times 10\% = 0.1\%$ or 1/1000. This simple example shows that when protection layers are truly independent, good safety levels can be achieved even with rather weak individual controls.

If applied to the scenario of data theft by an insider, we have, in a simplified setting, four conditions needed for the scenario to take place: (1) a dishonest employee, (2) access to confidential information, (3) the possibility to take a large amount of confidential information, and (4) the ability to sell this information to criminal parties (Figure 7.2).

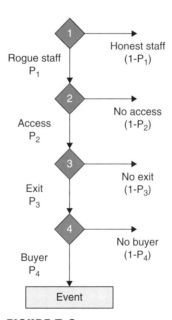

FIGURE 7.2 Criminal selling confidential data: a simple fault tree

In a simple case, let's assume that these four conditions are independent from each other; the likelihood of the scenario is thus the product of the four probabilities of these conditions realizing:

1. Percentage of dishonest employees in organizations: 0.5% (based on expert assessment in developed economies).
2. Percentage of staff having access to confidential data: highly dependent on the firm's business structure and access rights, but high in most financial firms where most information is sensitive and client-related.
3. Percentage of employees able to take large amount of data out of the organization: should be near zero but can be as large as 100% in firms that have not disabled their USB sticks. The monitoring of data outflow and the protection of sensitive data has been a focus for information security in firms in recent years. This in itself is the result of various layers of protection and depends on the type of information considered: a few pages of a strategic plan are much easier to remove than thousands of records of customer data.
4. Likelihood to be able to sell to criminal parties: we can assume that once a fraudster has gone to the trouble of accessing, copying and removing confidential data, it will be passed to a pre-arranged buyer. For many years, I used this example in training to illustrate fault trees and I always assumed that the likelihood of a ready-made sale would be 100%. However, events show that some information may still be stolen to order and some may be stolen opportunistically – for sale on the dark web. In 2017, an international health insurance company revealed that an employee had unlawfully removed more than 500,000 customer data records from one of the company's IT servers. The fraudster advertised the data on the dark web as "singles and bulk data from $25," which meant there was no agreed buyer when the crime was committed (Figure 7.3). However, the dark web provides a market and makes the information available to potential buyers. We do not know, publicly at least, whether the data in this instance has been bought and used. It seems very expensive to charge $25 for a single data record, whereas, as a matter of comparison, a credit card number is worth about 50 cents. I wouldn't be surprised if this fraudster, a rogue employee, failed to sell the data. He did, however, create mayhem for the company, triggered regulatory consequences for the firm and faced criminal charges himself.

Assuming these four conditions remain independent, the simple product of the individual conditions is: 0.5% × 50% (let's assume that 50% of the staff have access to confidential data) × 1% (likelihood to exit multiple confidential records in a context of imperfect controls) × 100% = 0.0025% = 1/40,000 ... per employee (Figure 7.4). The risk exposure is the number of employees in the firm. If it employs over 40,000 people, the expected probability is 1, which the health insurer that found its data on the dark web may now realize. Disasters are not necessarily improbable, but they should

FIGURE 7.3 Dark web advertisement of stolen data (real case, 2017)

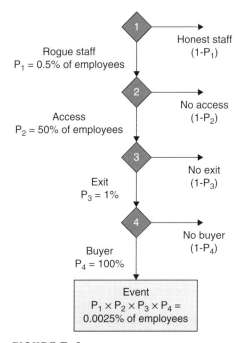

FIGURE 7.4 Likelihood estimation using fault trees

be improbable if appropriate controls are applied. This example also illustrates the importance of risk exposure, often neglected in risk assessment, as highlighted in previous chapters.

Fault Trees and Bayesian Models: Conditional Probability

The example of independent controls and conditions is a simplification for illustrative purposes. A common variation is to consider more realistic cases where control failures and other impact factors are partially dependent on each other. This leads to the use of conditional probability, i.e. the probability of an event occurring, conditional on something else having already occurred, or conditional on some previously unknown information coming to light. In the case of the health insurer, it would be the probability of accessing confidential data, given that the employee has malicious intentions, which is an important piece of information that changes the estimation.

Models using conditional probabilities are often called Bayesian models, or even Bayesian network, after Reverend Thomas Bayes (1702–1761), an English statistician and philosopher who gave his name to the Bayes theorem. The theorem provides the formula to determine conditional probability. Bayesian models in operational risk refer to measurements where likelihood assessments are updated by new expert opinions or because of new information.

Overall, I would recommend FTA or any of its variations for scenario assessment in order to generate meaningful discussions on the causes, preventive barriers and necessary conditions for extreme events. Of course, like every model, the results of FTA depend directly on the different faults identified and the probabilities attributed to each of them. However, breaking down scenario estimates into their different components of likelihood and impact increases the robustness of the results as well and the transparency of the process leading to those results.

Scenario analysis and assessment of extreme events are vast topics that go beyond the scope of this book. For more detailed discussions, please see the books and studies referenced in this chapter. The additional case study, inspired from real scenario assessment as part of an Internal Capital Adequacy Assessment Process (ICAAP) project, sheds more light on best practice scenario assessment techniques.

CASE STUDY: SCENARIO ASSESSMENT AT AN INVESTMENT FIRM

This firm needed to self-assess the capital required to cover its operational losses at 99.9% reliability. We used a scenario-based method and quantified each relevant scenario. Each scenario is decomposed into its risk drivers by the relevant business and risk specialists. Each risk driver is quantified, using a range of values and estimation of probabilities of all of these values. The method delivers a simple distribution of values for each scenario. The value around the 99.9th centile is the upper range of the capital need for a scenario.

Quantification detail – platform outage

The firm has an online trading platform and platform outage is probably the first operational risk scenario that comes to mind. A 30-minute outage is a relevant internal incident, while the worst-case scenario is evaluated at four hours by the IT team, with the firm reverting operations to the U.S. if its European data centers are both down.

Within a year, a third back-up center will be fully operational and the maximum outage time will be reduced to one hour. Further details on the management response to such a scenario and other extreme events are contained in the firm's disaster recovery plan. Complete policies and procedures are available to the regulator and relevant third parties upon request.

As mitigating action during an outage, customer detriment is reduced as the firm provides alternative ways for trading during an outage, such as conversations via email or telephone. The ability to trade is not interrupted, but is made less convenient. Clients may go dormant for a while but eventually come back. Permanent account closures are rare, as revealed by monitoring client numbers. The firm is insured externally against incidents related to platform outage. The cost of a previous event was claimed and reimbursed by the insurer. The table below presents the value range for each component of impact, associated with its probability of occurrence (numbers have been modified to protect the client's information).

Joint probability of occurrence indicates the likelihood of the loss, either direct or indirect. Results presented in columns combine all the low, medium, high and worst cases. A full distribution of the result can be obtained by running various combinations of low, medium and high versions of each driver, to generate a full distribution of scenarios. This is useful in capital modeling and is covered in the next chapter. The worst case is out of range since its likelihood is much lower than 0.1%. The relevant capital amount to cover from a scenario outage is around $32 million or just above.

This case is a simple, discrete, arithmetic case to estimate key points of what is in reality a continuous distribution of possible outcome. The continuous version can be easily achieved by running Monte Carlo simulations on the range of parameters. It can be run on Excel, using a program add-on, and requires some simple coding (Table 7.1).

(Continued)

TABLE 7.1   Running Monte Carlo simulations on Excel

Platform Outage Parameter of losses		L	M	H	Worst case
# minutes downtime	value (minutes)	5	30	120	240
	probability	60%	35%	3%	2%
revenue per minute	value ($/min)	100	300	500	750
	probability	20%	60%	15%	5%
Direct financial loss	**value ($)**	**500**	**9,000**	**60,000**	**180,000**
	Joint probability	12%	21%	0.5%	0.1%
number of clients active	value	12,000	16,000	40,000	60,000
	probability	25%	65%	9%	1%
% disgruntled clients	value (%)	5%	10%	20%	30%
	probability	50%	25%	20%	5%
revenue per client	value (S)	1,500	2,000	4,000	6,000
	probability	25%	60%	10%	5%
Indirect financial loss	**USD**	**900,000**	**3,200,000**	**32,000,000**	**108,000,000**
	Joint probability	3.13%	9.75%	0.18%	0.0025%

SCENARIO DOCUMENTATION AND VALIDATION

Scenario Sheet

The entire scenario analysis process and the methods used must be documented and explained in sufficient detail for the size and complexity of the business. Furthermore, each scenario should ideally be presented in a summary sheet that contains the title, description, rationale, assessment range and relevant internal and external incidents for the given scenario. Formats vary between firms but the nature of information presented is relatively similar in every organization (Table 7.2). Standard templates can help ensure that no item is missed and facilitate comparison and validation of the results.

TABLE 7.2 Common fields in scenario sheet

1. Admin: Owner, risk category, date
2. Scenario storyline
3. Relevant internal and external incidents and events
4. Assessment of relevant controls
5. Assessments of impacts, with rationale, for:
▪ **Assumptions (modeling approach, parameters chosen)**
▪ **Probabilities**
▪ **Range of impacts, direct and indirect (e.g. compensation to customers, fines and penalties, mark-to-market losses)**
6. Intangible impacts
7. Economic sensitivities – to be used for stress testing
8. Remedial actions, if the assessment results lie above risk appetite

Validation

After the assessment process, scenario lists and assessment values need to be reviewed and validated internally by independent parties. The validation team assesses the method and the consistency of the process that has led to the definition of scenarios, as well as their relevance to the risk and control environment of the business entity to which the scenarios relate. The function and size of the validation team depends on the size of the firm. Typically it will be the CRO in small firms, members of a central risk management function that has not led the process, or internal auditors. Sometimes an external validation is sought through an independent panel or a third party such as consultants.

The validation process is mostly based on the documentation from the scenario identification and assessment workshop, the documentation of the process and methodology used, and the results of the assessments.

Scenario Consolidation Based on Common Impact

When appropriate, scenarios with similar consequences can be merged into one and treated and assessed as such, especially for scenarios due to external events. The consequences of damage to an office building, for instance, can be treated the same way and be part of the same scenario whether the damage or collapse is caused by a terrorist attack, an earthquake or any other reason. Here, the severity assessment is the same regardless of the cause, and the assessed probability will be the sum of the probabilities of occurrence related to each cause (terrorist attack + earthquake + default in construction + etc.). Similarly, scenarios leading to IT systems disruptions can be grouped together whatever their cause: power surge, water leaks, roof collapse, internal failure, etc.

After selection, assessment and possibly grouping, the remaining list of scenarios should contain around 50 scenarios for very large institutions, 15 for mid-size firms and 6–10 for small businesses. The final approved list of scenarios will then be presented to senior executives and to the board or its risk committee for a final review and sign-off.

MANAGEMENT LESSONS FROM SCENARIO ANALYSIS

Scenario analysis is more about potential response and mitigation than exact probability. Grouping scenarios per type of consequence for the organization helps to focus on impact assessment and mitigation actions, as the ultimate objective of scenario analysis is to safeguard the organization.

If scenario analysis reveals breaches in the control environment or a risk level beyond the firm's comfort zone – in other words, its risk appetite – then scenario findings must lead to action plans for further mitigation.

If the results of scenario assessment are within the limits of the firm's risk appetite, then no further action is needed, except to make sure the situation doesn't change and to react if it does. Overall, even if the scenario seems unlikely, firms must have a planned reaction and mitigation. Part 3 presents internal controls, risk mitigation and action plans in more detail.

## CHAPTER 8

Regulatory Capital and Modeling

REGULATORY CAPITAL: RATIONALE AND HISTORY IN A NUTSHELL

Financial companies, like households and every economic agent, have two sources of funding: capital, also referred to as *own funds*, and debt. Bank debts are essentially made of retail deposits – the current and savings accounts familiar to most people. As with every economic agent, revenues generated on the asset side repay debts. If the activity slows down, revenues dry up, or if losses incurred are too large, assets are not enough to repay the debts. In the case of a bank, it is unable to repay people's deposits. Banks need own funds, or capital, to make sure that they can absorb whatever losses they may face without defaulting on their debt obligations on the liability side and disrupting the loan market and the financial market on the asset side, with terrible systemic consequences for the economy.

Since the Great Depression, which led to an estimated 15% drop in the US gross domestic product (GDP) between 1929 and 1932, government and public regulatory authorities have developed rules and regulations to restrict and monitor the activities of banks. The most important measure was the Glass-Steagall Act, separating commercial and investment banking. In particular, banks were forbidden to simultaneously lend and hold shares in the same company, in order to avoid conflict of interest and over-lending. In 1974, following serious disturbances in the banking market, notably the failure of the German bank Herstatt, a further supervisory step was taken when the Basel Committee was established by the central bank governors of the Group of Ten countries. Its first measures laid the principles for supervision of foreign banks by host countries and cooperation between banking authorities (Basel Concordat, 1975). In 1988, Basel I recommended a minimum level of capital to cover losses due to credit risk (the Cooke ratio at 8% of the risk-weighted assets). This was widened in 1996 to include market risk, followed in 2002 by operational risk.

Regulatory capital for operational risks therefore appeared for the first time in 2002, under the terms of Basel II. The reform introduced a three-pillars approach to banking regulation, going beyond the simple need for capital. Basel II became law in the European Community in 2007 and applies to all financial institutions. In the U.S., Basel II was mandatory for internationally active banks only, later on to be called systemically important financial institutions (SIFIs). The three pillars of the Basel regulation are as follows:

- Pillar 1: Regulatory capital: mandatory minimum level of capital to cover credit, market and operational risks.
  - For operational risk, additional managerial recommendations come in the form of the "Sound Principles for the Management of Operational Risk" (2003, updated in 2011 and 2014).
- Pillar 2: Supervisory review process (known currently as SREP): adjustments to the pillar 1 requirements based on the specific risk profile of an institution, its activities and the quality of its risk management, as assessed by the regulator and by the firm itself.
  - Over the years and especially since the crisis, this has resulted in capital add-ons, sometimes substantial.
- Pillar 3: Market discipline: body of rules on mandatory information disclosures yearly or quarterly by financial institutions regarding the financial situation and risk information.
  - The initial idea of pillar 3 was that the publication of certain financial and risk information would encourage market discipline, whereby shareholders of firms more exposed to risk would require the firms to hold more capital to compensate for the increased level of risk. It never quite worked as intended.

In the early 2000s the rule of thumb was that operational risk capital should represent 12% of the total capital held by the bank, the remaining 88% being covered by credit and market risk capital. Why 12%? Cynics like me will note that this percentage corresponds roughly to the expected drop in the credit risk capital introduced by the Basel II reform with the new diversification effect allowed in credit risk portfolio (a similar diversification effect was applied to subprime portfolios a few years later ...). With the market risk rules remaining unchanged, this led to a simple substitution effect between credit risk capital (down 12%) and operational risk capital (up 12%), but no increase in the solvency level of the sector. It made sense because according to some pressure groups, the Basel Committee at the time committed not to increase the regulatory capital requirements.

Although the rules for capital were strictly observed when implemented in the early 1990s, they weakened over time. Coverage became stretched and exceptions more common. Because the rules were not legally binding, each country applied them as it saw fit in its own jurisdiction.

The financial crisis of 2007/2008 was a painful reminder of what bank failures were like during the Great Depression. Several macroeconomic factors led to the recent financial crisis, such as the repeal of the Glass-Steagall Act in 1999 followed by a wave of other deregulations; the proliferation of new and misunderstood financial products, especially credit derivatives and synthetic derivatives linked to depleted underlying assets (the subprime loans); and, finally, the development of new and particularly ill-conceived accounting rules called the IFRS Standards. The rules required banks to mark-to-market their balance sheets, creating unnecessary volatility in the banks' valuations and forcing them to recapitalize in most adverse market conditions. The IFRS Standards created a terribly damaging pro-cyclical effect and were an underrated guilty party in the financial crisis.

The history, merits and flaws of banking regulation go beyond the scope of this book, but I encourage the interested reader to further explore the topic in order to understand the macro dynamics of banking activity, which are driven in part – possibly in large part – by reactions to regulatory rules and trends.

The crisis led to the reforms in Basel III but left operational risk rules untouched. Since 2015, the Basel Committee has been working on a reform of pillar 1 capital for operational risk. The standardized measurement approach (SMA) proposals have generated numerous debates and criticisms since the first consultative document was published in March 2016. I did not hide my reservations about the approach, which I expressed in several articles published with like-minded peers.[1] Even though the Basel Committee published in December 2017 the final regulatory revision including the new SMA regime, this one remains the object of intense industry debates between proponents and opponents. The SMA is a revised version of the standardized approach, where regulatory capital for operational risk is equivalent to a percentage of the firm's gross income plus an optional penalty – down to national regulators – for firms with a history of losses larger than the industry average.

Regardless of the reform, financial companies, especially the large ones, still need to assess, measure and model their capital requirements for operational risk. This chapter reviews the current structure of the regulatory capital requirements and some of the essential concepts and practices of operational risk capital modeling.

PILLAR 1 – REGULATORY CAPITAL FOR OPERATIONAL RISK

Standardized Approach

In standardized approaches, regulatory capital for operational risk is only determined by the average yearly gross income of the institution over the last three years, recognizing the loosely positive relationship between operational risk and size. Gross income is defined as the sum of the interest margin (interest received minus interest earned), the fee income and other revenues.

---

[1] The articles have been published as a collection in part 6 of the book *Reflections on Operational Risk Management*, A. Chapelle, Risk Books, 2017.

TABLE 8.1   Beta factors in the standardized approach

Business line	Beta factor
Corporate finance	18%
Trading and sales	18%
Retail banking	12%
Commercial banking	15%
Payment and settlement	18%
Agency services	15%
Asset management	12%
Retail brokerage	12%

In the basic indicator approach (BIA), the regulatory capital for operational risk is equal to 15% (called the alpha factor) of the gross income. BIA is allowed for local banks only.

In the standardized approach (TSA), the regulatory capital for operational risk is equal to the gross income of each business line, in direct proportion of a beta factor, where β is equal to 12%, 15% and 18% depending on the expected operational risk level of the business lines (Table 8.1).

These beta values were calibrated in the late 1990s through quantitative impact studies (QIS) of just 29 participating institutions, a sample that is hardly representative of today's banking world, two decades later. The increasing irrelevance of pillar 1 rules for operational risk justifies the increasing attention dedicated to pillar 2 by regulators worldwide. However, since the beginning, regulators have recognized the shortcomings of a sole regulatory capital to cover operational risks: no amount of capital can be enough to cover the losses generated by disasters due to operational failures in the absence of sound management. Unlike credit and market risk regulation, principles for sound management of operational risk are included in pillar 1, alongside the rules of regulatory capital. Good operational risk management is mandatory – not optional.

Principles for the Sound Management of Operational Risk

The principles were introduced in 2003 and revised in 2011 to incorporate lessons from the financial crisis. The last revision of the document, "Principles for the Sound Management of Operational Risk," published in October 2014, presents the results of a benchmarking exercise where 62 participating institutions rated their own compliance with 149 statements relating to the 11 principles of sound management

TABLE 8.2 Principles for the sound management of operational risk

Principle 1: Operational risk culture
Principle 2: Operational risk management framework
Principle 3: Board of directors
Principle 4: Operational risk appetite and tolerance
Principle 5: Senior management
Principle 6: Risk identification and assessment
Principle 7: Change management
Principle 8: Monitoring and reporting
Principle 9: Control and mitigation
Principle 10: Business resilience and continuity
Principle 11: Role of disclosure

(Table 8.2). For each principle, the supervisory authorities express their expectations on what represents "good." The document, free to download from the BIS website, is recommended reading for all operational risk professionals.

Advanced Measurement Approach (AMA)

In advanced measurement approaches for banks and internal modeling approaches (IMAs) for insurance companies, financial institutions are free to assess their own capital needs, provided that the regulatory authority of each country in which the firm is incorporated accepts their model. Using internal models, banks assess the level of capital sufficient to cover all possible operational losses up to a 99.9% confidence interval at a one-year horizon. In other words, they should cover for an amount of yearly losses up to the 999th worst year for losses, out of 1,000 years of simulation.

Internal modeling can result in lower capital requirements for the bank or the insurance company, compared with the standardized approach. Originally, the Basel Committee limited the capital reduction to 75% of what the standardized level would be. However, to my knowledge, no institution ever achieved savings anywhere near that magnitude; in fact, quite the opposite: many banks calculated higher capital levels with their own models compared with a standardized approach, which persuaded some not to apply for AMA. The intended motivation for AMA therefore fell through and it has never been adopted as widely as the supervisors initially hoped.

Most AMA adoptions came in the early days of the regulation and from European countries: France, Italy, Germany, the Netherlands and Belgium. Obtaining an

AMA approval takes on average three years to prepare, requires internal and external validation by independent parties and the fulfilment of around 30 criteria, both qualitative and quantitative. The criteria include:

- incident reporting history of five years (now ten years in the reform drafts)
- mapping of risks and losses to regulatory categories
- independent operational risk management function
- implication of the senior management in risk management
- written policies and procedures
- active day-to-day operational risk management.

Since the first publication of AMA rules by the Basel Committee, regulators around the world have published guidance documents on the models to be used and on the implementation of management principles and lessons learned from the models (use test). Interested readers in the U.S. should consult Fed and OCC publications, while readers in Europe should refer to the texts of the European Banking Authority (EBA) and the various national regulators.

The objective of advanced approaches for operational risk capital measurement is to have regulatory capital that fairly and honestly reflects the risk profile of the financial institution. Four types of input are required to build a qualifying model:

- internal loss data (ILD)
- external data (ED)
- scenario data (SD)
- business environment and internal control factors (BEICF).

Internal Loss Data Experience of internal events, incidents, losses and near misses is at the center of the institutional knowledge of operational risk and is the first step to improve the status quo. Internal loss data collection is essential because it provides management with information on past losses and future trends. If repetitive, losses can indicate control breaches and internal failures that could potentially lead to larger losses. Repeated losses that are inherently small due to reduced exposure or effective process controls can be included in pricing as the cost of doing business. From a statistical standpoint, internal loss recordings provide many data points for modeling the distribution, especially the "body" of the distribution, where frequency is high and losses are moderate. Comprehensive incident databases provide useful information on risk and control environments that can inform causal models, i.e., risk models based on causes of failures, and deliver parameters for scenario analysis and assessment.

From Internal Database to Calculation Dataset There is, however, a difference between the internal incident database maintained by the risk management department and the calculation dataset used by modelers; each institution must establish rules and rationales for when to include incidents in the calculation dataset, particularly for special cases such as near misses, accidental gains and rapidly recovered losses. The most conservative institutions will include those events both in frequency and in severity, considering the absolute value or potential loss as the severity. Others will include them in frequency but with zero severity, and some will simply exclude those records from the calculations and modeling. Other elements of data quality such as classification of events, risk categories, business lines, dates and amounts are obviously critical for the reliability of the model results.

However, the loss history of a single institution is not sufficient to reflect the full range of event possibilities and outcomes that might affect the institution; it needs to be supplemented by external data from incidents at peer organizations or in related industries.

External Data Loss data and event details from external parties are sourced from databases that gather public information on operational incidents, such as IBM Algo FIRST and Factiva. Industry associations and membership organizations also collect loss data information from members and share it anonymously with every member. ORX is the largest and oldest one, established in 2002, and has collected upwards of 600,000 incidents from 12 members initially, to nearly 100 members in 2018 – mostly international banks and insurance companies. ORIC International, founded in 2005, is the leading operational risk consortium for the (re)insurance and asset management sector globally. When choosing external sources to complement internal data, a firm considers many elements to ensure that the external losses come from comparable peers. They include geographical distribution of activities; sector or business lines concentration; length of data series by event type; the data classification and certification rule for data quality; the number, types and size of members; and the reporting threshold for incidents in the database. Information versus abundance is the tradeoff modelers face when choosing external datasets. Databases collecting publicly known operational risk events provide full information about the institution involved in each event, allowing you to compare contexts and judge the relevance of each event for the modeling firm. But they are less numerous than membership databases, which makes it statistically harder to model incidents. Although abundant, membership databases are anonymous and have very little information about each event.

Mixing internal and external loss data, for the calculation dataset that will be used to calibrate the models, requires several methodological decisions that may significantly influence the end results. There is extensive academic literature on this topic, with detailed discussions that go beyond the scope of this book. However, it is important for risk managers to be aware of the following three practices and to be able to discuss them with modelers:

- Scaling: the adjustment for the size of losses to the size of the institution, or to other dimensions. A loss recorded in a large international bank can be scaled down to fit a smaller national bank, for instance proportionally to the size of the institution. Other types of scaling include the correction for inflation if data span many years.

■ Cut-off mix: refers to the stage at which external data are included in the model; typically at a severity level where internal data become scarcer and more data points are needed to estimate a distribution, i.e., for larger losses.

■ Filtering: relates to the type of peer losses that will be filtered in or out of the calculation set of the modeling institution. Regulators require clear rules to be set for the selection of data in order to avoid "cherry picking" and manipulation of results.

Scenarios Operational risk disasters, whether due to systems failures or disruptions, cyber-attacks, physical damage or compliance breaches, have the potential to wipe out years of revenues, significantly damage reputation and damage the firm's long-term earning capabilities. Scenario analysis plays the important role of requiring organizations to consider the prospect of such disasters, which may never have happened to them before, or to their peers, and to assess their resilience if such disasters should occur. For modeling purposes, scenario analysis provides an important input to the tail of the distribution and an effective benchmark to judge the sufficiency of capital. To management, it provides information about the organization's large exposures, possible vulnerabilities and the necessary level of preventive controls and mitigating measures. Scenario analysis is detailed in the previous chapter.

Business Environment and Internal Control Factors Regulators require that operational risk models include updated BEICF regions/countries of operation, regulatory context, changes in the competitive landscape and level of external criminality. They also require information on the internal control environment, such as the design and effectiveness of controls, automated versus manual processes, evidence of control testing, and training and governance. The influence of BEICF is usually included in the model through RCSA results and scenario analysis. Regrettably, however, the AMA input still has the least explicit role in operational risk modeling, even though business environment and internal controls are two of the main drivers of operational risk.

CASE STUDY: MODEL STRUCTURE OF AN AMA BANK IN EUROPE

An AMA bank in Europe has been generous enough to share with me the details of its operational risk model methodology. Four national regulators have approved this model where the bank is supervised in Europe and overseas. The model explicitly includes the four inputs required by AMA, as illustrated in Figure 8.1. Two different statistical distributions are used to calibrate the body and the tail of the loss distribution. Overall, simplicity and transparency have been favored over mathematical complexity, which has the benefit of increasing model stability. The model also traces each contribution: every loss event, every scenario, has an identifiable impact on the resulting capital number. This remarkable traceability makes the model better accepted and actionable by the business.

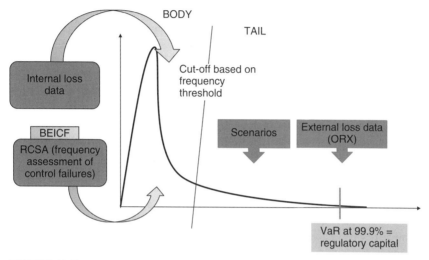

FIGURE 8.1   Model structure of an AMA bank
Source: Chapelle, A. University College London, 2015.

Types of Models

Over the years, four types of models have evolved: stochastic, scenario-based, hybrid and factor-based. Unfortunately, the last one is still in its infancy.

Stochastic Models   These models are part of the loss distribution approach (LDA); they are purely quantitative and based on past losses. Statistical techniques are used to extrapolate to a 99.9% percentile the future distribution of losses. LDA is the most widespread approach and is now increasingly mixed with scenario-based data.

Scenario-based Models   Models using scenario assessment were described in the previous chapter and are more qualitative. They are usually found in firms where the lack of internal loss data prevents the use of stochastic modeling. Scenario-based models tend to be more common in Europe and in the insurance industry, where collecting loss data is not as established as in banking.

Hybrid Models Hybrid models are currently the most common type of approach, and more in line with regulatory expectations and the four inputs for AMA model requirements. Hybrid models use a combination of data distributions from past incidents and prospective losses from scenarios to derive information operational losses distributions at a 99.9% confidence interval. Hybrid models are capital calculations based on incident data, with adjustments to account for scenarios and for risk management quality.

Factor Models Factor models explain the behavior of a variable from the values taken by its various influencing factors. They are common in equity pricing: stock market returns are predicted based on factors such as the risk of the asset (Capital Asset Pricing Model), the size of the firm and its level of financial distress (Fama–French), and the momentum of the price movement, upward or downward (Carhart). In 2000, during the early days of operational risk modeling, factor modeling was one of the possible paths for operational risk models: to determine operational risk losses by explaining their variables (size of the firm, economic context, internal controls, governance, culture, remuneration structures, etc.). A few academic studies were published, but the nascent trend was quickly overtaken by the LDA and the swathes of past loss data that were thrown at the issue. Additionally, the scarcity of data related to internal control, environment, governance and culture, less straightforward to capture, increased the difficulty of calibrating factor-based models. Personally I regret this turn of events. The current overall lack of stability and confidence in the operational risk models is certainly an argument for a fundamental revision of operational risk modeling methods.

Loss Distribution Approach in a Nutshell

Modeling activities require a lot of observation data points. Models are a simplified, theoretical representation of the reality, built on repeated observations to derive stable patterns and common laws governing the data observed.

When regulators decided to require banks to hold capital for operational risk, data on incidents were barely collected – except for external fraud – and so were particularly scarce. To increase the number of data points at their disposal to fit statistical distributions, modelers called upon an old actuarial technique: the LDA. The principle is to decompose risk events into two of their components: how often they occur (frequency) and how much they cost (severity). By decomposing a single event into its frequency and severity, it multiplies by two the number of observation points available for modeling. Modelers at the French bank Credit Lyonnais published a seminal paper[2] on applying LDA to operational risk and the approach has now become common practice.

---

[2]Frachot, A., Georges, P. and Roncalli, T. (2001) "Loss distribution approach for operational risk," Group Recherche Operationel Credit Lyonnais France, Working Paper.

Frequency and severity can be defined as follows:

■ Frequency: discrete distribution, counting the number of operational risk events per period of time, typically one year. Frequency in operational risk is most commonly modeled by a Poisson distribution. Poisson is the simplest frequency distribution, determined by a single parameter, λ that represents both the mean and the variance of the distribution. According to the Loss Data Collection Exercise of the Basel Committee in the last decade (2008), nine out of ten AMA firms model frequency with a Poisson distribution. Negative binomial distributions are usually a better fit and are used in about 10% of the cases.
■ Severity: continuous distribution, asymmetric and heavy tailed, to account for the dual nature of operational risk: a large number of small losses and a few very large incidents. The most common distribution used to model severity is the lognormal distribution, a log transformation of the normal distribution (Gaussian). More heavy-tailed distributions have been increasingly used over the years, in particular Weibull and generalized pareto distributions (GPD).

Frequency and severity distributions are then convoluted into an aggregated loss distribution, illustrated in Figure 8.2. The most common convolution method is Monte Carlo, where the aggregated distribution is generated by a million (or more) random draws of severity and frequency. Other methods such as fast Fourier transform and Panjer recursions are equation-based, requiring more coding and mathematical ability but less computer time. For the best and most detailed review of statistical techniques and recommended practices in operational risk modeling, please refer to Peters et al.[3]

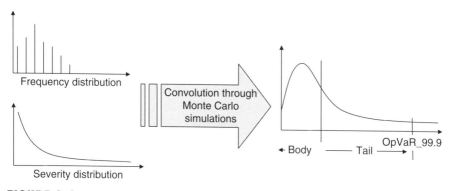

FIGURE 8.2 Frequency and severity aggregation – illustration

---

[3]Peters, G., Shevchenko, P. and Cruz, M. (2015) *Fundamental Aspects of Operational and Insurance Analytics: A Handbook for Operational Risk*, Wiley.

The LDA process is applied to each unit of measure (cluster of losses) that will then be aggregated into a total distribution where the 99.9th centile will correspond to the stand-alone capital for operational risk.

Units of Measure

The heterogeneous nature of operational risk events is a definite challenge for modeling and reporting activities. For modeling, a solution is to group events data into clusters of some homogeneity, called units of measure (UoMs). As an illustration, let's consider the following combinations of event types and business lines as possible UoMs:

- External fraud events, split by individual business line.
- Damage to physical assets events, grouped for all business lines.
- Internal fraud events, per business entity (under the same senior management and supervision).
- Processing error events, split by individual business line.

Good UoMs constitute clusters of fairly homogenous operational risk events, driven by the same types of factors and therefore having a similar dynamic and a similar distribution. There is a tradeoff, though, between the homogeneity of the data sets defined and data availability: finer segmentation leads to more homogenous data and more granular models, but it also reduces the amount of data available to estimate the models, leading to greater uncertainty in the results and increased complexity in the aggregation process.

Each UoM is modeled separately and aggregated into a standalone capital for operational risk. The choice of UoM thus has important consequences for the model dependency structure and results. It is, unsurprisingly, the object of attention for model validation teams and regulators alike. In principle, modelers should demonstrate that the units of measures follow the way the business is organized and in line with the final use of the model. This intra-risk aggregation of UoM into operational risk capital most commonly uses copula techniques, as required by the regulator. Copulas are generalizations of correlations and can be used to model advanced dependency structures, including tail dependence and dependence between extreme values.

PILLAR 2 – SUPERVISORY REVIEW PROCESS

SREP, ICAAP and CCAR

The SREP enables the regulator to evaluate risks to which the firm is or might be exposed and assesses the risks that the firm may pose to the financial system, should the firm fail. The regulator also evaluates the measures taken by the firm to identify, assess and mitigate risks. In particular, it will "review the arrangements, strategies, processes and mechanisms implemented by a firm to comply with its regulatory requirements" (Prudential Regulation Authority, supervisory statement 31/15), taking into account the nature, scale and complexity of a firm's activities. Finally, it will evaluate any further risks revealed by stress testing.

As part of a SREP, regulators evaluate the sufficiency of the firm's capital to cover its risk. Common across the U.S. and Europe, the evaluation has different names and varies depending on the realities and processes in each geography and each industry:

- In Europe, the evaluation of capital sufficiency for banks and financial firms is called ICAAP (internal capital adequacy assessment process).
- In the insurance industry, it is called ORSA (own risk and solvency assessment).
- In the U.S., the process is CCAR (comprehensive capital analysis and review).

For all risks, operational or otherwise, the solvency assessment of a financial firm requires the identification of key threats and scenarios for large loss events, and the assessment of the firm's resilience to internal and external shocks that would lead to changes in the operating environment and to the business plan and profitability. This is what the market refers to as stress testing, presented in the next section.

Alongside solvency assessment, regulators use the SREP to form a view of the firm's governance arrangements, its corporate culture and values, and the ability of managers to perform their duties, namely through effective, comprehensive and reliable risk reporting.

CASE STUDY: ICAAP OF AN INVESTMENT FIRM

Figure 8.3 is a replicate, with changed numbers, of the summary table of an ICAAP report prepared by one of my clients. The firm is mid-size, active in the UK, and its main exposure comes from market risk. With the management and a team at my firm, we reassessed the firm's capital for all risks – credit, market and operational – both in day-to-day conditions and in stressed market conditions. We compared the results to the firm's pillar 1 capital requirements, calculated in standardized method for all risks. The results showed a comfortable level of capital surplus, even when accounting for stressed market conditions, and an additional capital buffer for other risk types not covered by pillar 1, such as concentration risk, group risk and reputation risk. The regulatory outcome of the assessment did not lead to any additional capital from the firm.

(Continued)

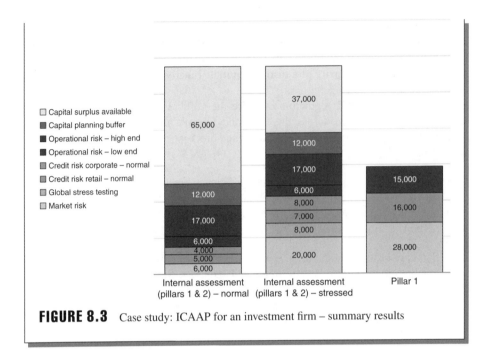

FIGURE 8.3   Case study: ICAAP for an investment firm – summary results

STRESS TESTING

Stress testing in operational risk can be confusing as it potentially refers to four different types of exercise: sensitivity stress testing, risk scenarios, macro-economic scenarios and reverse stress testing.

Sensitivity Stress Testing

This relates mainly to testing the robustness of a model by changing the value of the parameters. In pillar 2 or SREP exercises, sensitivity stress testing can be applied to the parameters underpinning projections of sales and revenues; a change in those parameters may very well affect the business plan of the firm and its future profitability and, hence, solvency.

Scenario Stress Testing

This focuses on possible yet unlikely tail events – in every risk type – for which the losses would need to be covered by capital. In credit risk, it can relate to the failure of a large institutional client; in market risk, to a crisis; in operational risk, to a business disruption or a large systems crash. Scenario stress testing is very similar to the process presented in the previous chapter. In CCAR, the analysis and review process used in the U.S., more attention is dedicated to legal risk and compliance scenarios than in Europe – a consequence of the legal and regulatory differences between the U.S. and Europe.

Macroeconomic Stress Testing

Each year, regulators provide international financial institutions – those which face potential systemic impact – with one or two macroeconomic shock scenarios, in order for them to assess their solvency level should these scenarios materialize. This is the core of the CCAR exercise in the U.S. Smaller regulated firms are also encouraged to stress test their capital level in case of a global economic shock. The stress-testing structure adopted by one of these firms for its SREP is illustrated in the case study.

CASE STUDY: EUROPEAN ICAAP – EXAMPLE OF STRESS-TESTING STRUCTURE

Figure 8.4 outlines an example of stress testing on global, financial and non-financial scales.

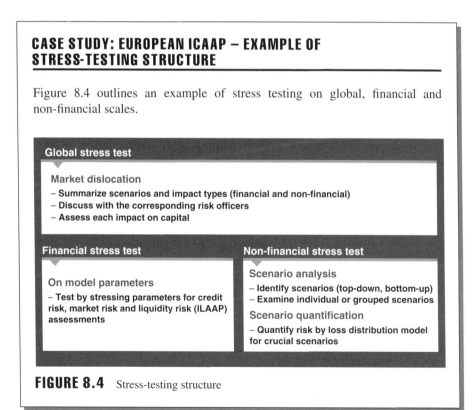

FIGURE 8.4 Stress-testing structure

Reverse Stress Testing

In comparison with the other methods, reverse stress testing is slightly different conceptually. It is the exercise of reviewing the eventualities that could halt the firm's operations, bringing it to a close. If these eventualities are manageable, the aim is to make sure that they are as unlikely as possible and definitely beyond the 99.9% confidence interval required. If the eventualities are about external shocks beyond the control of the firm, then it relates to wind-down planning scenarios. Wind-down planning means the orderly closure of the firm, with minimal disruption to its stakeholders and to the financial system.

WIND-DOWN PLANNING

There may be situations that render the firm no longer viable. The wind-down scenario planning exercise requires the firm to identify these situations – for example, large financials losses, loss of key clients without prospect of recovery, or loss of critical infrastructure.

The identification exercise involves a review of the business model and the exposures to change, the vulnerabilities to the business model and operating model as well as the key revenue drivers. As part of wind-down planning, the firm needs to decide and present the indicators in favor of winding down and to perform an impact assessment of the effects of closure on the firm's internal and external stakeholders. Then it must consider measures to mitigate those effects. The wind-down planning must also foresee a transition period and must be sensitive to the needs of all parties, who will naturally be anxious, and take account of reduced resources. Planning must include an assessment of the resources needed for an orderly closure in terms of liquidity, solvency, personnel and infrastructure.

PART
Three

Risk Mitigation

"Anyone who has never made a mistake has never tried anything new."
Albert Einstein

Operational Risk Governance

RISK GOVERNANCE AND THE ROLE OF THE BOARD

Firm governance starts with a definition of the roles and responsibilities of the different stakeholders in the firm. Similarly, proper risk governance must ensure that the roles and responsibilities of those involved in the firm's risk management – arguably, everybody – are clearly defined, understood and executed accordingly.

Effective governance can be described as clearly defined roles and responsibilities across the organization with an executable decision-making process and enforceable discipline.

Worldwide, corporate governance codes use similar terms to express that the board is responsible for determining the nature and extent of the significant risks it is willing to take to achieve its strategic objectives and to maintain sound risk management and internal control systems. In other words, the board is responsible for setting the risk appetite of the firm and for making sure that it operates within the limits of its risk appetite.

Following the development of non-financial risk management and the recommendations of regulators and large consultancy firms, most banks and insurance companies have now articulated their risk governance according to the three lines of defense model (3 LoD). Originally derived from risk management organization in the military, the 3 LoD model is now commonplace in the financial industry.

Although straightforward in theory, risk governance and the 3 LoD model are not always easy to implement in practice, and for years the topic has generated huge debates and many publications. The next section describes the model and some of its challenges.

THREE LINES OF DEFENSE MODEL

First Line: The Business (or Risk Owners)

The first line of defense, or front-line risk management, typically covers all the commercial and front-office operational functions; in one word, the "business." *Risk is managed where it is generated* is a common risk management adage and is useful as a reminder that risk is – ironically – *not* managed by the risk *management* function but by the business itself.

Yet, in referring to the "business" as the first line of defense, a common question arises regarding the support functions: are the Human Resources, Communication, Legal or Finance departments first line or second line? The answer is "both," depending on the tasks at stake. For its own risk-taking, a support department should be considered as a first line of defense: HR, for instance, is on the first line to manage the risks within its own department, so is Legal or Finance. However, for the assessment and management of risks in other departments, support functions are second line. HR is the second line of defense for the assessment and mitigation of people risk in the organization, although the power and responsibilities of HR departments vary widely from firm to firm, and Legal is the second line of defense for legal risks borne by other departments (unless specified otherwise within the firm).

Overall, when defining the first line of defense, it is better to refer to *risk owners* rather than to the *business*. Risk owners are those impacted by the consequences of the risks (the consequences owners, to be precise); as such, they must be in charge of the risk management: assessment and mitigation.

The roles of the first line of defense with regard to operational risk management (ORM) include:

- complete and accurate collection of relevant risk events
- regular self-assessment of risks and controls linked to the activity
- reporting on issues, key risk indicators and other risk metrics
- definition of appropriate actions, based on the limits of risk appetite and on the information reported
- corresponding follow-up on action plans and further mitigation initiatives.

RISK OWNERSHIP – A SIMPLE REMINDER

Having worked in so many firms for so many years across different continents, I find that the notion of risk "ownership" is often misunderstood or at least understood differently according to the firm and the people involved.

A risk owner is responsible for the consequences of a risk materializing. A risk owner generates the risk and therefore should assess its possible consequences and manage or mitigate the possible impacts. Just like when someone owns a phone, a car or a dog, he or she is responsible for its value, its usage and the impact it creates.

Line 1.5: The Risk Champions

Over the last 15 years, risk management has become a formidable discipline in the financial sector, with increasing levels of technical sophistication, jargon, codes, compliance requirements and quantification techniques. The old days of classic credit risk management are over. Financial risk management is centralized in most large organizations and is handled by dozens, if not hundreds, of quant specialists who maintain complex quantification models. Non-financial risk management – operational risk – is more decentralized by nature. However, it is also centrally reported and assessments are aggregated and communicated to senior management and the board by a central function. Not everybody in the business has the vocation to be a risk specialist and to understand risk management methods and terminologies. This is why, early on, many firms stipulate that in first-line departments the so-called "risk specialists" or "risk champions" should interact with the risk function. These "specialists," "champions" or "risk correspondents" are also referred to as the line "1.5" or "1.b." They are particularly common in larger organizations.

The roles of risk specialists within the first line of defense include:

- being the main correspondent for risk issues
- collecting and recording the risk events and losses
- mapping the risks and controls in line with the group definitions (when appropriate)
- following up on the control rules defined, in the context of the risk profile of the entity, and the quality of the operational environment
- being part of the redesign of procedures if needed
- being part of the follow-up of audit tracking and risk management action plans.

Second Line: The Risk Function

The second line of defense is the risk function. I purposefully refer to this line as the risk function rather than the "risk management" in order not to reinforce the common confusion arising from a poor choice of words at the time that operational risk management emerged as a discipline in the financial sector. Unlike financial risks, ORM cannot be centralized; instead, the ORM department should be called the risk *methodology* department because this is where the methods for managing operational risk are developed and communicated, not where risk is managed.

The risk function should fulfill three roles:

- To help define the risk appetite for the business and the board.
- To monitor the risk exposure within risk appetite and to own the risk management framework.
- To challenge and to advise on strategic business decisions with regard to risk-taking.

For these three roles, risk professionals must have expertise in conceptual and technical aspects of risk identification, assessment, mitigation and monitoring. They also require excellent knowledge of the regulatory demands and of the environment to ensure business compliance. In addition, role holders should understand the business processes and their application, constraints and vulnerabilities.[1]

The first and most important role of the risk function is to establish a process for the business to define its risk appetite. Defining a relevant, specific and actionable risk appetite results from a mature risk management process. To assess the risks that a business is willing to take, and to maintain sound risk management and internal control systems, requires the identification and assessment of the key risks that may negatively impact the business objectives, the evaluation of the current exposure to those risks, and the definition of additional controls if this exposure is judged excessive. It is the role of the risk function to provide a consolidated view of the risk profile of the business, to inform the executive committee about staying within risk limits and to report instances when the business's risk limits are breached. Part 4 of this book, dedicated to risk reporting, provides more detail on this topic.

The risk function requires great visibility over the conduct of business operations, as well as a deep understanding of the risk drivers impacting the business. It also requires a firm grasp of the most suitable metrics to capture the risk drivers so that a successful key risk indicator program can be created to ensure proper monitoring of the risk appetite.

Another major contribution of the risk function is business decision-making, by providing an informed view of the possible risks and mitigating options available to the business. The risk function should act as a sounding board to the business for decisions that may modify risk-taking and the risk profile of the institution. Such business decisions may concern new ventures, commercial accords or acquisitions, new products or new markets, investments or divestments.

To achieve an effective challenging role, the risk function needs to have enough delegated authority to freeze some business decisions that may contradict regulatory requirements or upcoming possible regulatory scrutiny, or that exceed risk appetite without proper acknowledgment from the board.

Third Line: Internal Audit

The third line of defense is internal audit – probably the line with the clearest boundaries. Internal audit is the independent party to the risk management process.

---

[1] For more detail, please read "Building an invisible framework for risk management," A. Chapelle and M.Sicsic, risk.net, 2014; also in *Reflections on Operational Risk Management*, Risk Books, 2017.

It independently assesses the risks to and compliance with the policies and procedures of the different departments and activities in an organization, including the risk function.

Both the risk function and internal audit use risk assessment tools. These tools differ in all the organizations I have worked with, except for one or two firms. In some firms, audit and risk coordinate their agendas in order not to overload the business with redundant visits and risks assessments. Sometimes, the second and third lines of defense also exchange information and findings. In a recent publication,[2] the Institute of Internal Auditors expressed its view on the interaction of internal audit with risk management, compliance and finance functions:

- Effective Risk Management, Compliance and Finance functions are an essential part of an organisation's corporate governance structure. Internal Audit should be independent of these functions and be neither responsible for, nor part of, them.
- Internal Audit should include within its scope an assessment of the adequacy and effectiveness of the Risk Management, Compliance and Finance functions. In evaluating the effectiveness of internal controls and risk management processes, in no circumstances should Internal Audit rely exclusively on the work of Risk Management, Compliance or Finance. Internal Audit should always examine, for itself, an appropriate sample of the activities under review.
- Internal Audit should exercise informed judgement as to what extent it is appropriate to take account of relevant work undertaken by others, such as Risk Management, Compliance or Finance, in either its risk assessment or determination of the level of audit testing of the activities under review. Any judgement which results in less intense Internal Audit scrutiny should only be made after an evaluation of the effectiveness of that function in relation to the area under review.

SECOND LINE: BETWEEN GUIDANCE AND CHALLENGE

The relationship between the first and second lines of defense is probably the aspect of the 3 LoD model to have generated the most debate. Many regulators require a second line to be "independent" from the first line, to provide "oversight and challenge" of the risk management activities performed in the first line. Yet, pure independence of the second line of defense raises the question of the duplication with internal audit. More fundamentally, it is close to impossible to operate effective oversight and challenge before risk management activities are both embedded and mature in the business.

---

[2] *Guidance on Effective Internal Audit in the Financial Sector*, second edition, Institute of Internal Auditors, September 2017.

Therefore, the first role of the operational risk management function is to educate all internal parties on the essentials of ORM. The key considerations in the first instance are: what is operational risk, how to recognize and report operational incidents, what are the benefits of good operational risk management and what are the pitfalls of poor risk management. Next, risk training can focus on the description and implementation of risk management tools for risk identification, assessment and root cause analysis or scenario workshops. Effective, engaged and widespread training on operational risk is an important prerequisite for any implementation of a risk management framework.

Yet, the risk function can still maintain its independence from the first line, even when providing thorough guidance on risk management methods: the key is in asking questions without suggesting answers. For instance, a risk manager from the second line of defense may very well run a risk and control self-assessment workshop with the business, triggering reflections on risks and effectiveness of controls, while also remaining independent. However, the manager must collate the responses and challenge the answers and their justifications, without influencing the content of the answers and their assessment. It is important to avoid the first line delegating the risk assessment and risk sign-off to the risk functions: this is neither a role nor a responsibility that the risk function should take or endorse. The risk function owns the methodology; the first line owns the risks.

On one end of the spectrum, risk and business work in such close collaboration that the lines of defense are blurred and risk ownership is unclear. This is more common in small firms, sometimes when the small size of teams makes it difficult to clearly separate the roles. At the other end of the spectrum, this time more often observed in larger organizations, first and second line develop a somewhat conflicted relationship, where the risk function cannot demonstrate its added value to the business and is perceived as a hindrance rather than an asset.

I have met a handful of firms where the relationship between the business and the risk function is positive, respectful and constructive. A couple of these firms define their relationship as a "partnership model." One of them is an insurance company, whose model is represented in the case study here. Cooperation and joint decision-making are a powerful way to embed risk management in the business.

CASE STUDY: THE PARTNERSHIP MODEL

Figure 9.1 lists the roles and responsibilities of the first and the second lines of defense in an international insurance company. The "partnership model" highlights an area of explicit cooperation and joint decisions between the risk function and the business. In this firm, line 1 and line 2 have a good working relationship.

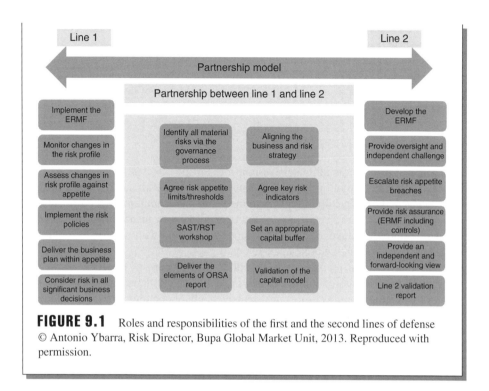

FIGURE 9.1   Roles and responsibilities of the first and the second lines of defense
© Antonio Ybarra, Risk Director, Bupa Global Market Unit, 2013. Reproduced with permission.

RISK COMMITTEES AND ORGANIZATION

Governance also means committees taking collegial decisions, based on reporting and escalated information. This section briefly reviews the main committees in relation to operational risk. Often, the size and complexity of the organization significantly influence the size and number of committees addressing the governance of operational risk.

The Board of Directors

This is the ultimate committee. The board of directors sits above the three lines of defense model and it is where the three lines join. In corporate governance, the board is in charge of all the administration of the firm. In practice, it delegates its powers to various committees. For example, executive management is delegated to the executive committee, risk management to the risk committee, and the audit to the audit committee. Boards are made up of executive directors (active in the management of the firm) and non-executive directors (non-active in the firm), and dependent directors (representing the interest of certain shareholders) and independent directors, with the composition depending on the country, tradition and corporate governance code under which the firm operates.

The vast literature on boards and board effectiveness is beyond the scope of this book. True board value is as precious as it is rare. Board effectiveness in matters of operational risk requires profound knowledge and understanding of the business, besides a strong background in risk management.

Risk Committees

The board of directors is ultimately responsible for the effective identification, management and oversight of operational risk. Oversight of operational risk identification and management is typically delegated to the board's risk committee, as is the review and assessment of the effectiveness of the operational risk management framework. The risk committee makes recommendations to the board with regards to risk-based decisions, risk exposure and risk management.

The risk function prepares regular reports to the board of directors and to the risk committee. The risk committee reviews and investigates larger incidents. The frequency of meetings should ensure consistent oversight of operational risk and adequate representation and escalation of potential issues to the board.

Operational Risk Committees and Other Specific Risk Committees

Larger organizations have specific risk committees, either per risk type, such as credit, market and operational risk committees, or committees at local, regional or business unit levels. All these structures are fine, as long as they are justified by the size and the complexity of the business. Operational risk itself is often split into several main non-financial risk categories such as fraud, information security, and legal and compliance. Sometimes, but less frequently, it includes business continuity and third-party risks. In many large organizations, each category of risk usually has its own committees, subordinated to either the risk committee (or enterprise risk committee) or the operational risk committee, reporting in turn to the enterprise risk committee. Figures 9.2 and 9.3 illustrate the two types of structure commonly observed, especially in the U.S. and Canada.

POLICIES AND PROCEDURES

Policies, procedures and other written guidelines or terms of reference are the backbone of corporate governance for committees. Policies describe – or should describe – the rules and principles according to which a company runs its business and organizes its processes. Procedures and guidelines provide more specific guidance on how to execute

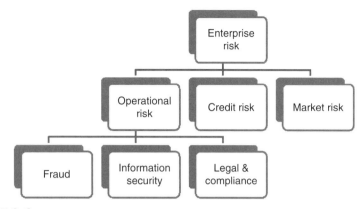

FIGURE 9.2   Operational risk sets the framework for all non-financial risks

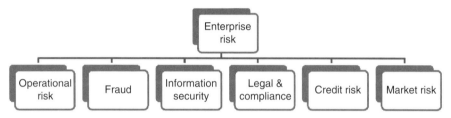

FIGURE 9.3   Specialized risk types all equally coordinated by the risk committee

certain tasks or processes. This documentation constitutes the core of a company's governance structure, attributing roles and responsibilities to the different parties.

Policies and procedures are important as long as they are lived in the company; they should apply in daily practices and be meaningful. Policies should reflect business realities. This is the best way to embed them in a company and they can then evolve gradually to complement the business, unless new activities or new processes require a fresh start.

Who likes reading policies? Who likes writing them? Let's be honest, policies and procedures are often the poor parent of a risk management framework and are often painful to write and even more so to read. They do not need to be. Specialist teams and skilled technical writers can create short, well-crafted and clearly presented documentation that can serve as a useful guide. It is a sensible investment for firms that can afford external help. Communicating policies is another challenge. Embedding a policy does not mean posting it on the intranet; it requires proper communication, in focus groups, through face-to-face sessions and tests or exercises, and it must be appropriate for the topic and the specific risk.

Policies, procedures and other guidelines are a form of internal controls, known as directive controls. The next chapter is dedicated to internal controls.

## CHAPTER 10

Risk Mitigation

DEFINITIONS

In the International Organization for Standardization (ISO) vocabulary, risk mitigation is defined by the four Ts: Tolerate, Treat, Transfer, Terminate. Tolerate means accepting the risk as it is. Treat refers to internal controls, aimed at reducing either the likelihood or the impact of a risk (or both); it is the most common form of risk mitigation. Transfer means to move the consequence – or the causes – of a risk to another party, typically an insurer or a third-party supplier. Terminate means to remove risk exposure altogether, when none of the other options is acceptable. This chapter concentrates on the two most common mitigation solutions: internal controls and risk transfers.

TYPES OF CONTROLS

There are many different classifications for controls. Given my background in internal audit, I tend to adopt the following simple classification used by the Institute of Internal Auditors (IIA):[1] preventive, detective, corrective and directive controls.

The aim of preventive controls is obviously to reduce the likelihood of an event happening. The controls are executed before possible events and address their causes. A car seat belt is an example of a preventive control in everyday life, while the segregation of duties, where different people are in charge of initiating, approving and settling a transaction, is probably the most common and effective preventive control for internal fraud.

Detective controls take place during or just after an event and, thanks to early detection, can reduce the impact. An example is a smoke detector, which will alert

---

[1] For further references, please refer to the note "Control" from the Chartered Institute of Internal Auditors, 31 August 2017.

you to a fire. Detective controls can become preventive if they detect a cause of an event. File reconciliations, for instance, which detect gaps, can be considered either as a detective control if the error is already made and recorded, or as a preventive control if it allows the detection and correction of an error before a transaction is executed.

Corrective controls take place after the incident, to mitigate net impacts. Redundancies, backups, continuity plans and crisis communication strategies are all part of corrective controls that firms use to mitigate the consequences of unexpected events and accidents. Backing up data will not prevent a server from crashing, but it will significantly reduce the pain should it happen. Similarly, to take an example from everyday life, a car airbag will not prevent an accident from happening but it will limit the damage if one occurs.

Lastly, directive controls cover all the required actions and rules to execute a process: policies and procedures, training and guidance, governance structure, roles and responsibilities. Figure 10.1 lists some of the most common examples of the various control types.

Another important feature of internal controls is key versus non-key or, to use vocabulary from internal audit, primary controls versus secondary controls. A key control is sufficient to prevent the risk on its own. In contrast, non-key or secondary controls are present to reinforce or to complement key controls, but they are unable to prevent a risk on their own.

Preventive controls

- Segregation of duties
- Access controls (digital or physical)
- Levels of authorization

Detective controls

- Exception reports
- File reconciliations
- Smoke detector
- Intrusion detection systems

Directive controls

- Procedures and guidance manuals
- Induction training
- Team supervision

Corrective controls

- Complaints handling process
- Communications and compensations to affected parties
- Backups and systems redudancies

FIGURE 10.1 Types of controls and examples

There is a large body of literature on internal control design, setup and testing. Interested readers can refer to publications from the IIA and COSO, among others. The impact of Sarbanes–Oxley (SOX) regulations on internal controls for financial and accounting information has played an important role in maturing the organization of processes, internal controls and control testing in financial firms. Operational risk managers subject to SOX can take inspiration from these regulations when assessing or advising on internal controls in their firms.

CONTROL TESTING

Control testing is traditionally the responsibility of internal audit. In addition, the first line of defense (the risk owners) will routinely test, or should test, internal controls. In most firms, the risk function does not test controls, except during thematic risk reviews, "deep dives" constituting detailed assessments of a given risk type across the firm or in a department – for instance, information security, third-party management or project risk management. Risk managers should understand the essentials of control-testing specialists, without necessarily being topic specialists themselves. Increasingly, the focus of risk management in the financial industry is moving toward controls and control assessment rather than risk assessment. Indeed, controls and control effectiveness are observable and, to a large extent, measurable, whereas risks are not.[2]

Controls can be tested with various levels of scrutiny. PRMIA,[3] in line with the related literature and practice, recognizes four types of control testing, which I summarize here:

- Self-certification or inquiry: not exactly a type of testing but the results of an interview with the owner of the control processes. Given the lack of evidence involved, this type of assessment should be limited to secondary controls or to control related to low inherent risk environments.
- Examination: requires supporting evidence and documentation of the controls, both in the form of written process and in written evidence of results. The effectiveness of this testing method depends on the relevance and adequacy of the documentation. It provides moderate assurance and is better suited for automated controls.
- Observation: this involves real-time oversight of the execution of the control process to judge its design and effectiveness in practice. It is a more stringent type of testing, suitable for key controls.

---

[2]For more discussions on these issues, please read *Antifragile*, N. Taleb, Penguin Books, 2012.
[3]*Operational Risk Management Handbook*, pp138-139, Professional Risk Managers International Association (PRMIA), 2015.

- Reperformance (also called reproduction or parallel testing): the strongest form of testing, where the tester reproduces the control process on a sample of transactions and compares the results with those previously obtained by the process. Mystery shopping to assess the quality of customer service or the effectiveness of call centers is a form of reperformance testing. So are the fake transactions inserted in trading systems to assess the effectiveness of the controls in middle office and back office, or in accounting and treasury in financial markets activities. Reperformance provides the highest level of assurance of control effectiveness; it is recommended for high inherent risk environments.

Table 10.1, inspired by the PRMIA handbook,[4] illustrates the principle of risk-based control testing. Risk-based control testing is commonplace in internal audit methodology. However, in my experience, this is still news to many operational risk managers. I believe that the operational risk function would benefit from exploring the methods and practices in internal control departments and internal audit departments. It could gain useful insights and identify synergies to improve risk and control self-assessment workshops or to challenge the results of the RCSAs performed by the first line. Internal control is a fairly well-established discipline and should closely complement the risk function.

Several elements influence the effectiveness of control testing:

- Independence of the tester: obviously, to avoid conflict of interest and biases, the tester should be independent from the owner of the control process.
- Frequency of testing: the frequency of control assessment will ideally be aligned with other control testing programs in the organization (such as SOX) and prescribed in company policies. Like everything else in risk management,

TABLE 10.1 Risk-based control testing

Control Attribute	Risk-Level		
	Low	Medium	High
Manual	Inquiry	Observation/ reperformance	Reperformance
Automated	Examination	Examination	Reperformance
Key	Examination/ observation	Observation/ reperformance	Reperformance
Non-key	Inquiry	Examination	Examination/ observation

[4]PRMIA Handbook for the Certificate in Operational Risk Management, op. cit, p139.

the approach to control testing should be proportionate, with more frequent assessments for higher risks or unstable risk environments.

- Scope and sample size: the scope of testing and the size of the sample tested are important, yet it can be difficult to find the right balance. The reliability of the results must be judged in relation to the time and effort committed to testing. Over the years, I have seen control effectiveness undermined by numerous operational incidents resulting from insufficient sampling or biased sample tests.

Assessment results for controls are usually rated on a 2-, 3- or 4-point scale, depending on the firm. Controls are usually assessed for design and effectiveness. Control effectiveness relates to their application, while design focuses on how well they have been conceived and how fit they are for purpose. Control design is particularly important and is presented in the next section.

Beware of Poor Control Design

Experience shows that many controls in firms are ineffective by design. This leads at best to a waste of resources and at worst to a false sense of security in vulnerable environments. There are three common types of poor controls:

- *Optimistic controls*: these require either exceptional ability or exceptional motivation from the controller to be effective. Because they are cursory rather than thorough, they are often referred to as "tick-box" controls. One example is sign-offs for large volumes of documents just before a deadline.
- *Duplicative controls*: "four-eyes check" is the most common form of duplicative control. Though widespread, having more than one person check the same information can dilute accountability. Also, because too much trust may be placed in collective control, individual attention and focus may be less rigorous, increasing the overall risk. Four-eyes checks are more effective when carried out by a manager and a subordinate, or by people from different departments, and more generally when accountability is clearly attributed to those performing the tasks.
- *More of the same*: this means responding to a control failure by adding a control of the same design, even though the previous one has failed. Two real-case examples clearly illustrate the flaws of this approach:
  - A firm sent the wrong mailing to a group of clients, due to failure of the four-eyes check between the mailing third-party supplier and the firm. In response to the incident, management added a third person to the process control, turning the four-eyes into six-eyes. Unsurprisingly, the process failed again and the incident reoccurred. Adding a third person simply diluted the accountability and weakened the process even further.
  - A firm with sensitive customer information built a strict process for third-party onboarding. But the process was so cumbersome that employees tended to

bypass it to onboard suppliers more quickly. In response, the firm made the onboarding process even more stringent, further encouraging employees to bypass it. As a result, large volumes of the firm's client data ended up being held by a third party without a proper, enforceable, third-party contract.

More controls do not necessarily mean less risk. Poor control design can increase the vulnerability of a process to various risks. Conversely, proper process design reduces inherent risk by the simple fact of organizing tasks properly, without the need to add controls. In the field of health and safety, the concept of "prevention through design" (PtD) focuses on minimizing occupational hazards early in the design process. The next section explores the more general issue of preventing non-financial risks by using better design of processes.

PREVENTION THROUGH DESIGN

"We cannot change the human condition, but we can change the conditions under which humans work."

James Reason[5]

If we accept human fallibility, we need to rely on well-designed systems to support us in the workplace and remove error traps wherever possible.

James Reason, Professor Emeritus of Psychology from the University of Manchester, is considered by the healthcare sector to be "the father of patient safety." He is a leading researcher and scholar in human error,[6] still active and publishing in the domains of healthcare safety and aerospace safety. This section highlights different types of human errors, based on Reason's work. I suggest how his findings can be applied for risk mitigation in the financial industry. For further details, interested readers can refer to the academic literature on human reliability analysis (HRA).

Typology of Human Error

It is a puzzle to me to see how little risk managers in the financial industry have investigated the causes and mechanisms of human error, given how exposed banks and insurances companies are to it. Maybe it is because in finance people don't die when they make mistakes? While the various types of human error are well known

---

[5]J. Reason, "Human error: models and management", BMJ, 2000 Mar 18; 320(7237): 768–770. Available on: https://www.ncbi.nlm.nih.gov/pmc/articles/PMC1117770/#

[6]His book *Human Error*, published in 1990, had been cited by 11,410 scholarly publications as of January 2018.

in transport, emergency services and the energy industry, for example, they are little known in the banking sector. However, they generate a vast amount of interest when revealed.

The first difference to be aware of is between slips and mistakes: a slip is an involuntary error, due to such things as inattention, distraction, noisy environment or tiredness. Better or more training is typically put forward by risk managers as a response to human error, but it is not a universal solution, far from it. Responses to slips should include a better work/business environment, a more appropriate work space, reduced noise levels, clearer accountabilities and clarity about the consequences of every action. The type of appropriate response depends on the root cause of the slip leading to an incident.

Unlike a slip, a mistake is the result of a voluntary action: what Reason calls "strong, but wrong." Here, a person intentionally takes action in good faith but it is the wrong action. Mistakes can be "rule based" or "knowledge based" (Reason, 1990). Rule-based mistakes are caused by flawed rules, or rules inducing conflicts of interests. A classic example of a rule-based mistake in financial services is mis-selling to retail customers due to aggressive commercial incentives by the sales force. It comes as no surprise that many regulators are tracking conflicts of interest in incentive and remuneration structures as causes of poor conduct. Here again, lack of training is often cited as a mitigation measure, but changing the rule, in the case of rule-based mistakes, makes a lot more sense.

Knowledge-based errors refer to the wrong choice of action when confronted with a new situation, illustrated by the well-known saying: "for a man with only a hammer, every problem looks like a nail." Knowledge-based errors are due to a lack of knowledge, a lack of familiarity with a process, or a lack of training or guidance. In this case, training is a relevant answer, whether in the form of help files, scripts, escalation procedures or training on the job.

Finally, the last type of error is violations: in fact, rather than an error, this is a voluntary misdeed. The person knows the right course of action, knows the rule, but chooses not to follow it. Supervision is commonly recognized as one of the most effective ways to mitigate violations, together with culture.

Another important distinction for human errors is the difference between active errors and latent errors (Reason, 1990). Active errors are perpetrated by the operator: they are caused by an action such as pressing the wrong button, forgetting to send a document, keying the wrong amount. Latent errors are invisible as direct causes; they materialize only when certain actions take place, and are linked to poor process or control design, flawed rules or erroneous management decisions. In engineering, it might be two types of screw that could fit in the same plane wings, when only one screw is appropriate, the other one representing a hazard. In the financial sector, examples include misconceived sales incentive schemes that lead to internal fraud or mis-selling; misleading capture screens in equity brokerage; and underinvestment in IT or people, leading to increased operational risk. There are countless examples for latent errors, but they are almost invisible in superficial analysis of operational risk incidents. This underlines the importance of root cause analysis for proper diagnosis and proper remediation of incidents. Root cause analysis is presented in the next chapter.

Prevention by Design

In risk management in engineering, "human error is a symptom of a safety problem, not a cause."[7] In other words, if people make mistakes, it is the fault of the process, not vice versa. As a risk manager with a food retail process background put it: "There is no such thing as human errors: they are either poor processes, or processes that are not followed." I believe that the financial industry still has some room for progress in exploring the causes of human errors and preventing errors by design. This would mean redesigning some of the processes and controls to support the reliability of actions and to minimize the chance of error. Checklists, strong communication protocols, standardization and better work environments are all part of the solution.

Risk Transfer

Risk transfer, like risk avoidance, is another type of mitigation. Insurance is a common and dependable type of risk transfer; outsourcing is potentially another powerful way to transfer risk. The validity of risk transfer from outsourcing will depend on why a risk is transferred and to whom. If it is to reduce costs – like transferring call centers to a less costly labor environment – then the strategy is more one of risk acquisition (hopefully, consciously). Conversely, a firm might want to outsource some non-core activities to better specialist parties: using the services of the best call center provider in the country, delegating its payment and settlement systems to a prime player, transferring its data center storage and maintenance to a safe cloud company. In these cases, the costs of the service may not be cheaper than the in-house solution, but the strategy should result in a net risk reduction. However, outsourcing is not always considered as a risk transfer strategy, maybe because important elements such as reputation risk cannot really be outsourced. Even so, it is arguably similar with external insurance: it can cover losses from operational incidents, but it can't repair reputational damage.

External insurance essentially reduces profit and loss volatility: the firm pays a premium every year for being compensated for damage should certain events materialize. Several firms I know either self-insure small losses via captives, or just absorb the volatility and take external insurance to cover only very large events. The underlying assumption is that the insurance premium for small losses will be about equal to, if not

---

[7]Leveson, N. (2011) "Risk management in the oil and gas industry testimony: senate committee on energy and natural resources", May. Some of the best pages I ever read in risk management. Highly recommended.

higher than, their average annual losses. They would rather face the limited volatility of smaller losses but are ready to pay to avoid the larger swings in profit and loss caused by significant events. In the December 2017 Basel III paper on the standardized measurement approach for operational risk, insurance recoveries are deducted from gross losses to calculate the net loss amounts, part of the loss multiplier of regulatory capital that will influence – in some jurisdictions – the amount of capital held by banks. The future will tell whether this is an incentive for banks to take operational insurance in regulatory environments and enforce the loss multiplier.

CHAPTER **11**

Root Cause Analysis and Action Plans

GENERALITIES AND GOOD PRACTICE

Performing root cause analysis of significant operational risk events and near misses is covered in *The Principles for the Sound Management of Operational Risk* by the Basel Committee on Banking Supervision (BCBS) in its third edition of 2014.[1] BCBS states:

"A noteworthy practice identified by only a few banks was the establishment of an internal threshold (eg $100,000 or €100,000) whereby any operational risk event (ie losses, near-misses and profitable events) was subject to an exhaustive and standardised root cause analysis by the first line of defence, which in turn was subject to independent review and challenge by the second line of defence. These banks noted that the operational risk management function provides the business line with supporting guidance and a standardised template to ensure a consistent approach. Some banks also noted that the process involved embedding the bank's operational risk taxonomy into the template, so that this information could inform the use of the other operational risk management tools.

Additional noteworthy practices include the first line of defence leading the root cause analysis and creating action items to address any identified control deficiencies, the second line of defence closely monitoring and tracking those action items, and escalating the details of the root cause analysis and resulting action plan for items above a higher internal threshold to senior management or an operational risk committee for review. Another noteworthy practice was the establishment of a common operational risk event template and supporting guidance to ensure a consistent approach is taken by the first line of defence across the bank's divisions. In addition, some banks have developed a process to share details of operational risk events across business lines

---

[1]Bank for International Settlements, Basel Committee on Banking Supervision, *Review of the Principles for the Sound Management of Operational Risk*, October 2014.

and geographies and encourage a similar approach to remediation where applicable. Also, one bank noted that it uses its operational loss data to assess the quality of other operational risk tools such as the RCSA, and to review whether the associated risk or control assessment may have been evaluated improperly."

In short, good and recommended practices include consistent and systematic root cause analysis performed by the first line following incidents or near misses above a given materiality threshold and supported or challenged by the second line. Even better practice is to draw links across incidents to generate a systematic solution across the organization. The bow-tie analysis presented in this chapter is in my experience an excellent tool for root cause analysis.

BOW-TIE TOOL AND SYSTEMIC PATTERNS OF FAILURE

The bow tie is a root cause analysis tool commonly used in heavy industries, such as oil and gas, and is now slowly making its way in the financial sector. It is a form of "5-whys" analysis, encouraging investigators to identify several levels of causes for operational failures.

In the bow-tie diagram, the risk or event to analyze lies at the center of the figure, with the left-hand side detailing its direct and indirect causes until all roots are identified. The right-hand side of the figure expands into all direct and indirect losses and impacts, forming the shape of a bow tie. Preventive controls are labeled in front of each cause; detective and corrective controls are documented on the impact side to the left (Figure 11.1).

Even today, many of the forms of root cause analysis employed by firms are limited to a first level of incident causation, often focusing on general "human error" and "lack of training." Bow-tie analysis for risks and events is a powerful way to help organizations look beyond what meets the eye and to identify indirect and root causes of their risks and incidents. It is also an effective method to reflect on and identify leading key risk indicators. I will return to this particular application of the bow tie in Chapter 14.

An obvious direct benefit of a root cause analysis is a deep understanding of the causes of an incident, leading to recommended action plans in the form of improved processes or better controls. In addition, there are even more powerful benefits to unlock when performing systematic bow-tie analysis in firms. When you perform bow-tie analysis of seemingly unrelated incidents in the same organization, you are more likely to develop a structural risk profile of the business, with a clearer picture of the recurrent types of control failures. Repeated incidents may be due to certain features in the organizational culture – in other words, a business style that exposes the firm to a pattern of causes leading to operational risk events. In my years of experience in performing this type of analysis with firms, I almost always found

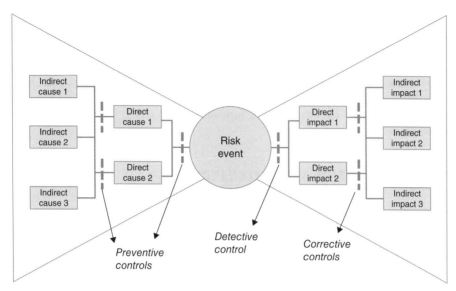

FIGURE 11.1 Bow-tie tool

common features between operational incidents in a given firm, regardless of how dissimilar they looked at first. For example, common features included:

- imbalance between preventive and corrective controls, leading the firm to "fire-fight" and remediate, while feeling overwhelmed by workload
- defective internal communication flows, leading to disparate incidents such as a misstatement by the CEO in the press, business disruption caused by drilling through ethernet cables, double spend on insurance policies, etc.
- excessively low red KRI thresholds in a firm new to the discipline and overly strict about operational risk management, leading to reporting dashboard mostly red, meaning it becomes impossible to distinguish real red alerts from petty issues, the signal from the noise
- a risk-averse and mature organization in risk management, but with chaotic third-party management processes: most events were caused by poor selection or mismanagement of vendors.

So far, I have rarely encountered firms that compare the results of several forms of root causes analysis to identify their pattern of failure. In my view, this is the largest untapped opportunity in operational risk management today.

Risk managers from the second line of defense should facilitate bow-tie analysis, especially when it requires a transversal analysis and the involvement of several departments or divisions. Successful bow-tie analysis depends on a deep knowledge and understanding of the various causes and consequences of an event, of the controls that were missing or defective, and of the strengths and weaknesses of the incident management and response. One individual or even one team rarely attains this breadth of awareness and abilities, which requires the coordination of different parties in the business. The risk function plays a beneficial coordinating role, especially when it comes to identifying patterns of causes across various incidents and to rolling out firm-wide action plans.

ACTION PLAN DESIGN AND GOVERNANCE

An action plan is a remediation program to reduce the risk level of a product or an activity, either by reducing the risk exposure or by improving processes or controls. Action plans typically follow an incident or near misses whose potential impact appeared to be above risk appetite. Actions plans should ensure that unacceptable events would not reoccur. Alternatively, action plans can be made of forward-looking, preventive measures aimed at keeping a risk within the acceptable limits of risk appetite.

Each operational incident does not necessarily trigger an action plan and neither should it. Action plans are additional mitigation steps when events, near misses or ex-ante risk assessment reveal potential impacts or likelihood above risk appetite. However, many times I have observed in a firm a certain disconnect between risk appetite and the decisions to initiate action plans. Regrettably, this can lead to a waste or a misallocation of resources.

Deadlines and follow-up are also important elements of action plans, alongside the need for consistency with risk appetite, governance and ownership. Action plans are like mini projects, and sometimes even large projects, and should be managed as such. Each action plan must have an owner, accountable for its timely and accurate execution. Large plans need to be phased and reported on periodically. Risk managers in the second line of defense can be particularly helpful here in assisting with the design of the plan and, of course, the follow-up of deliverables and timeliness. Operational risk managers should support and guide the business, and not let risk owners feel alone in resolving issues and events. Without effective support from the risk function, business lines tend to underplay the nature and size of the risks they face in order to avoid dedicating scarce resources to action plans.

## CHAPTER 12

Conduct and Culture

"Laws control the lesser man.... Right conduct controls the greater one."

Mark Twain

DEFINITIONS

Conduct

From a regulatory perspective – especially in the UK but increasingly also internationally – a conduct event is any event that breaches the three conduct regulatory objectives of consumer protection, market integrity and effective competition. Therefore, conduct goes beyond customer treatment, quality of information, product design or sales practices. Failure to properly perform anti-money laundering (AML) checks, for instance, is a conduct issue that does not involve sales, but it breaches market integrity. Also, when business disruption negatively impacts customers, perhaps because of negligent maintenance of IT systems, it can be regarded as a conduct issue. Conduct issues – like reputation issues – can arise from incidents classified in any of the seven Basel operational risk categories. This is why regulators mention "conduct" rather than "conduct risk." Conduct is not a risk category in its own right: it is a possible consequence of other risks materializing, like reputation damage.

It follows that the quality of a firm's management of conduct is directly linked to the quality of its risk management framework. Importantly, because conduct is not a standalone risk type, it does not have to be managed in a separate department, by a specific management team, with a different database and yet another silo. In every activity it undertakes, a firm needs to ask whether the activity could negatively impact any of the regulator's statutory objectives. It is essential for a firm to recognize the possible consequences of its actions on conduct objectives and demonstrate that the management considers risks arising from internal behaviors and practices and then mitigates those risks. Some common metrics of conduct, demonstrated by certain behaviors and outcomes, are presented in Chapter 15, dedicated to risk reporting. Before moving on to the concrete aspect of measuring and reporting on conduct, we must focus on target culture and ways to identify and drive desirable behaviors.[1]

Culture

To use the phrase popularized by Bob Diamond, CEO of Barclays, at the height of the Libor-rigging scandal: "Culture is what happens when no one is looking." Culture underpins behaviors of people, driven by individual values and beliefs. To a large extent, culture will drive conduct, i.e. behaviors. Culture, as a set of values that matters to individuals, is not measurable. Behaviors, however, are observable and therefore traceable. We cannot measure values, but we can track behaviors; we cannot measure respect, but we can observe respectful language – and we can measure the frequency of respectful versus disrespectful communication. Equally, we cannot observe integrity, but we can measure fair pricing. Over the last few years, regulators have developed the trend for behavioral regulation. By influencing good behaviors, good conduct is encouraged and can be monitored.

Key Behaviors

Objective Target culture and desirable behaviors depend on the firm, its history, its ethos, its vision and its top management. Risk culture is part of a wider corporate culture and intimately linked to it. The tools and the research mentioned in this chapter are not limited to risk management in the financial sector. However, the way they apply to other corporate cultures is beyond the scope of this book. This chapter focuses on desirable behaviors for better risk management and on some concrete ways of influencing them.[2]

Defining the objective is the first step for any action. Whether you want traders to respect their risk limits, staff to speak up about risks or issues, or incidents to be reported as soon as they arise, define your goals as clearly and precisely as possible.

Concentrate on Key Behaviors Research and experience show that focusing on one or two key behaviors to promote change is effective because it reinforces and simplifies the message. Key behaviors are central to unlocking the path to the desired objectives.

---

[1]Much of this chapter is inspired by a highly recommended book: *Influencer: The Power to Change Anything*, Patterson et al., McGraw-Hill, 2008, 299p. Further worthwhile reading includes *Willful Blindness: Why We Ignore the Obvious at Our Peril*, M. Heffernan, Simon & Schuster, UK, 2011, 391p.
[2]For a more general overview of influencing techniques and their applications, please refer to Patterson et al., op. cit.

Some are obvious, like key behaviors for succeeding at school ("work hard, be nice") or for staying healthy ("eat well, exercise"). Another example is the familiar warning in hospitals to prevent the spread of infection ("wash hands between every patient"). Less well known in the hospital context is the principle of "200 percent accountability." This means that in addition to being 100 percent responsible for their own actions, every member of a team should be 100 percent responsible for the actions of others. For example, they should feel compelled to speak up in the event of safety breaches: if anyone, regardless of his or her grade – assistant, nurse, consultant – notices a breach of safety procedures, he or she is 100 percent accountable for reminding the offender of the procedure, while the offender is 100 percent accountable for thanking the person for the reminder and then complying with the rules. This particular behavior, one of empowerment, has proved necessary in U.S. hospitals, where a strong sense of hierarchy may prevent people from speaking up.[3]

Similarly, in the many risk culture workshops that I have run with firms, the most frequently cited behaviors to improve proactive risk management are speaking up about issues and risks, reporting incidents and raising alerts to allow early intervention. "Blame culture" and fear are most often cited as powerful hurdles to these desired behaviors. The most common aspiration of the risk function is to build a relationship of trust and respect with the first line. Knowledge and understanding of the business, competence in risk management and empathy are the recommended behaviors to achieve this objective. The case study below presents more behaviors and the language used to describe them.

CASE STUDY: KEY BEHAVIORS FOR BETTER RISK CULTURE IN FINANCIAL FIRMS – INTERNATIONAL BANK AND INTERNATIONAL ASSET MANAGEMENT FIRM

I have conducted numerous workshops where risk functions and first-line managers reflect on the key behaviors required to achieve a better risk culture. Most answers relate to transparency of information, particularly in case of risk events or anomalies.

The phrases below emerged from some of these workshops. The international retail bank, based in Northern Europe, was responsible for the first-line behaviors, and the international asset manager, based in the U.K., was responsible for the second-line behaviors.

(Continued)

---

[3]Patterson et al., op. cit. For a case application by one of the authors in operating rooms, please visit: https://www.beckershospitalreview.com/or-efficiencies/6-steps-to-build-of-a-qculture-of-safetyq-in-the-hospital-operating-room.html

Key behaviors to adopt by risk owners (first line):

DO YOUR BEST – excellence as a standard.
COME FORWARD – call for help, put your hand up, when there is an issue.

Key behaviors to adopt by the risk function (second line):

GET TO KNOW YOU – gain credibility through knowledge of the business and competence in risk management.
HERE TO HELP – support to the business before oversight, and risk management as an enabler of better management.

HOW TO ACHIEVE CHANGE

Willingness and Ability

Willingness and ability are necessary conditions for action. One can be willing but not able to act, or vice versa. Influencing behaviors requires training and guidance just as much as encouragement. Ability is often overlooked or taken for granted by change managers. At the same time, recipients of the message are reluctant to admit ignorance. Indeed, on several occasions I have been invited to firms to train the operational risk "champions," the so-called line 1.5, who are in charge of reporting business incidents to risk managers, and the firms have generally insisted on reporting all operational risk events. The first question I hear is often: "What is an operational risk event?" Going back to basics is often a good thing. Do not hesitate to restate the obvious, to explain and to show. Make sure you resolve every misunderstanding before pressing ahead.

Levels of Incentives

Research in psychology identifies three levels of motivation: personal, social, structural. Personal motivation relates to individual preference: what we like doing. Social motivation arises from peer pressure: doing something because everyone around us is doing it. Structural motivation comes from formal incentive schemes: we do it because we are paid or rewarded in other ways. One method of creating desired behaviors is to address all three levels of motivation in combination with adequate training and support. Culture translates into taught behaviors and those behaviors are driven by personal values, the influencing environment and the rules.

Personal Values

To unlock change, people will need to like the new behavior. To make them like reporting incidents, flagging issues and raising risks, they need to envisage and believe in the benefits of this transparency: better support, future prevention, smarter ways of working, better business performance. Positive aspirations, business-driven objectives and concrete benefits at the process level are far more engaging than the prospect of regulatory compliance to avoid fines or possible losses. Highlighting the positives – the business benefits of good risk management – is more effective than focusing on negatives.

Sustainable change requires consultation. Businesses often complain that risk management is done *to* them rather than *with* them – a view that I share. In the majority of risk functions that I encounter in financial companies, business managers are not sufficiently involved in the design and implementation of operational risk management frameworks, particularly when it comes to risk assessment and event reporting.

Influencing Environment

People Environment: Influencers and Mentors
You must consult the influencers (i.e., opinion leaders) in a business before deciding on and rolling out the changes. Once they have agreed to the changes, opinion leaders can be a significant help in implementing recommended behaviors. Their behavior will set the tone and standard for the rest of the group. *Do as I do* is much more effective than *Do as I say*.

Leading by example is arguably the most powerful form of leadership. Influencers are recognized and respected for their competence and their empathy, but they are not necessarily among the top managers in the business; however, if senior managers are also influencers, so much better.

Management attitude is fundamental to support risk culture changes or improvements. This is why I prefer to focus on what is *Done at the Top* rather than the *Tone at the Top*. Risk culture must be more than just lip service and the attitude of senior management toward conduct and risk management is the foundation for a strong culture.

Physical Environment: Propinquity and Consistent Message
Physical environment plays an important role alongside human influence. Even so, it is grossly neglected in many workplaces. Teams and divisions who share the same process, or who need to work collaboratively, may be located next to each other: it shortens processing time, improves communication and leads to mutual acceptance, even if the relationship is not good at first. Propinquity recognizes the effect of repeated exposure on attractiveness. Occupational propinquity analyzes the psychological effect of proximity and liking in working environments: proximity breeds familiarity, understanding, acceptance and liking. This phenomenon has been studied for a very long time, sometimes with consequence outside of the workplace. For example, an academic paper published in 1918 examined the link between occupational propinquity and the selection of marriage partners.[4] In more recent years, the

---

[4]Marvin, D.M. (1918) "Occupational propinquity as a factor in marriage selection," *Publications of the American Statistical Association*, 16, 123, 131–150.

development of instant messaging and video conferencing has seen the emergence of virtual propinquity. However, in my opinion, virtual exposure is not as compelling as geographical proximity, though maybe younger generations would disagree.

Consistency between messages and facts is another feature of supportive physical environments. Office spaces and practices should facilitate the development of the target culture and fit the message. For example, if management has an "open door" policy, then doors need to be open in practice as well as in principle. As for risk reporting, everything should be done to make the process as clear and simple as possible. Arguably, when operational incidents are underreported, it is mainly because people don't know what to report, or because the reporting process is too onerous. Chapter 13 has more details on incident-reporting processes and features.

Rules

Incentive structures are strong and proven drivers of behaviors. Logically, financial regulators request firms to identify and eliminate any conflict of interest between remuneration structures and conduct or risk management, within the limits of risk appetite. Risk-based performance measures have long been common in banking sector, in credit risk as well as in market risk and are now beginning to appear in operational risk. Even though operational risk is less easy to measure than financial risk, risk-taking boundaries can be set through qualitative statements about the type and intensity of impacts that a firm can tolerate. Companies must eliminate any remuneration and incentive structure that encourages behaviors that exceed risk boundaries.

When rules are violated, negative reinforcement must be used unsparingly. This is best applied to repeated violations and poor behaviors that are committed intentionally. Negative reinforcement must be predictable and credible: rules must be clear and consistent. Random and indiscriminate punishment only creates withdrawal, fear and resentment: the commonly cited "blame culture" as the major hurdle to open and honest communication in firms.

Meanwhile, positive reinforcement is vastly underestimated and underused in the industry. There is great value in thanking people for reporting incidents, praising departments that demonstrate good conduct, and appreciating all examples of risk management progress and commitment. These simple, non-financial rewards provide powerful incentives to adopt good risk management behavior.

Assess Progress

Like a benchmark for a portfolio of assets, we cannot measure success if we do not first define what success means. Target behaviors are observable, so progress is measurable when objectives are clearly stated from the outset. Regularly tracking progress, to record the successes and the obstacles, will enable managers (or, specifically, risk managers) to adjust their programs accordingly. Behaviors do not change overnight, so it is important to be patient and to monitor and assess progress. The case study presents a one-year culture definition and transformation program I initiated and ran with a local bank in London.

CASE STUDY: CULTURE CHANGE PROGRAM AT A LOCAL BANK

A mid-size bank in the U.K. felt the need to review its messages around values and behaviors for better regulatory compliance. Starting from a conduct and risk culture perspective, the project quickly transformed into a full revision of the corporate culture, as culture and risk culture are hardly dissociable.

Using the Influencer methodology, we adopted a consensus approach, starting with an observation phase of the current practice and behaviors at the bank, continuing to a wide consultation on the strong and weaker points of the organization through focus groups and workshops with members of staff attending voluntarily. Next, we ran a bank-wide survey – with an 84% participation rate – asking people to rank by order of importance the issues and recommended solutions raised during the focus groups.

The consultation phase led to the selection of three values and corresponding behaviors to reinforce to make the firm stronger:

- Transparency: *we maintain an open and honest communication among colleagues, from top management to staff and with our stakeholders (customers and regulators).*
- Empowerment: *we appreciate work well done and celebrate success.*
- Anticipation: *we plan ahead to respect deadlines, we adapt in the face of change.*

Everyone in the organization now refers to these values and behaviors as the TEA values.

Defining key behaviors is only the first step of the change program. Acting on the different drivers of behaviors to change them in a sustainable way is the make or break of culture change programs.

To leverage on social incentives, we have identified a handful of Influencers who act as role models, each in their field of activities, to impersonate those values and lead by example. In particular, the middle management is keen to live the Empowerment value by *standing up*, rising to take new initiatives to facilitate decision-making and take some of the load off a slightly overburdened executive team. In turn, executive directors impersonate Transparency by multiplying

(Continued)

direct interactions to staff, town halls and presentations, to communicate clearly and honestly on strategy, good news, bad news and decisions made. Project managers and risk managers take the lead for the embedding of the Anticipation value, reinforcing planning and timelines and deploying preventive action plans to avoid repetition of mistakes.

At the individual level, reinforced training programs and coaching plans develop and support personal ability in living the values and demonstrating the expected behaviors.

To leverage on the structural incentives, the compensation structure has been profoundly reviewed to recognize and reward employees demonstrating behaviors according to the values of Transparency, Empowerment and Anticipation. It also incorporates sanction mechanisms in case of violations of conduct rules and gross negligence leading to material incidents or missed deadlines on audit recommendations and regulatory actions.

Finally, plans are underway to modify the physical environment of the workplace to fit the TEA value message: glass doors for Transparency, creative rooms and planning tools for Empowerment and Anticipation, social events and outings to celebrate success.

Risk Monitoring

"Perfection is not attainable, but if we chase perfection we can catch excellence."

Vincent Lombardi

Incident Data Collection

IMPORTANCE OF LOSS REPORTING AND REGULATORY REQUIREMENTS

As a regulator once said: "Operational risk is the risk of loss resulting from inadequate or failed internal processes, people and systems or from external events; and if you don't know your losses, you miss an essential point of operational risk management." Rightly so, most firms consider incident data collection as the bedrock of their ORM framework. In 2000, the bank-insurance company ING created its first representation of the ORM framework. It comprised four concentric circles: the loss database formed the center circle, RCSA the second circle, with KRIs forming the third circle. The final, outer, circle was "lessons learnt" from large incidents (Figure 13.1). This was a simple and effective representation of four essential activities in non-financial risk management.

Internal loss data are a component of the advanced measurement approach and together with external loss data are the largest driver of regulatory capital for many firms. The Basel Committee on Banking Supervision has refocused attention on the incident data collection process and data quality, and the standardized measurement approach reform, finally published in December 2017,[1] applied an internal loss multiplier to the capital charge of banks, penalizing those with a history of large losses.

The role and use of loss data go much beyond regulatory capital requirements. It is fundamental for risk management: in order to improve an organization's profitability, business performance and internal control environment, you must know where loss events occur and be able to identify control breaches and weaknesses. Loss data also inform scenarios, as internal loss data and near misses help scenario identification and assessment. It finally relates to pillar 2 because the collection, knowledge and analysis of loss data enhance the management and good governance of operational risk. This is part of the pillar 2 regulatory requirements for the supervisory review process.

---

[1] BCBS, "Basel III: Finalising Post-Crisis Reforms," December 2017.

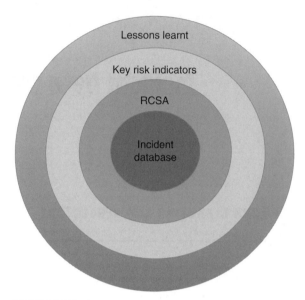

FIGURE 13.1   ORM framework

Comprehensive, high-quality data collection and analysis reduce the occurrence and size of regulatory capital add-ons under pillar 2.

BCBS lists eight criteria for the data quality and collection process under SMA. They include a required history of ten years; a minimum collection threshold of €20,000; mapping to Basel event-type categories; and the requirement to report dates of occurrence and recovery and processes "to independently review the comprehensiveness and accuracy of loss data." However, national regulators have the authority to waive the internal loss multiplier component for the institutions under their supervision.

LOSSES VERSUS INCIDENTS AND THE FALLACY OF NON-FINANCIAL IMPACTS

Interestingly, the Basel Committee still considers "loss" data in the same way that banks did in the early part of this century. Indeed, regulators only make it a requirement to consider the directly identifiable negative financial impact of operational incidents as losses for regulatory purposes. In contrast, firms consider operational "incidents" rather than "losses" because most organizations also collect other types of operational incidents: unintentional gains, incidents without direct financial impacts and near misses.

A near miss is a loss avoided by sheer luck or due to accidental prevention outside the normal course of controls. Losses avoided because a control worked are not near misses and neither are events with only indirect financial impacts. The nuance can be subtle and I have met many firms where near misses are confused either with the normal course of controls or with other types of incidents. For instance, delays or corrections leading to client dissatisfaction should be captured as operational risk *incidents* with *indirect financial impacts*. The event does not lead to a direct loss, i.e., a cash outflow or impaired future budgeted revenues, except if the dissatisfied customer cancels a contract or an expected business transaction. From a regulatory perspective, firms must only report losses that are directly and identifiably linked to the incident. From a management perspective, it is good practice to record indirect impacts, which are often called "non-financial impacts." This term is particularly misleading because so-called "non-financial impacts" have real financial consequences. Regulatory scrutiny, customers' dissatisfaction, remediation plans and management attention all have concrete and often costly consequences for organizations. When these consequences are not evaluated properly, the cost of operational risk and, more generally, the cost of poor operational performance will be significantly underestimated.

Direct losses result from the event itself. Examples include direct remediation, time lost, client compensation, regulatory fines and money lost in wrongful transactions. These losses are usually well captured, or at least firms attempt to estimate them. Indirect losses result from the consequences of the event: loss of customers because of poor service; damage to reputation through negative referrals; low employee morale affecting productivity; regulatory scrutiny leading to increased compliance costs; and increased insurance premiums. Indirect losses are often captured as a vague 1 to 4 impact rating, in line with the impact assessment matrix. Only the most mature firms monetize their indirect losses – a behavior that is necessary to produce accurate management information to inform proper decision-making.

THE FALLACY OF NON-FINANCIAL IMPACTS

"When I see a frown on a customer's face, I see $50,000 about to walk out the door."

A grocer evaluating the loss of revenue from a $100-a-week client over ten years. Cited by Tom Peters (*Thriving on Chaos*, 1988) to illustrate the long-term effects of customer profitability.

Many financial organizations still grossly underestimate the opportunity cost of losing clients through poor service quality and inefficient processes.

"We incurred a regulatory fine of £20 million. Remediating the issue cost us about £200 million."

(Continued)

From a conversation with the head of compliance at a U.K.-regulated financial firm. Remediation costs are often far bigger than the cost of the incident itself.

"The incident itself was small, but it triggered so many meetings that it captured management attention for about 30 hours."

Management attention is another type of impact that is usually unaccounted for. Capturing these "hidden" costs is likely to create a better risk-based view, enabling you to avoid micro-managing petty but more frequent and visible issues and instead concentrate on events and near misses with larger indirect but less obvious impacts.

INCIDENT DATA COLLECTION PROCESS

Data Fields

Every firm typically reports the same set of core data for operational incidents, but some firms will collect many more data fields than others. From experience, sticking to the minimum meaningful set of data avoids excessive reporting and wasting resources. Table 13.1 shows a typical set of useful operational incident data. Incident records must follow the taxonomy of risks, causes, impacts and controls. Drop-down menus, or formatted labels of risks, causes and event types, are essential because free-text fields lead to information chaos when slightly different narratives are created for similar types of events.

Net losses and gross losses vary because of the amount of money that is recovered through insurance or other reimbursements. Minimum reporting thresholds vary largely across firms. Some set it at zero in an attempt to capture everything or to simplify instructions to the people in the business who do not need to estimate a loss before deciding to report incidents. At the other end of the spectrum, some firms set a reporting threshold at 10,000 dollar, euros or pounds, more rarely at 20,000, a limit now validated by the SMA incident data collection criteria. Commonly, reporting thresholds are set at 1,000 or 5,000 monetary unit. From a regulatory perspective, the choice of threshold should not impact the credibility of the process or impair management information; the reporting threshold chosen by a firm must be justified and should not suggest cherry-picking or manipulation of capital requirements.

There are four important dates relating to incidents: date of discovery (when the event is first identified); date of occurrence (when it actually happened – which may be long ago); date of reporting (when the event enters the reporting database); and date of accounting (when the financial impact enters the general ledger). Impacts can

TABLE 13.1 Common and useful fields in operational risk incident reporting

Unique Incident ID
Place of occurrence (Business Unit/Division) – should be mapped to the risk assessment units
Event type (level 1, level 2) – aligned with taxonomy – formatted types
Event title + description (as standardized as possible)
Cause type (level 1, level 2) – aligned with taxonomy – formatted types
Controls failures – aligned with control library
Date of occurrence/discovery/reporting/settlement
Expected direct financial loss (may evolve until closure)
Impact type: loss/gain/near miss
Indirect impacts (per impact type): often on a impact scale
Recovery (insurance and other recoveries)
Net loss (gross loss minus recovery)
Actions plans (when appropriate): measures, owner, time schedule
Link with other incidents (if any) – for grouped losses and reporting
Other comments if necessary

materialize over long periods, up to many years for very large incidents. Some banks may also include a date of settlement in their reporting, when all the impacts have been accounted for. Dates must be used carefully and consistently when reporting incidents because mixing several dates can create large discrepancies between reports. It is advisable to choose one date type and to stick to it for all reporting.

The difference between the dates of occurrence and discovery reflects the visibility of issues in the organization. The difference between the date of discovery and reporting shows how diligently operational incidents are reported in the organization. Most organizations have a policy for incident reporting, specifying the maximum time that should elapse between discovering an event and reporting it. Best practice dictates a risk-based approach that will not waste resources in petty risk management. Material incidents should typically be reported within 2–5 working days, while minor incidents can simply be included in periodic summary reporting. The required speed of reporting is often part of the escalation criteria, or "escalation matrix," where events are escalated to different levels of management depending on their size.

The size of an incident is commonly judged by its potential impact rather than its actual materialized impact – which is good practice. The most prudent firms treat near misses and unexpected gains as if they were both actual loss events. This is because unintentional gains of, say, £500,000 will trigger the same type of reaction and action plan as a loss of similar size. The same goes for near misses: events should be judged by how much they could have cost, not what they actually cost. These criteria relate to gross losses, before recoveries and other mitigating controls that are part of incident management.

An alternative practice is to judge the severity of an event based on expected losses, with the caveat that expected losses can be hard to assess at first. There may also be a reluctance to report large expected losses, for incidents that could trigger strong reactions, before knowing for sure that the losses will materialize. To overcome this type of reluctance, I would recommend simplifying the reporting of expected or potential losses to severity bands corresponding to different escalation criteria or triggering different types of reaction, e.g., >10k, >100k, >1m. A FTSE 100 firm adopted this "banded reporting" in 2012 with good results. When incidents close, actual losses are reported with their precise value. The next section examines the causes of resistance to loss reporting and the ways to overcome them.

Finally, grouped losses are different events linked together by the same operational risk failure – for example, the same wrong advice to a group of clients, an IT failure impacting various departments in different ways, or product mis-selling or misconception impacting many sales. Different events that materialize from a single failure should be grouped as a single loss to reflect the same underlying cause.

Reporting: Overcoming Resistance

There are a number of reasons why comprehensive reporting is still a challenge for the vast majority of firms. For example, business lines (and even risk correspondents) may not know what to report, or how to recognize an operational risk event, let alone how to assess the impacts of a risk event. Even if people are comfortable with these actions, they may not know how to report, where to find the intranet link that will open the recording page, how to use the reporting system, or who to call and ask for help. Finally, if they know what to report and how to report it, they may not bother because they are put off by a cumbersome process or simply don't see the value, or both. Having worked as head of incident data collection in two large banks and observed and advised the sector for 15 years, my experience tells me that people don't take the time to report incidents if they feel that the process is unnecessarily complicated and bureaucratic, even more so when they don't see the value in it, and rarely because they want to hide something. To overcome underreporting, my advice is to make the reporting process as easy as possible for the business units. Charity websites provide a good example to follow, as they usually have impossible-to-miss "donate" buttons and make donating swift and easy. As industry practice in firms goes, the reporting process ranges from tedious and cumbersome form-filling by the business lines to a no-fuss, lean and efficient centralized recording by the ORM team. The case study describes one example of good practice.

CASE STUDY: NORDIC BANK'S "THANK YOU" NOTE

To facilitate reporting, a large Nordic retail bank centralizes the recording of operational incidents, with four people in the ORM team dedicated to filling out operational incident forms. When incidents arise, a call or an email to the ORM team suffices. The operational risk manager talks through the incident details and completes the form. This straightforward process has two main advantages. First, because it is not too much bother, it overcomes one reason why people are reluctant to report. Second, it ensures far better data quality, in particular regarding categorization of risk events, causes and various impacts.

In addition, the risk team will thank anyone who reports an incident or sends information about risk and issues. Because risk managers respond with "thank you" notes, it creates positive reinforcement and encourages future cooperation. This is the best practice I have witnessed so far. And because it is in a large bank, it demonstrates that corporate size is not an impediment to a centralized recording process and effective communication between business lines and risk function. The excellent relationship between the first and second lines of defense in this bank is no coincidence.

If it requires effort and openness from the business lines to report incidents and near misses, people are entitled to get some recognition in return. The risk team must provide clarity on how the collected data will be treated and analyzed and should provide feedback on the data. Feedback from the risk function to the business, preferably with benchmarking across similar departments and in comparison to firm-wide values, is a powerful encouragement to report. Finally, the overall value for the business will depend on how the risk function responds to the data collected, for example by assisting in the design of action plans, supporting risk mitigation when needed or advising on how to improve processes so that events do not reoccur. Only mature risk functions inspire high levels of transparency and voluntary reporting.

Process: Incentivizing Timely Self-Reporting

In terms of incentives to report, practice ranges from soft encouragement to stringent oversight. I know at least one bank where internal audit scans emails to identify unreported incidents. Soft incentives are more often present in small organizations or where senior management is insufficiently supportive of ORM.

More commonly, self-reporting of incidents is required, with the threat of consequences/disciplinary action if unreported events are subsequently discovered. This may include escalation to the executive committee, to the risk committee and to internal audit, and possible penalties on the management's balance scorecard. In the early 2000s, a bank was incentivizing management to report incidents and penalizing entities where events reported were suspiciously low. This practice has become rare now, but incentivizing self-reporting is a good practice.

Most organizations now include risk metrics in the balanced scorecard of their managers. The design, relevance and enforcement of the scorecards will vary from firm to firm, so even if the intention is commendable, you must be wary of poorly designed incentives leading to unintended consequences. Examples of operational risk metrics in scorecards include existence and frequency of risk committee meetings, overdue action plans, overdue audit recommendations, timeliness of incident reporting, KRI status and number of risks above appetite.

Sophisticated banks have been using a system of economic capital allocation since the late 1990s. Economic capital is allocated to business lines according to their risk profiles, which in turn are influenced by a number of metrics in credit, market, liquidity and operational risks. The higher the risk profile, the higher the consumed capital, which means higher funding costs and therefore lower profits when higher risk-taking is not properly compensated by higher returns.

BOUNDARY EVENT REPORTING

Boundary events are those that materialize in a different risk class than their cause, such as a credit loss aggravated by the wrong recording of collateral or a market loss due to an unintentional error in booking a position. The pragmatic view is to leave the recording of the events where they materialize, without trying to disentangle the cause. This is the view adopted by the Basel Committee, at least for credit risk, as long as the credit loss recorded is covered by the risk-weighted asset credit capital.[2] The position of Basel is understandable because regulators focus on the sufficiency of capital coverage, regardless of whether the losses are recorded as credit or operational risk. From a management information perspective, however, the more common practice is to insist on reclassifying boundary events into their original risk class, digging out the causes of credit and market incident, at least for losses above a given threshold. Although this makes sense in theory, in practice it can generate considerable resistance from the business lines, which may question the value of the exercise and possibly feel unfairly investigated, especially when the recording applies to small recurrent losses and without a regulatory requirement. Therefore, I recommend striking a balance between the resistances generated by the reclassification of boundary events

---

[2]BCBS, "Basel III: Finalising post-crisis reforms," December 2017, p 131. Market risk losses due to operational risk though must be recorded under SMA, the reason being that market risk capital calculations are based on value-at-risk and not on past losses.

and the value of the information collected. At the very least, firms should limit the reclassification of events, and the investigation of causes, to major events (according to their respective definitions of "major").

REVIEW AND VALIDATION

Data Quality Reviews

Data quality is naturally of prime importance and risk data are no exception. Regulators pay attention to the completeness and accuracy of key fields such as dates, classification of losses, consolidation of group losses and the amounts of expected losses versus settled losses. Comprehensiveness of data collection is, arguably, the main point of quality assessment by the regulator. How comprehensive is the loss collection exercise and how many incidents have not been reported and with what impact? These questions are almost impossible to answer, but some regulators will ask them nonetheless. More reasonably, they will check whether the data collection process has been reviewed and validated by reconciling it with the general ledger, internal audit or a third party.

Feeding from Existing Sources: A Case Against Standalone Databases

Most organizations possess – sometimes without realizing it – several databases that can directly feed the operational incident data collection process and improve data quality, comprehensiveness and reconciliation, as well as simplify the overall exercise. Figure 13.2 presents an example of such databases.

   The general ledger (GL) is the first information source that comes to mind as a loss data feed; every amount lost by a firm should be entered in the GL. In a perfect world, all direct operational losses would be identified directly and fully in accounting. Regrettably, in practice, the usability of the GL for operational risk strongly depends on whether the ledger rubric allows you to identify operational risk events. I was fortunate to start my career in operational risk in a group where the GL had a rubric labeled "miscellaneous inflows and outflows." It comprised all the money flows in and out of the bank that were not justified by an accounting document, from cash imbalances in retail banking to goodwill gestures in private banking. This acted as a wonderful proxy for operational incidents. After spending three days with the accounting team, I had sufficient records to make my case to the risk committee and, as the new head of operational risk for the region, I received the green light to recruit my first collaborator for the ORM team, much to the amazement of several of my older colleagues. However, some GLs are not as easy to exploit and this strategy does not always work. Some tier 1 banks have profoundly reorganized their GL so they can isolate operational risk losses and reconcile them with the operational incident database. GL data can provide direct,

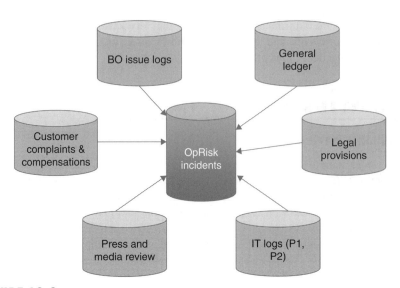

FIGURE 13.2 Data-feeding sources in an operational incident database

settled, financial losses from incidents and will often need to be complemented by other management information about indirect losses and other so-called non-financial impacts.

IT logs are probably the most common form of incident collection used in recent years to feed operational risk incident databases, either automatically or by manual transfer. IT issues rated Priority 1 (P1) and Priority 2 (P2) are generally considered as operational risk incidents. Other types of data, such as the list of provisions made for pending lawsuits, are excellent sources of information about large past incidents that are yet to be settled. Customer complaints and customer compensations are obvious data sources for operational events. Many firms use them and those that don't, should. Many firms also use information feeds from the marketing and media department, which provide alerts about bad press and other types of reputational risk incidents. Sometimes, back offices and other departments maintain their own log of issues and incidents. Using these logs to build operational incident data is efficient and much more acceptable to the business than asking it to log the same type of information again on a different system.

Good practice does not include standalone incident databases in operational risk: incidents emerge from all parts of the organization and in many forms; they are present in operations, processes and communications, and are captured by various systems in different logs and departments. Most of the information needed by the ORM team already exists in the organization, so it is a question of capturing it in the most efficient way and then filtering into the ORM database whatever is needed for the incident details. The aim is to minimize effort and avoid duplicating information from disconnected systems. Integrated data collection is less effort for the business, requires fewer corporate resources overall and frees more time for intelligent analysis and valuable risk management.

This intelligent analysis includes causal analysis of loss events to identify failure patterns and preventive KRIs. Event and trend gaps in severity data are useful to inform thresholds. Key indicators are detailed in the next chapter.

CHAPTER 14

Key Risk Indicators

INTRODUCTION

Key risk indicators are the heart of monitoring, of performance, of risks and of control effectiveness. This chapter explores these indicators and focuses on preventive risk indicators, which in several instances are the same metrics as performance and controls indicators.

KRIs for operational risk have attracted considerable attention in recent years. The need for predictability and control is a priority in the business world, and many boards of directors now ask their senior managers and risk managers to compile a list of leading KRIs. KRIs were identified as primary information in 68% of the operational risk profile reports of the institutions surveyed by Protiviti and risk.net at the end of 2014.[1] The majority of respondents (60%) also use KRIs to assess their control environment and operating effectiveness and to gain confidence in the risk profile of their organization.

Many organizations struggle to gain a clear view of what constitutes an efficient suite of KRIs. We can count on one hand – maybe two – the number of financial firms that are fully satisfied with their KRIs.

ROLES OF RISK INDICATORS

KRIs are used for a number of purposes in the management of operational risk and the overall management of an organization. In relation to operational risk, KRIs have the following essential roles:

- monitor risk-taking and the potential impacts of risk events on the organization
- translate risk appetite, defined at board level and possibly also at the operational/ business unit level

---

[1]Protiviti, "Forward march – Op risk integration strides on – survey results," Dec 2014, risk.net

- provide an objective and documented way of demonstrating effective risk monitoring and mitigation in the organization.

Risk Monitoring

Risk indicators are used to track changes in an organization's exposure to operational risk. When selected appropriately, indicators should flag any change in the likelihood of a risk occurring or its possible impact. Leading indicators, i.e., indicators that flag a risk before it crystallizes, are most useful in this regard. Therefore, leading KRIs will concentrate on the metrics of risk drivers, also called risk causes or risk factors. Figure 14.1 illustrates well-known leading KRIs of car accidents: speed and lack of vigilance, through tiredness, medication of alcohol, all legally regulated. Risk drivers can increase the likelihood of a risk, its impact, or both. So-called "lagging KRIs," tracking events that have already occurred, are a specific form of incident reporting that flag weaknesses that need to be corrected in the control system.

Giving Assurance to the Board

The UK Corporate Governance Code of May 2010 states that "the board is responsible for determining the nature and extent of the significant risks it is willing to take in achieving its strategic objectives (...) and should maintain sound risk management and internal control systems." Defining a relevant, specific and actionable risk appetite results from a mature risk management process. Assessing the risks that a business is willing to take and maintaining "sound risk management and internal control systems" requires the identification and assessment of the key risks that may negatively impact the business objectives, the evaluation of the current exposure to those risks and the definition of additional controls if this exposure is judged excessive. Because KRIs

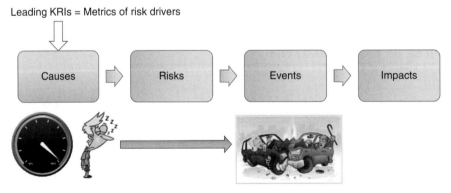

FIGURE 14.1   Preventive KRIs Illustrated

enable a firm to monitor risk-taking in relation to risk appetite, essentially by overseeing the exposure to risk and the effectiveness of controls, they help to achieve this objective.

RISK APPETITE KRIS

Risk appetite KRIs are now common in a majority of firms. Risk appetite statements are complemented by metrics quantifying risk appetite limits set by the board, but these metrics are rarely leading or preventive KRIs. Instead, they represent the performance of the firm's control environment, which adds to the confusion and debate over which metrics are KPIs and which are KRIs. They are often the same, but viewed from a different perspective.

Many risk appetite KRIs are obvious, such as the number and severity of incidents, and some are common but not very useful, such as turnover and customer complaints. Turnover is meaningless when reported on average: it hides the turnover of high performers and of key people in control functions, such as the cybersecurity team. Client complaints are strong lagging metrics, and if there are numerous complaints, it will be the tip of an iceberg of customer service and operational issues that have been neglected. Leading KRIs, even at risk appetite level, relate to increased exposure to risk, shortages of resources and control failings. Near misses also are important KRIs but rarely considered as such.

Reflecting BEICF

The strength of an organization's KRI program reflects the strength of its risk management function. When KRIs are comprehensive and can reliably monitor the level of key risks faced by an organization, they are a useful indication of the organization's level of risk management and control. In this context, they can be included as part of the modeling of operational risk for the AMA and IMAP (internal model approval process), reflecting the fourth mandatory components of modeling methodology: BEICF.

For financial institutions that calculate and hold operational risk capital under more advanced approaches, there is a specific requirement to include BEICF in their capital estimation and allocation processes. While the definition of BEICF differs from one jurisdiction to another, and in many cases is specific to individual organizations, these factors must:

1. be risk sensitive
2. provide management with information on the risk profile of the organization

3. represent meaningful drivers of exposure which can be quantified
4. be used across the entire organization.

KRIs are a good way of meeting BEICF requirements.

KEY INDICATORS: PERFORMANCE, RISKS AND CONTROLS

In an operational risk context, a KRI is a metric that provides information on the level of exposure to some operational risk, at a given point in time. Preventive KRIs measure a rise in the causes of risk, either in probability (KRI of likelihood) or in potential impact should the risk materialize (KRI of impact). Key performance indicators measure performance or target achievement, establishing how well a business entity contains its operational risks. Examples of performance indicators are cumulative hours of IT system outage, the percentage of transactions containing errors, customer satisfaction scores, and the quality and application of service level agreements (SLAs). Key control indicators (KCIs) support the effective control of information, either in design or in performance. KCIs measure the effectiveness of a particular control at a certain point in time and they demonstrate their worth when a key control fails a test.

In practice, the same metrics can often be considered as performance indicators and risk indicators, or control indicators and risk indicators, or they may share elements of all three. KPIs, KRIs and KCIs overlap in many instances, especially when they signal breaches of minimum standards. A poor performance will often become a source of risk; for instance, poor system performance such as repeated downtime can signal worse to come. An example is the 24-hour meltdown of British Airways' reservation system in May 2017, which had been preceded by six short-term interruptions over the previous 12 months. In other areas, poor customer service increases the risk of bad referrals and commercial losses, and poor performance of the finance function increases the risk of delays in the publication of information, or errors and legal impacts.

Failing controls are even more obvious candidates for preventive KRIs: a key control failure always constitutes a source of risk; examples include incomplete due diligence, reduced IT testing, missing reconciliation steps and overdue maintenance. Furthermore, the failure of a control function is jointly a KPI, a KRI and a KCI. For example, overdue confirmation of financial transactions indicates poor back-office performance (KPI), increased risk of legal disputes, processing errors and rogue trading (KRI) and signal control failures in transactions processing (KCI).

When undertaking a KRI program, organizations should start with an inventory of the KPIs and control tests that are already in place and could play the role of KRIs. Many potential risk indicators will often be present but are hidden under other names.

TEN FEATURES OF LEADING KRIS

Leading KRIs are, in short, metrics of risk drivers. Indicators are also a type of reporting, hence reporting rules apply: KRIs must improve decision-making and bring more value than they cost. More specifically, preventive KRIs should have the following ten characteristics:

1. Early warning devices: they signal changes in risk levels, either an increase in the likelihood of an event, or impact, or both (like car speed, where an increase in speed will increase both the risk of a collision and the damage if a collision occurs).

2. Must address risks, not events: KRIs are proxies of risk drivers; indicators addressing events are "lagging." Lagging KRIs are signals of missing controls: once they turn red, the answer is not to keep capturing the metrics but to put an appropriate control in place (see the box on British road signs).

3. Specific to each activity and risk profile: only few KRIs can be common to all activities in the firm, and the thresholds will certainly vary with the nature of each business and activity. Moreover, to maximize efficiency and to keep reporting short and useful, KRIs should be filtered according to each firm's risk profile, tracking what a firm is not so good at rather than the non-issues.

4. Best identified via data analysis and experience: in many aspects of operational risk and especially for HR risks, data alone are insufficient to prove the relationship between risk factors and events. Often, business intuition and experience are useful guides if there is a lack of data. When data are available, they should be used to confirm intuition and to identify other causes and other effects.

5. Have a business owner who relies on the metric: it is good governance that KRIs are used and owned by the business. In particular, it reinforces data quality and continuity of maintenance.

6. Be worth more than they cost: KRIs, like many other types of reporting, may need heavy data collection, which can be costly. You must ensure the right tradeoff between the value of information collected and the cost of collection.

7. Timely: monitoring KRIs (as distinct from reporting) should match the cycle of the activity, from real time (like in IT or financial markets trading) to quarterly or even yearly for some HR metrics. Automated KRIs are the only option for high-frequency activities and automated data capture is a better option all around.

8. Must help business decisions: like any type of information reporting, KRIs need to support and improve decision-making.

9. Thresholds linked to risk appetite: higher tolerance for risk is reflected in higher thresholds triggering intervention on rising KRIs and vice versa. Thresholds are examined later in this chapter.

10. Must be back-tested for validity: like every other part of the framework, KRIs must be assessed, refreshed and replaced when necessary. A good practice is to revisit each section of the framework once a year.

LAGGING INDICATORS AND BRITISH ROAD SIGNS

Despite the demand for preventive indicators, the number of organizations still using lagging indicators, such as the number of incidents as KRIs, is puzzling. The rationale behind British road signs helps us understand the role of lagging KRIs. Lagging KRIs are useful just once, to understand the severity of the risk before proper prevention takes place. Many of the speed limits and warning signs we see on our roads relate to past accidents: the worse the accident, the stronger the corresponding prevention. SLOW signs painted on British crossroads – and costing about £1,500 ($1,800) in paint and labor – are the result of past accidents at the crossroads, justifying the investment in further awareness and prevention; a STOP sign or a mirror are the response to a more serious, possibly fatal, collision.[2] It is the role of lagging KRIs to assess risks in the first instance only. Once the risk is assessed, it is pointless to keep counting the crashes; you have to move to prevention. In an operational risk management context, lagging KRIs above accepted incident thresholds must trigger the move to better controls, process redesign or other action plans. Relevant preventive KRIs will then focus on the effectiveness of the new controls and proper execution of the reviewed process.

Issues are usually synonymous with leading KRIs. For example, a large international bank calls an issue a control gap or an overdue action. A KRI is an issue overdue for resolution. This is an excellent forward-looking approach. Another example of a forward-looking approach is when a company reports project delay KRIs in the color expected for the next reporting period, e.g., "We are still on time now but we will be late next quarter" – so this will be reported "amber," meaning "approaching problems."

CATEGORIES OF KRIS

In 2013, I proposed a classification of KRIs[3] to help risk managers and firms reflect on leading indicators top-down and bottom-up, and to identify a comprehensive set

---

[2]Source: UK road safety awareness program.
[3]Chapelle, A. (2013) "Unlocking KRIs", *Risk Manager Professional*; Chapelle, A. (2013) "Preventive KRIs", *Operational Risk and Regulation*. Both articles reproduced in Chapelle, A. (2017) *Reflections on Operational Risk Management*, Risk Books.

TABLE 14.1   Categories of indicators and examples

Indicator type	Description	Examples
Exposure indicators	Monitor changes in an organization's exposure to one or more risks, either in likelihood of occurrence or potential impact	Changes of resources exposed to risk, changes in political or regulatory environment
Stress indicators	Capture the stretch in organizational resources in human capital, equipment or IT	Rise in transactions handled per staff, long-term vacancies in small teams; percentage of machine time operated at capacity limit, reduced buffer system capacity, overdue maintenance, missed intermediary deadlines, etc.
Failure indicators	KRIs derived from failing organizational performance and/or control weaknesses; typically captured by a KPI or KCI breaching their thresholds	Unconfirmed back-office transactions, incomplete client files (AML), incomplete due diligence check (suppliers/staff), poor customer services ratings
Causal indicators	Metrics that provide information about the causes and root causes of key risks	Pay under market rate (for key man risk), financial pressure (for internal fraud), abnormal trading pattern (for rogue trading), abnormal behavior pattern (for all types of fraud)

of risk indicators (Table 14.1). The four categories – Exposure, Stress, Failure and Causal – have been adopted by firms I had not even met personally and have been reproduced in a number of publications on the topic. This section discusses these four categories.

Exposure Indicators

Exposure indicators relate to the nature of the business environment and to its critical dependencies. The business environment may be volatile or stable, growing or mature, regulated or free. Critical dependencies include main suppliers and vendors, large clients, essential systems or key staff. Accepting a given business environment and critical dependencies are risk appetite decisions. Next, monitoring any changes to this accepted level of risk is part of a comprehensive KRI program. Exposure KRIs capture significant changes to the business environment or to its exposure. For example, an increase in financial markets volatility is an appropriate KRI for errors in the back offices of trading floors, due to the increased volumes of trades it commonly generates. Critical stakeholders monitoring is another important part of exposure KRIs.

As a director of a small business I won't tolerate a single client generating more than 50% of my turnover for longer than three months. This is a risk appetite decision about critical exposure to key clients. Reporting of exposure KRIs can be regular or ad hoc, depending on their nature and the type of business.

Stress and Stretch

Stretch KRIs reflect the overusage of business resources, whether human or physical. Tiredness is a well-documented cause of accidents, mistakes and slip-ups, whether in medical services, road safety or other areas. Many human resources departments record the number of hours of overtime per staff member, and some organizations have introduced overtime limits after realizing that overworked staff members make more mistakes, damaging productivity.

Overused equipment and IT resources are likely to lead to equipment losses, downtime or crashes. Care is therefore needed to protect the infrastructure. An example is a messaging company that closely monitors the number of messages passing through each of its network hubs and then reroutes messages before a hub reaches a critical threshold. Stress indicators may be reported regularly or exceptionally, whenever there is a significant change in the use of resources. IT resources and usage are typically monitored continuously, with flags raised when critical points are reached or approached.

Failure Indicators

Failure indicators are another name for failing performance and failing controls. Put simply, a KPI is a performance indicator when it is green and become a KRI when it turns amber. The same goes for control indicators. Any indicator of a key control failure is a good potential KRI, either as formal KCI reporting, unsatisfactory control testing or low rating on control effectiveness. Poor performance also often leads to risk increases, leading to the common ambiguity between KPIs and KRIs. This is why many organizations avoid confusion by calling all indicators KPI or KI (key indicators), or KxI (x being either performance, control or risk), or simply key metrics.

Causal Indicators

At the heart of preventive KRIs, causal indicators focus on risk drivers. They capture the direct causes and the root causes of key risks. In practice, the three other indicator categories can also be causal indicators, in the sense that they capture the causes of events rather than the incidents themselves. Causal indicators capture the causes of risks that have not been addressed by exposure, stress and failure. This residual category ensures a comprehensive range of indicators.

CASE STUDY: PREVENTING KEY MAN LOSS

Staff turnover is all too often mentioned as a KRI. It is a lagging indicator for key man risk and loss of institutional knowledge, and it can be a leading or current indicator of productivity drop and human errors, since lack of familiarity with processes is a main driver for slow work and errors. Preventive KRIs for key man risk relate to the causes of the risk – for example, where key information is limited to too few associates and there are no backups for key staff (exposure indicator and KRIs of impact), or where there is a risk of key staff resigning due to a bad boss or poor pay (causal indicators and KRIs of likelihood). Figure 14.2 lists some of the most relevant KRIs for key man risk.

> **Drivers of resignation (KRIs of likelihood)**

- Bad pay
  - KRI: pay gap to market rates (for high performers and key functions)
- Bad career prospects
  - KRI: nbr of promotions/theoretical nbr; internal mobility (in years)
- Bad boss
  - KRI: 360 review results; engagement survey results

> **Drivers of exposure to key people risks (KRIs of exposure)**

- Number of key people
  - Without alternate/cross trained substitute
  - Without succession plan
  - Without fully documented process

FIGURE 14.2   Preventive KRIs for key man risk

The best practice I have observed to prevent key staff exposure was from a newly appointed CEO who gave each key manager three months to designate and train an alternate. Had the managers simply consolidated their own positions, thus making themselves indispensable, they would have run the risk of not being promoted. All substitutes were trained within the deadline. This is risk management by reducing exposure.

A large banking group provides another example of an inspiring practice. It focused on pay as a way to reduce the risk of losing key staff in the risk management function. After it identified who to retain and any pay that was below market rates, the bank offered overnight pay rises to a number of surprised and delighted employees.

KRI DESIGN: NUMBER, THRESHOLDS AND GOVERNANCE

KRI design relates to the detail of data capture and the frequency, thresholds and governance of who reports and who acts on KRI breaches.

Selecting KRIs: Number and Data

How many KRIs should you use? I suggest the *minimum meaningful*: preferably no more than one KRI per main risk driver of likelihood and driver of impact. To avoid redundancy and information overload, do not capture the same type of information under different forms.

Most operational risk drivers are common knowledge. Internal fraud drivers include financial pressures, lax environment, resentment toward the company and non-segregation of duties. IT disruption drivers relate to overcapacity, overdue maintenance of systems or rushed testing. However, the many validated KRIs that specialists use every day are labeled differently depending on where they are collected. They might be called logs, issue logs, breaches, key performance indicators, control breaks, concentration factors and events, without risk managers realizing that most of the KRIs they need are already monitored in specialist departments.

The first task for a risk manager in charge of KRI selection and reporting is to make an inventory of what exists in the firm, to avoid duplication and identify any gaps. This requires understanding the mechanisms behind incidents and near misses, or at least a few conversations with specialists, to identify the risk drivers and their metrics. However, not all causes need to be monitored by KRIs, nor will they all be suitable as proxies and measures. As tempting as leading KRIs may be, they need to be filtered to achieve maximum reporting value and must be validated by experience. To save costs and efforts in reporting, firms should preferably choose KRIs among the metrics that are already captured as part of the monitoring and possibly under a different name. Moreover, data captured automatically are preferable, to save costs and efforts.

Even so, before drafting the list of possible indicators, it is good to have an open mind when considering all the possible risk drivers without restricting oneself by the availability of data. Indicators should aim to track issues and vulnerabilities, in order to fix them and increase the firm's resilience; their primary role is not demonstrating a steady performance of the business. In many firms, directors and senior managers become nervous when indicators keep flashing green. Their suspicion is often justified, or at least understandable: either they live in a perfect world, the organization doesn't know what to track, or the design metrics are calibrated so that they produce a green report all the time. I remember a manager in a U.S. organization who handpicked KRIs in a way that ensured his department reported 100% green KRIs at every period. His green-fingered approach earned him the nickname "the English Garden."

Selected KRIs should have three qualities – they must:

- capture a risk cause
- have data that are already available in the organization (or easily collectable)
- measure a risk cause to which the organization is vulnerable.

For instance, if a firm pays well but doesn't have very good managers and this is affecting staff retention, there is no point tracking a KRI for pay gap to market rate, but there is value in tracking the 360 review of team managers and other staff survey results. This is the main reason I don't recommend using commercial databases with thousands of possible KRIs. Because they are broad-brush, with so many possible metrics, it would take a long time and much effort to filter information so that it is relevant to the risk profile of your firm. Rather than run the risk of being overwhelmed by unfocused metrics, I encourage firms to network with peers. Membership-based risk associations are a good example and the entry fees are cheap compared with the wealth of information they offer. In addition, some websites provide open-source risk management tools. Finally, data consortia offer services way beyond data pools, including benchmarking and guidance around scenario methodology, modeling, taxonomy, risk appetite, and meetings and surveys with members.

Figure 14.3 presents a fictitious example of a KRI dashboard for human error in credit processes, although it was inspired by a real case study. KRIs of human error typically relate to experience, proxied by time on the job, and workload. KRIs on results of key control testing are also valuable.

Thresholds and KRI Definitions

KRI thresholds are one way of expressing risk appetite throughout the organization, with a lower threshold typically linked to lower risk appetite.

Options for KRI thresholds include:

1. Zero for risks for which firms have the lowest appetite; or x% above zero, 'x' depending on appetite; this requires defining KRI as an issue, not a simple exposure number.
2. Deviations from normal (upwards and downwards): observe historical trends over 3–18 months depending on the activity.
3. Cluster-based: a jump in data may constitute a natural threshold.
4. Gradually reaching an ideal objective (e.g. control effectiveness): when a control fails, say 30% of the time, setting up gradual quality criteria may be more realistic than demanding high performance from day one.

In my experience, the reason firms struggle with KRI thresholds is often linked to the definition of the metric itself rather than the choice of threshold. Many KRIs

	Key risk errors in credit handling process						
KRI #	Risk cause/sub risk	KRI	Measures required	Thresholds	Actual score	KRI	Comments/action
1	Legal risk/late involvement of legal	Process stage at which legal is contacted by credit department	Credit process structure, time of contact between legal and credit department	Stage 2	Stage 3	A	Plan a resolution
2	Legal risk/legal complexity	Multiple jurisdictions per deal	Group structure and geographical spread of clients	5	3	G	
3	Legal risk/exposure/pace of change	# updates in rules and regulations impacting Dpt per quarter	Legal and compliance update log	TBD with legal		G	If elevated: reinforce resources in legal team
4	Legal risk/familiarity and expertise	Number of similar deals previously executed	Deals categorization and recording	2 (if 0: yellow)	0	A	Elevate controls
5	Legal risk/ missing documentations	# of missing documents in file	Sampling	3%	20%	R	Investigate and solve for the future
6	Process/data capture error	# missing reconciliations between processing stages	Control testing – sampling	5%	25%	A	Plan a resolution
7	Process/data capture error	# reconciliation breaks between processing stages	Control results	2%	15%	A	Improve processes and training
8	Human error/competency (mistakes)	Drop in average # years' experience in the business	Years' of activity in the dpt, per staff member	<25% drop	Stable	G	
9	Human error/competency (mistakes)	# of key client to inexperienced (<1yr) account manager	Key client identification, account manager, years of activity	0 (red: 3)	1	A	Provide support/ mentoring
10	Human error/overload (slips)	# of key clients per account manager	Key client identification, account manager	10 (red: 20)	10	G	

FIGURE 14.3 Example of a KRI dashboard – errors in credit handling

are defined in numbers: number of sick days, turnover ratio, number of vulnerabilities, number of administrative rights, and so on. So where do you begin and where do you end? When KRIs are defined across such a wide spectrum, thresholds are very hard to define. The rule of thumb I recommend in these instances is "Your metric is a KRI when even one is an issue." Let's take IT vulnerabilities: is 10 the right number? What about 100, or 1,000? I know an organization with 50,000 IT vulnerabilities. Even if 50,000 seems a bit much, KRI thresholds on absolute numbers of vulnerabilities seems like shooting in the dark. A better KRI would be: number of critical vulnerabilities unpatched within the required deadline. Even one is an issue: it is a control breach and a breach of policy. Equifax's internal policy is to patch critical vulnerabilities within 48 hours, which is pretty standard in the industry. However, it identified a vulnerability that was then left unpatched for *two months*, which allowed hackers to access the personal details of 145 million customers.

A U.S. regulator on one of my courses in New York was investigating KRIs around IT administrator rights. An absolute number of those rights would be unhelpful. Instead, as a KRI, we considered using the number of rights beyond what the organization might need – say one or two per department. KRIs related to access management, a key control in IT security, are very relevant, such as overdue access revision or unchanged access following a change of job, to mention just two examples. Table 14.2 shows some of the ways KRI metrics could be transformed to make the definition of threshold easier and more linked to risk appetite.

Governance

Governance around indicators is common and simple, and broadly aligned with the response to colors in the RCSA matrix (green: do nothing; amber: monitor; red: act). Some firms have four colors and some act on amber. The practice has moved away from the shades of red concept, where the severity was judged according to the department or the type of metric considered. Nowadays, red means red for all KRIs: there are no levels of severity – at least in best practice. This underlines the importance of selecting the right thresholds for indicators. Thresholds can vary per department or business unit when risk appetite varies, but governance must be uniform across the firm; a red is a red.

Like all directives, governance and control must be defined ahead of time. It's not when an indicator turns red that firms should wonder who is in charge of what. Typically, KRIs are identified and designed in collaboration with the business and the risk function, and thresholds are signed off by the business. Indicators have an owner, in charge of taking actions when the value of the indicator enters a risky zone – which will be amber or red, depending on the firm. To avoid conflicts of interest, KRI values ideally should be captured automatically, or be directly and objectively observable, so that the indicator owner is not tempted to report a value slightly under the threshold, to avoid having to take action.

TABLE 14.2   Examples of more risk-sensitive KRIs for easier thresholds

Classic KRI	Recommended
# sick days	▪ Number of/% rise in short leave (Mondays and Fridays) – signal of absenteeism ▪ Number of long-term sick leave (>3 months)/in small teams – risk of overstretch of resources
% downtime	▪ # of systems interruption > x minutes in a row over the last 3 months (x depending on the nature of the activity)
# vulnerabilities	▪ # critical vulnerabilities unpatched within policy deadlines
Turnover rate	▪ # of talent/high potential staff resigning over the last 3 months (lagging but more specific) ▪ leading: # talented individual underpaid/without substitute/unmanaged/expressing dissatisfaction at work
# recommendations following a penetration test	# delays in actions plans following the penetration test
# customer complaints	# customer complaints unresolved within x days (x depending on the firm's policy and tolerance for customer dissatisfaction)

VALIDATION KRI FRAMEWORK

The validation stage is essential to maintain a reliable and valuable set of KRIs. A number of advanced organizations, in terms of operational risk, use a simple method to validate their key risk indicators: their loss-reporting databases include fields to document the colors of the related indicators when an incident occurs. A green indicator at the time of an incident does not say much for its usefulness. And while a red indicator may prove its worth, it could also reveal a breakdown in governance, since the red signal did not aid prevention, at least in this example. Conversely, it is useful to check the situation after indicators have turned red or amber: has it led to events? If not, it can mean that KRIs are inappropriate, or too strict, or you just got lucky. More positively, if action was taken to avoid incidents, it can mean that KRIs play their role fully.

Defining preventive KRIs requires continuous effort and is extremely useful for understanding how operational risk is generated. It helps to address the top challenge identified for the operational risk function in recent years – namely, management's poor understanding of the value of the ORM program.[4] Chapter 16 will explore further ways to demonstrate the value of operational risk management.

---

[4] 22% of respondents to a risk.net survey on the challenges faced by operational risk function, 2015.

SUMMARY: FRAMEWORK FOR PREVENTIVE KRIS

To summarize this chapter, Table 14.3 presents a six-step method to identify, design and validate preventive KRIs.[5]

TABLE 14.3   Six steps for preventive KRIs

1. Identify	Key risks to the organization
2. Understand	Causes and root causes of these key risks
3. Recycle	KPIs and KCIs that can be treated as KRIs
4. Define	Missing metrics of key risk drivers
5. Design	Data capture, frequency, thresholds and reporting governance
6. Validate	The preventive nature of KRIs

---

[5]Chapelle, A. (2014) "Six steps for preventive KRIs." Operational risk, risk.net.

## CHAPTER 15

Risk Reporting

This chapter presents the principles of reporting and the types of content that are common in risk reporting in financial institutions. It explores the main challenges of reporting on non-quantitative data, presents options to address risk aggregation and gives examples of conduct reporting. Finally, it proposes solutions to deal with the heavy tail nature of operational losses while turning data into reporting stories.

GOLDEN RULES OF REPORTING

Except for regulatory reporting, which is a mandatory requirement, firms should consider a few golden rules for efficient reporting:

- The value must exceed the cost of collection: there is no point collecting and reporting information when the cost is greater than the intrinsic value of the information.
- Know how you will use the information: if you have a clear purpose – usually to help make or confirm a decision – it helps you decide whether the information is worth knowing.
- Reporting influences decision-making, even if the decision is to confirm the status quo. Rule 3 connects rule 1 and rule 2; a piece of information is valuable if it influences decision-making, even if the decision is that the findings are good and nothing needs to change.

These rules are variations of the "so what?" approach to reporting, ensuring that everything reported has a purpose.

TYPICAL CONTENT OF RISK REPORTING

Reporting packs in operational risk commonly include the following:

1. Incident reporting: this covers number and size of events, and trends and top loss events. Monthly reporting is the usual frequency, although some firms do it weekly, but I believe that's too much and unnecessarily time-consuming, unless it's in a large bank.

2. Top risks (usually ten): these are reported to the board and to the risk commit-tee. Whether the organization actually does something about these top ten risks is a different matter: the more mature the organization, the more it acts on risks assessed above risk appetite. Poor practice, still too common, is to go through risk reporting with very little decision-making; as a CRO commented once: "Are we taking decisions here, or are we looking at pictures?"

3. KRIs and issue monitoring: these are dashboard tables with thresholds and corre-sponding status and colors.

4. Risk appetite KRIs: now a general practice in firms, risk appetite statements are complemented by KRI metrics, as detailed in the previous chapter.

5. Emerging risks/horizon scanning: this practice became general 3–5 years ago. It is commonly applied to regulatory risk and changes in the compliance and regulatory environment but should not be limited to that.

6. Action plans and follow-up: tracking mitigating action plans, following large incidents or for risks assessed above appetite, is essential in risk monitoring and reporting.

Best practice includes clear accountability and time frames for each action and action owner, with regular documenting and tracking, typically monthly. Most disciplined firms have a "big zero" objective: zero overdue action plans and zero over-due audit recommendations. Overdue ratios are rightly called "discipline indicators." Examples of poor practice include firms that commonly miss deadlines or continually postpone planned dates.

RISK REPORTING CHALLENGES[1]

Management reporting is challenging – risk reporting even more so. It is often hard to find the right balance between too much information and too little. When you have too much, you may end up with 200-page risk documents that are seldom read, which means important insights are lost. If you have too little, information becomes so thin that it is meaningless.

One of the challenges of risk reporting is how to filter risk information upwards and what form it should take. Group management and different departments and business units don't all need the same type, or amount, of risk information. Reporting information to the next level of management implies choosing what to escalate and what to aggregate. Some key information deserves to be communicated to the next decision level without alteration, when the rest could be summarized

---

[1] A previous version of this section was published in Chapelle, Oct 2015, "Have your cake and eat it", risk.net, reproduced in Chapelle, 2017, *Reflections on Operational Risk Management*, Risk Books.

in aggregated statements. High risks, near misses, defective key controls will typically be escalated without alteration, while other information will be summarized in aggregated reporting.

Separating Monitoring and Reporting

There is a difference between risk monitoring and risk reporting: not everything that is monitored needs to be reported. Monitoring typically remains at operations level and only alerts to be escalated, alongside summary data, are reported to the next level of management.

Monitoring applies to risk assessment units (RAUs), either per business line or per process. Increasingly, institutions try to operate process-based risk assessments, even though they are organized vertically, in order to analyze the risks at the touch point of these processes. Best practice for operational risk monitoring focuses on controls (design, effectiveness and control gap) more than on risks. Controls are observable while risks are not. Mature banks require evidence of control testing to rate a control "effective" and do not solely rely on unevidenced self-assessment. In some banks, risk control self-assessment is simply called risk control assessment (RCA).

Risk registers containing risk assessments are not necessarily included in the centralized reporting. The risk function maintains the risk register for all risks at inherent levels, controls and residual levels. Best practice in reporting follows clear risk taxonomy, e.g. categories of risk, causes, impact and controls to assess and report against this taxonomy. Risk taxonomy does not have to follow the Basel categories, which are now fairly outdated given the evolution of the sector. The only requirement, from a regulatory perspective, is for it to be possible to map the firm's risk categories with the Basel categories.

Best practice in mature firms is to select and report risk information on a "need to know" basis, depending on the audience and the level of management:

- Process management and risk management levels: "All you need to know to monitor."
  - Process management and risk management access a full set of metrics to perform their day-to-day tasks of monitoring activities and risks. Only alerts needing escalation and synthetic data are reported to the next management level.
- Department heads: "All you need to know to act."
  - Out of the full set of monitoring metrics, division heads receive only the information that requires them to take action, such as process halts needing intervention or incidents needing early mitigation. The rest is periodically summarized to show the global picture, but this will not raise any particular concerns or require any particular action.
- Executive committee: "All you need to know to decide."
  - Executive directors and board members take the decisions that will influence the direction of the firm. They need the most appropriate type of information to

help them fulfill their mission – for example, a set of leading indicators telling top management where to focus more attention and resources; trends showing deteriorating performance; information on progress against plans; and any unexpected good or bad results reflecting the materialization of risks against objectives. Where top-down environment screening impacts the firm's strategy, it should also be part of the risk reporting to executives.

I would advise against reporting solely on red flags without the balance of a summary report, as it can give a biased, overly pessimistic view of the firm's risk level. If 80% of the indicators are green, this should be reported, alongside the more problematic issues, to give a balanced view of the situation. Most firms now adopt this approach.

Aggregating Risk Data

Unlike financial risks, operational risk reporting faces the additional challenge of aggregating qualitative data. Risk scores, red-amber-green ratings and other indicators are discrete, qualitative and completely unfit for any arithmetic manipulation. A risk rated "5" (extreme) alongside a risk rated "1" (low) is not at all equivalent to two risks rated "3" (moderate). Calculating sums on ratings brings to mind the old joke about recording a fine average body temperature when your head is in the oven and your feet are in the refrigerator. Even when expressed in numbers, risk ratings are no more quantitative or additive than colors or adjectives.

Three options are worth considering for aggregating qualitative data:

- Conversion and addition: qualitative metrics are converted into a common monetary unit, which can then be quantitatively manipulated. Some large banks convert non-financial impacts results of their RCSA (reputation, regulatory, etc.) into financial data to be able to sum the impacts and aggregate risks. It is the approach followed by a number of firms which prefer converting impacts into monetary units, for additivity. A variant of this approach is presented in the case study, where KRIs are converted into percentage score above risk appetite. This approach requires a number of assumptions and approximations that some firms find uncomfortable, while others happily apply it.
- Worst-case: the worst score of a dataset, such as a group of key risk indicators, is reported as the aggregated value, e.g., all is red if one item is red. It is the most conservative form of reporting. This is appropriate when tolerance to risk is minimal, when data are reasonably reliable and when indicators are strong predictors of a risk. This approach has the advantage of being prudent but the disadvantage of being potentially over-alarming and even unsafe if it generates so many alerts that management simply disregards red alerts or is unable to distinguish the signal from the noise.

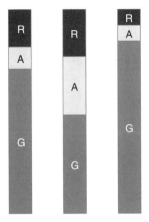

FIGURE 15.1 Categorization: candle reporting

- Categorization: rather than averaging and summing risk scores, which is a common but regrettably misleading way of reporting risk data, an acceptable alternative is to report the risk scores per percentage of categories: percentage of red, amber and green, or percentage of low, medium and high risks. The Basel Committee took this approach when reporting on the Review of the Principles for the Sound Management of Operational Risk (October 2014): color bar charts denoted the proportion of firms that were mature, in progress or immature in relation to each principle. This avoids the misleading collapse of heterogeneous information into single data and presents a balanced view of the situation while still being concise in display. Figure 15.1 provides an example of categorization reporting, with red scores (marked R) positioned at the top of the bar chart. I named this bar chart "candle reporting," highlighting that the longer the flame, the higher the danger. The image speaks to imagination and several companies I know have adopted this format of reporting.

CASE STUDY: CONVERSION AND ADDITION: AGGREGATING KRIS AGAINST RISK APPETITE

I am no great fan of scoring mechanisms, even less so in risks. Yet, when facing a homogenous set of KRIs and clear thresholds linked to risk appetite, a scoring mechanism for each color of a KRI set gives an overall result of percentage level above risk appetite, ranging from 0% when all indicators are green to 100% when all are red (R). It has the advantage of summarizing the scores of all KRIs for given risk types of activity into a single percentage score. This method

(Continued)

AML and onboarding risks

KRI #	Risk cause/sub risk	KRI	Measures required	Tolerance level	Actual score	KRI	Comments/action	Risk score
1	Exposure/activity	Volume of operations in high-risk countries	Country rating, volume of business	0	5%	A	Investigate and solve	4
2	Exposure/compliance breach	# clients with operation in high-risk countries (i.e. rated >5 on a scale 1 to 8)	Client's group structure with countries of operation	1	3	A	Investigate	4
3	Human error/mistakes	Drop in average # years' experience in the business	Years of activity in the dpt, per staff member	<25% drop	Stable	G		0
4	Human error/mistakes	# of key client to inexperienced (<1yr) account manager	Key clients account manager, years of activity	0 (Red: 3)	1	Y	Provide support/mentoring	1
5	Human error/mistakes	% of staff with less than one year's experience	Years of activity in the dpt, per staff member	<15% (Red>1/3)	10%	G		0
6	Human error/slips	# of key clients per account manager	Key client identification, account manager	10 (Red: 20)	10	G		0
7	Legal risk	# files with missing documentation	Sampling	3%	20%	A		4
8	Legal risk/control weakness	# uncomplete due diligence	Sample control checks	0	1	Y	Reinforce process/checklist/awareness	1
9	Compliance breach/control weakness	# of credit files without compliance validation	Sample control checks	0	1	Y	Extend sample check/review file compliance	1
10	Compliance breach/control weakness	# missed updates of OFAC files	IT trail	<1%	2%	Y		1
							Total score	**16**
							Max score	**100**
							Excess risk (%)	**16%**

Ratings

G Within risk appetite
Y Slightly elevated, tolerated risk
A Above risk appetite
R Requires immediate action

Risk score (excess of risk appetite)

Within risk appetite 0
Slightly elevated, tolerated risk 1
Above risk appetite 4
Requires immediate action 10

FIGURE 15.2 KRI dashboard for AML/onboarding risks

applies only if all metrics have the same relative importance, of course, and their collective score paints a meaningful global picture, like an index.

The dashboard in Figure 15.2 displays a KRI dashboard for AML/ onboarding risks developed for an AMA bank; the combination of scores leads to a risk excess of 16% out of a theoretical maximum of 100%. If all KRIs scored yellow (Y), the score would have been 10%.

Governance
- CRO on the board
- Risk specialist in risk committee
- Frequency of risk committee meetings

Supervisory skills and training
- Training of team managers
- Guidance and policy for managers and team leaders
- Face-to-face awareness sessions

Staff conduct
- Behaviours against prior set objectives
- # information security breaches
- # disciplinary cases
- # policy violations

Culture and timeliness
- # self reported issues
- Occurrence date vs. reporting date of loss events
- Overdue risk management actions against plan
- Overdue audit recommendations against plan

Business model
- Client sophistication/information asymmetry
- Pricing structure vs. cost and quality

Post-sales review
- Complaints handling and customer satisfaction
- Product cancellations

Onboarding process and screening
- Employees and contractors
- Third-party onboarding
- Client onboarding

FIGURE 15.3 Themes and metrics for conduct risk reporting

REPORTING ON CONDUCT

Conduct and behavior have attracted considerable regulatory attention since the financial crisis and firms are now taking great care to monitor conduct in their businesses. Figure 15.3 presents the common themes and metrics reported in the context of a conduct-monitoring program. A case study presents an abbreviated example of metrics used to monitor conduct in financial firms, from a regulatory and operational risk perspective.

Culture is measurable as long as it is defined by behaviors, measured and tracked by proxies. Methods to influence and change risk culture are addressed in Chapter 12. Culture reporting is specific to the culture of each firm and exceeds the scope of risk reporting.

CASE STUDY: EFFORTLESS CONDUCT DASHBOARD

Table 15.1 is an abbreviated example of a real conduct dashboard (thresholds and scores are fictitious). It is a sanitized version of a reporting dashboard we created for a bank that needed to start reporting quickly on conduct. Using metrics already available in the firm is the fastest and easiest way to put together a reporting set. This is what we did: out of all possible metrics, we ask the firm to select the ones that were both relevant for their business model and already available. This led to a dashboard quite seamless to create with the additional significant advantage of displaying past data and trends over the last four quarters.

TABLE 15.1 An abbreviated example of conduct metrics

Department/ Metric supplier	Indicator	Value Q-1	Current value	Trend	Target (illustration)	Score (illustration)	Action plan
HR	% missed mandatory compliance and risk training (all staff)				0		
	# of actions and sanctions against staff				0		
	% response in staff survey				85%	▓	
	% of late reporting of operational incident (as per policy)				5%		
Operational risk and compliance	# incidents not self-reported by the risk owners				0		
	% overdue action plans				5%	▓	
	# of unreported conflicts of interest				0		
	# days missed regulatory deadlines				0		
	% overdue regulatory actions				5%	▓	
Customer service	% complaints addressed within timeline				95%		
	% complaints resolved within policy timeline				95%		
Audit	% overdue high-risk audit recommendations				5%		
	# days overdue for high-risk audit recommendations				30		
Company secretary	% of time of board meetings dedicated to risk discussions				25%		

ADDRESSING ASYMMETRY OF OPERATIONAL LOSS DATA

Rare and Large, Frequent and Small Losses

Operational loss data are particularly fat-tailed. This means that most of the loss severity is concentrated in a handful of incidents and the mass of small incidents accounts for only a tiny part of the annual loss budget. These statistics are very stable over time and across firms. The data below, from the largest operational risk data consortia, show proportions of losses from aggregated data from their members:

ORX (Operational Risk Data Exchange) 2012–2016[2]

- Largest losses (>€10 million): 0.5% of the occurrences, 74% of the total severity.
- Smallest losses (€20,000–100,000): 55% of the occurrences, 3% of the total severity.

ORIC International 2016[3]

- Largest losses (>£10 million) 2008–2012: 1% of the occurrences, 55% of the total severity.
- Smallest losses (£50,000–100,000): 56% of the occurrences, 2% of the total severity.

Large European bank (2007–2010)[4]

- Largest losses (>€10 million): 0.04% of the occurrences, 43% of the severity.
- Smallest losses (<€5,000): 65% of the occurrences, 2.2% of the severity.

These enlightening statistics have important consequences for risk management priorities: managers and risk managers must focus on the prevention and remediation of large incidents and not be caught up in the management of daily volatility – those minor and insignificant events whose frequency and visibility can easily become a preoccupation and distraction for novice risk managers.

I encourage every institution to run those statistics on their own database if they have not done so already (and please let me know if you find anything different – I would be very surprised). The firms that manage to avoid or even reduce one or two of their largest operational incidents will significantly reduce overall loss severity for the year.

---

[2]ORX Annual Report, 2018.
[3]ORIC International's own calculations, 2017.
[4]Real data from an anonymous source.

Large accidents and small day-to-day losses are different and so need different responses. Large events and large near misses are typically known immediately throughout the firm as they come as a shock. They are, or should be, the object of root cause analysis and should trigger actions plans. They are also outliers in the loss distribution and need to be isolated and reported separately, in order not to contaminate other summary statistics about small losses, as I will detail further.

Small and frequent losses are usually limited in size, especially if they relate to small processing errors in an operations-type environment. If they are structurally limited, stable and repetitive, their cost could be passed through to the customers as part of the cost of services. In any case, they should be known. Additionally, small losses need to be checked regularly to see whether they were structurally small, limited by design, because controls kicked in at a higher stage or because exposure is limited. More worrisome cases are small losses limited only by sheer luck. These come from uncapped risks, incidents with small materialization so far but large loss potential in adverse circumstances. These include consequences of trading errors (when trading limits are large or exceeded), rogue trading losses (when unnoticed until spiraling down to disasters), gaps in IT security or, generally, any event signaling weaknesses in key controls mitigating high inherent risks.

No Averages in Risk

Asymmetry of operational losses has more than managerial consequences – it impacts data treatment and reporting as well. The impact is reflected in four words: "no average in risk." Averages are meaningful only in very specific circumstances: for symmetrical, concentrated (low variance) and uniform (without data clusters) distributions; these are typically Gaussian (normal) distributions, such as weight and height in populations. For most managers, arithmetic average is the first metric that comes to mind when they attempt to describe a dataset. However, averages make no sense in the following cases:

- For binomial distributions, where data take only two values: e.g., the old statistical joke "on average, human beings have one breast and one testicle."
- For qualitative distributions, where data represent qualities, such as risk ratings: on average, the color of the rainbow is black.
- For asymmetric distributions (skewed, fat-tailed): on average, the gain per player at the National Lottery is 39.7 pence[5] (about 50 cents).

In risk, the frequency of events is binomial: there is an operational event or there is not, like for credit defaults. For severity, most operational risks are assessed qualitatively on a rating scale and losses are heavily fat tailed: concentrated in a few tail

---

[5]Own calculations based on the distributions of prizes by the U.K. National Lottery.

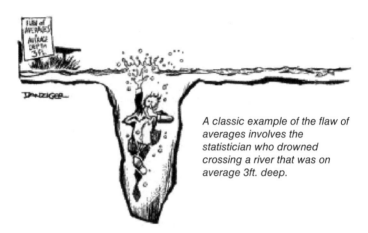

A classic example of the flaw of averages involves the statistician who drowned crossing a river that was on average 3ft. deep.

FIGURE 15.4   Flaw of averages – illustration
Source: Cartoon by Jeff Danziger from *The Flaw of Averages: Why We Underestimate Risk in the Face of Uncertainty* by Sam L. Savage, John Wiley & Sons, 2012. © John Wiley & Sons. Reproduced with permission.

incidents. As a result, risk managers should refrain from reporting losses, ratings and frequency of events, *on average*; it just produces misleading results.

Sam Savage's book *The Flaw of Averages* is dedicated to the misuse of averages in risk management.[6] It includes the cartoon in Figure 15.4, which neatly highlights why averages can be dangerous. Think of the riverbed as the distribution of operational loss events: for the most part they are very limited, but sometimes they can be large enough to sink the firm. Averaging operational losses can be dangerously misleading.

Alternatives to Averages

Managers usually look puzzled when told not to average data. Better alternatives to averages are the median (the mid-point of a distribution) and quartiles (P25 and P75, the first and third quarters of the data values), as they can be selected and presented easily.

But if averaging *all* operational losses can be misleading, it is usually caused by a handful of outliers, a few very large events. If loss data are split between the expected losses (EL: small and frequent risk events) and the unexpected losses

---

[6]Savage, S.L. (2012) *The Flaw of Averages: Why We Underestimate Risk in the Face of Uncertainty*, John Wiley & Sons. Sam Savage has been a consulting professor at Stanford University since 1990.

(UL: large, infrequent, severe incidents), the EL distribution is more concentrated, more symmetric and more suitable for averaging. Large loss events need to be reported individually, while EL can be the object of classic descriptions, with minimum, maximum and average.

Benchmark to Gross Income   Reporting the losses to a benchmark, typically the gross income, can be very effective to attract the attention of senior management. In my experience, firms that have developed a high-performing operational risk management practice experience a total volume of losses between 1.8% and 2.2% of operational losses to gross income. Between 2.2% and 3% is common and above 3% are higher levels of operational losses, often due to environments with many manual and complex processes or a history of underinvestment in people and systems. A ratio of operational losses to gross income inferior to 1.5% is more likely to originate from underreporting rather than from good operational performance. Interestingly, firms for the food retail and telecommunication sectors told me they are experiencing operational losses around 2% of gross income as well and working hard to reduce those losses.

TURNING DATA INTO STORIES

In risk reporting, like many other forms of reporting, the value of information lies in deviations from the norm. For example, credit card frauds are detected by abnormal spending patterns, excellent traders (positive outliers) have unusually long performance records, rogue traders (negative outliers) display unusually low volatility in performance, the best managers have greater staff retention and the highest productivity levels, and poor suppliers have the largest number of operational mishaps. The value of information lies in data patterns, in concentrated parts of the distributions and in distances between observations. You need to pinpoint where the most or least number of events are, what the variations are in performance, the record highs and record lows, and how to interpret everything. To turn data into stories, by all means look at the individual data points, graphically and numerically, clean obvious entry errors and missing fields, and then look for outliers, clusters and patterns. Next, seek interpretation for these behaviors before distilling the points into summary statistics. Adjust your analysis to your data.

Risk reporting is the opportunity to investigate the reality behind numbers and to determine what is going well and what might go wrong. Remember that positive outliers carry just as much information as negative ones. Sadly, most firms still dedicate more attention to reporting problems than highlighting and explaining success stories. *Positive risk management* is how I like to call a risk management style dedicating at least as much attention to positive deviations as to negative ones. I will return to this in the conclusion.

## CHAPTER 16

Valuable ORM

In the introduction, I highlighted the importance of feedback assessment as part of a risk management framework.

The international standard for risk management (ISO 31000) highlights the necessary feedback loop in the framework, starting with mandate and commitment of the risk function and closing with monitoring and review of the framework, followed by continuous improvement. In 2017, COSO published a new enterprise risk management (ERM) framework, positioning ERM as the enabler of corporate performance. This chapter reviews some useful criteria to assess the maturity of an operational risk management framework, discusses risk-based priorities in the implementation of a framework, and proposes ways to quantify and demonstrate the value of risk management.

HOW DO YOU KNOW IT WORKS?[1] CRITERIA FOR A MATURE FRAMEWORK

Some organizations use maturity models, either developed in-house or sourced externally, to assess the performance of their risk management frameworks. These models use scaling tables that rate the design and implementation of each part of the framework on a 4- or 5-point scale, ranging from "beginner" to "expert." Firms self-assess their current maturity level against their own objectives. They do not necessarily need to be at "expert" level for all elements of the framework. The box presents a simpler, yet effective alternative to a maturity model, in the form of a list of quality criteria for each part of a risk management framework.

---

[1]This question is reported by Douglas Hubbard in the opening chapter of his excellent book *The Failure of Risk Management* (Wiley, 2009); it is my favorite question for risk managers and directors alike.

IN PRACTICE: SOME KEY CRITERIA TO ASSESS ORM QUALITY

A simpler option than a maturity model is to use a set of key criteria to judge the quality of each part of the framework. I suggest the following tests:

- Incident data collection is comprehensive across the firm.
- Risk reporting is fed back to the business lines with benchmarks and comparisons across similar entities.
- Risk assessments are comparable across businesses.
- Action plans and mitigating actions are based on risk assessment, not just in response to incidents. They are linked to risk appetite.
- Results of scenarios identification and assessments are used to improve management decisions.
- KRIs are preventive and actively used; they help to avoid or limit incidents.
- Executive directors understand the concept of risk appetite and purposefully agree on limits of exposure and necessary controls.
- Business line managers own risks responsibly and take risk-based business decisions.
- Risk management culture is valued throughout the organization, with the risk function and risk management activities having the explicit support of senior management.

A RISK-BASED APPROACH TO ORM

Firms that are at the beginning of their journey in non-financial risk management need to address their top risk priorities first before deploying an ORM framework one department at a time and reaching the steady state of business as usual in operational risk. Such a state takes years to achieve. "Tell me where it burns," the COO of ING South West Europe said to me on my first week as head of operational risk. "I don't care about petty issues." I never forgot the lesson. The group in my remit had 11,000 employees and I was alone. Prioritizing was not optional. Before addressing day-to-day risks, operational risk managers need to identify, address and mitigate some of the most pressing issues and risks generated by the firm's activities.

DEADLY SINS AND GOLDEN RULES

A deadly sin in ORM is to roll out a framework uniformly, without adopting a risk-based approach. It exhausts resources and, at worst, allows bad incidents to materialize before high exposures are uncovered and mitigated. Priority areas for risk identification and assessment should include back-office operations, IT and finance functions, and anywhere with large numbers of transactions and/or high financial flows. Another deadly sin, just as common, is to spend inordinate amounts of time assessing risks and reporting incidents without leaving enough time to mitigate the former and learn the lessons from the latter. When too granular, RCSAs are time consuming and so detailed that key messages are impossible to draw, high risks are hidden in the mass of assessments and results are often made more chaotic by the absence of a proper taxonomy.

Golden rules, however, include:

- Being accepted by the business in order to gain access to information, risks and incidents. The worst outcome for a risk manager is to get pushed back or ignored and so become irrelevant to the organization.
- To get accepted and respected, risk managers being able to demonstrate the value of better risk management and, more specifically, the individual benefits it brings to the teams.
- Focusing on top risks and their mitigation while not wasting rare resources on minor issues or confusing risk with daily volatility and accepted variations of performance (and setting limits for these accepted variations).
- Operating a framework that supports the risk priorities and facilitates risk management activities and reasoning without driving them.

Finally, regulatory compliance in ORM follows good risk management and does not precede it: organizations able to demonstrate mature, risk-based operational risk management practices are de facto complying with the principles of the ORM regulation. However, firms sticking to the letter of the law do not necessarily deliver valuable risk management to the business, nor are they necessarily fully compliant with regulations.[2]

IN PRACTICE: SEVEN ORM PRIORITIES FOR STARTER FIRMS

1. Firm-wide screening to identify all high-risk areas: top-down risks assessment and, depending on the business, review of all areas combining high

(Continued)

---

[2] See also Chapelle, Dec 2015, "What do regulators expect?" risk.net. Reproduced in *Reflections on Operational Risk Management*, Risk Books, 2017.

money flows with high numbers of transactions, as they are natural breeding grounds for operational risk.

2. Action plan design and follow-up on high residual risks identified above appetite or above management's comfort zone if risk appetite is not precisely articulated. Mitigating risks as they are uncovered makes a lot more sense than doing a firm-wide assessment first and mitigating next – if a pipe is leaking in your house, you will not run a full assessment of all the other rooms before calling a plumber.

3. Taxonomy of risks, impacts, causes and controls: categorizing risks and controls in a formatted list is a necessary prerequisite for any useful risk assessment. A proper taxonomy and definition of risks, controls and impacts is often lacking, especially in tier 2 and tier 3 institutions.

4. Risk and incident reporting analysis and thematic action plans: reporting is fair, analysis and diagnosis are good, acting on diagnosis is best practice. Make sure reporting matters for decision-making and actions.

5. Risk training for the business and lean risk function: lean risk management departments are in line with best practice – mature banks delegate most risk management activities to the business, keeping only a central team specialized in risk assessment methodology, monitoring and reporting. To achieve this, organizations need to train business lines on the scope of operational risk, the benefits of risk management, key methods to identify and assess risks, and how to reports incidents. It does not happen overnight.

6. BAU ORM: once these priority activities are completed, you can start deploying business as usual in operational risk. This includes completing incidents reporting, finalizing a bank-wide risk register and refining risk appetite limits, generalizing key risk indicators, and establishing regular risk and event reporting and analysis.

7. Selection or development of an IT ORM solution, integrated with existing systems: it is only when ORM has reached a steady state that I would recommend considering risk software solutions. The "nice to have" of ORM software may not be so nice and may even be detrimental if implemented in an unprepared environment. Just as importantly, the solution needs to fully integrate the existing systems and feed from other data sources in the organization to avoid multiplying data capture.

DEMONSTRATING THE VALUE OF RISK MANAGEMENT

It is not an easy task to get risk managers accepted by the business, never mind liked, and the threat of regulatory non-compliance is no great incentive. A far better approach is to demonstrate the value that risk management adds. It is optimistic at best, and somewhat unrealistic, to try advocating to the business the value of risk management without any hard evidence. Resources and investments in risk management should follow the same logic as business investments: build a business case for operational risk management before arguing its benefits. Despite what some may think, measuring the value of operational risk management is not synonymous with the impossible task of demonstrating what has not happened. True, a key role of operational risk management is to prevent incidents and accidents, but that is not the only role.

Beyond the minimum requirements of capital and compliance, it is now generally accepted that operational risk management brings value to the business by allowing better decision-making. Over time, risk management matures and becomes an essential element of business performance.

The business value of better decision-making takes different forms and can be measured in many ways (Table 16.1). Reducing large losses, one of the most obvious goals of ORM, brings business stability that is reflected in, amongst other things, the share price for listed firms (after correcting for general market movements), besides a count of losses and severity trends compared with those of peers. General profitability is improved by reducing recurrent losses, provided there is a necessary cost-benefit analysis of controls: expected loss avoidance needs to be larger than the cost of the controls and other risk mitigation mechanisms. In 2008, an international AMA bank asked me to assess the value generated by the review of its operational risk management framework. The case study presents the substance of this baselining exercise.

A third important component of business value is productivity increase. With fewer incidents, less time is spent on impact mitigation and remediation, freeing resources for more productive activities. Project management also is now systematically included in the scope of operational risk management, helping to reduce project failures, as detailed in Chapter 17. Finally, one of the key roles of the risk function is to advise on the strategic and investment decisions of the firm, balancing risk with reward and offering a cost-effective solution for risk mitigation. Mature organizations include risk in all their decisions, in order to achieve better outcomes, higher success rates and sustainable long-term growth. Building a business case for risk management by evidencing its benefits beyond the default argument of capital reduction and regulatory compliance empowers risk managers to fulfill their true corporate role.

TABLE 16.1   Metrics for business value of risk management[3]

Business value of ORM	Metrics
Reduced large losses: Business stability	- Peer comparisons of tail risk losses - Count of large incidents - P&L volatility - Share price volatility compared to equity market volatility
Reduced expected losses: improved profitability	- Trend of loss frequency per type - Trend of loss severity per period - Profitability trend and volatility
Improved business performance: productivity and success rate	- Trends in cost/income ratio - Success rate of internal projects
Better investment selection: long-term growth	- Operational losses in new investments - Investments success rates trends - Investments profitability - Volatility of growth rate over long period

CASE STUDY: BASELINING OPERATIONAL RISK

Years ago, a large European bank asked for a benefits assessment following the implementation of an extensive and ambitious reform of its ORM framework. The bank wanted to know whether the investment was paying off. The operational loss data was the only accessible source of information to answer this question. To correct the asymmetry of operational loss data, I took the largest losses (above the threshold set by company policy) from the rest of the sample and treated them separately. I used a four-quarter moving average to eliminate the seasonality effect in the data, which is always strong in reported operational incidents. I investigated the two measurable benefits from improved ORM: reduction of everyday losses in frequency and severity, and reduction of the frequency of

---

[3]Table previously published in my risk.net column, "Measuring the business value of operational risk management" (June 2015), and reproduced in the compendium book *Reflections on Operational Risk Management*, op. cit.

large incidents (severity of large incidents can strongly bias analysis, so I worked on the assumption that better management will prevent large events more than impacting their size).

The results showed the encouraging effect of the new ORM program:

- Reduction in severity of both gross and net losses at group level: the revision of the ORM program had paid for itself in loss reduction after one year.
- Reduction in frequency of losses.
- Reduction in frequency of all event types except one.
- No recording of large events over four reporting quarters following the start of the program (at the time of the baselining exercise), whereas the last three years recorded one or two significant events per quarter and no more than two quarters in a row with any.

A graphic representation is given in Figures 16.1 and 16.2 (severity is expressed in negative numbers, upward slopes are good news).

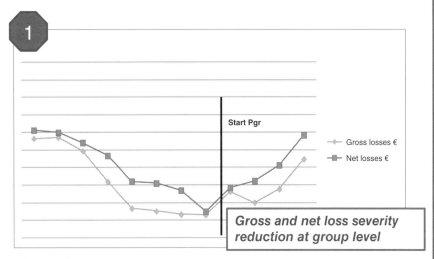

FIGURE 16.1   Severity reduction – group level

This simple study shows why impact assessments of risk management activities are easy, useful and recommended.

(Continued)

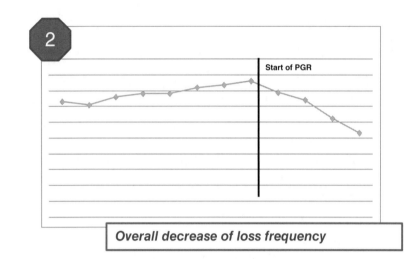

FIGURE 16.2   Average loss frequency

Rising Operational Risks

"Nothing novel or interesting happens unless it is on the border between order and chaos."

R.A. Delmonico

Project Risk Management

CONTEXT

Projects and change are some of the most commonly cited sources of risks in organizations. Beyond the multitude of risks brought by new processes, new technologies, lack of familiarity and resistance to change, we have all experienced projects overrunning and exceeding budget, if not failing completely due to causes such as weak governance, unrealistic deadlines, short-sighted budgeting, poor synergies, lack of internal skills or team stamina, and conflicted interests.

PRINCE 2 lists the most common causes of project failure (Table 17.1). Each project failure can cost an organization thousands or millions in wasted resources and untapped future revenues. Yet these sums are usually overlooked and not recorded as what they are: severe crystallizations of operational risk.

It is therefore good practice for the risk function to be involved at the start of a project and to remain present throughout the project life cycle, right through to debriefing. The actual level of involvement should depend on the risk exposure and criticality of the project.

This chapter is based on my experience of assisting firms in framing or improving collaboration between the operational risk function and the project teams.

STAGE OF INVOLVEMENT OF THE RISK FUNCTION IN PROJECT MANAGEMENT

Initial Stage, Before Kick-off

Although the project decision-making and stage-gate processes are well established in many organizations, they are not as embedded and rigorous as they should in some tier 2 or tier 3 firms. In these instances, risk management should play the role of gatekeeper and enforce a sound decision-making process prior to each non-trivial project launch. Even in firms where project decision-making and governance are well established, the

TABLE 17.1   Common causes of project failures (PRINCE 2)[1]

1. Invalid business case.
2. Insufficient attention to quality at the outset and during development.
3. Insufficient definition of the required outcomes, creating confusion.
4. Lack of communication with stakeholders and interested parties.
5. Poor definition or acceptance of roles and responsibilities, resulting in lack of direction.
6. Poor estimation of duration and cost.
7. Inadequate planning and coordination of resources.
8. Insufficient measurables and lack of control over progress.

project team or the business don't always dedicate sufficient attention to the additional risks generated by a new project beyond the project delivery risks themselves. What is missing is proper involvement of the second line of defense. When project risk management matures, the role of the risk team is to help the project team with project and execution risk identification and assessment. This includes mitigation action plans and regular assurance and reporting, much like an RCSA. The RAU here is the project itself and its consequences for the day-to-day business operations.

When this is absent, the risk team should establish a full project approval process (Table 17.2), much like a new product approval process. Indeed, launching a product is a particular type of project.

The risk level of the project will dictate the degree to which the risk function is involved and the extent of the mitigation requirements. This risk-based approach can typically follow a risk-rating methodology common to non-financial risks. Examples of risk-rating scales and criteria are detailed in the next section.

Project Life: Monitoring and Risk Update

The monitoring structure introduced at the beginning of the project should remain during the project life – again, much like RCSA monitoring and updates. There should be quarterly or six-monthly updates of the risk identification and assessment workshop with the risk team and the project team, which amongst other things will cover project risks that may affect business as usual operations. The project team itself usually manages the typical project risks of time, budget and delivery quality, without intervention from the risk function. A regular project report on both execution risks and project risks is sent to all project stakeholders, including the risk function.

---

[1]Modified table from PRINCE 2, cited in Chapman, R. (2014) *The Rules of Project Risk Management*, Gower.

TABLE 17.2 Information requirements before project approval, from a risk management perspective

1. Project motivation and objectives	Qualitative and quantitative assessment of expected benefits
2. Budget	Expected external costs (third-party fees and equipment) Internal costs (man-days from existing resources)
3. Cost-benefit analysis	From the analysis above
4. Impact scope (direct and indirect)	People (staff, customers, stakeholders) and processes impacted directly and indirectly by the project
5. Top risks for the outcome of the project	*What could go wrong?* Scenarios with likelihood scale (H – M – L in a simpler form) + quantified approximated impact for all *important* and *critical* projects (see rating scale further below)
6. Planned mitigating actions for top risks	E.g., internal controls, insurance policy, backup plan and/or exit strategies
7. Reporting to the risk function and the business	▪ Evolution of risks ▪ Mitigating actions ▪ Action owner and timeline ▪ Milestones and deliverables ▪ Benefits expected or produced ▪ User satisfaction
8. Reporting to project team	▪ Timing, delays and contingencies ▪ Spending against budget ▪ Rules of descoping/rescoping and reporting of breaches ▪ Progress report
9. Steering committee, sponsor and designated project manager	Risk-based rule, e.g.: ▪ Fully dedicated (100%), professional and experienced project manager (with relevant experience) for *critical* and *important* projects ▪ Part-time dedicated (50%) professional with relevant experience for *important* (non-complex) project and *moderate* projects ▪ Internal, non-specialized project manager for modest projects

Project Portfolio View

Project portfolio view, interactions and interdependencies are other important elements of project monitoring and are not always fully grasped by organizations, even though most of them aspire to it. Project interdependencies include:

▪ Reliance on similar resources such as people or systems. Common dependencies can create single points of failure and a domino effect. If resources used by one project get overstretched, it can affect other projects. A common example of vulnerable dependencies is when key subject matter experts or key project managers are involved in several projects in a firm.

- Path dependency: a project may depend on deliverables from another project and delays may compound when the deliverables are late. Path dependency is a common cause of project delays in firms, with multiple dependencies increasing the chance of delays. Removing dependencies as much as possible is likely to improve timeliness.

Examples of monitoring tools and reporting formats are covered later in the chapter.

Project Closure and Debriefing

Post-delivery review, quality evaluation and debriefing are what differentiate mature organizations and sectors from beginners. Systematic debriefing is common practice in the military, and the financial sector would benefit by adopting a similar level of discipline. Some firms maintain a database of post-project evaluations, debriefing and lessons learnt in order to avoid repeating the same mistakes or to benefit from past success stories. Once again, the risk function has a role to play, either to prompt the development of such a database or to make sure it is used effectively.

Summary and Policy

From design to debriefing, the requirements above apply to all projects. However, to keep an efficient allocation of resources, the active involvement of the risk function should be limited to larger and riskier projects, while smaller projects are simply framed by a project and risk management policy, as presented in the case study.

Table 17.3. summarizes the stage and nature of involvement of the risk function during a project life, in function of its risk rating. The next section presents common ways to attribute risk ratings to projects.

CASE STUDY: PROJECT AND RISK MANAGEMENT POLICY

Like many firms, one of my clients needed to frame the nature and criteria of involvement of the risk function in project management. We determined the risk-rating criteria for the project, met with the project teams and agreed on the stages of collaboration between the project managements teams and the operational risk team, as well as the minimum business case content required for a project to be evaluated. The result of these discussions was documented in a short and simple policy and the table of contents is shown below.

Project and risk management policy outline

1. Risk rating of projects
   - Rating structure
   - Classification criteria

2. Minimum requirements per project
   - Components of the project business case
   - Requirements per project type

3. Project governance and involvement of the risk function
   - Projects types requiring the involvement of the risk function
   - Stages and nature of involvements of the risk function
     1. Initial stage (before kick-off)
     2. Project life: monitoring and risk update
     3. Project closure

TABLE 17.3 Stage of involvement of the risk function – summary

Initial stage (before kick-off)
■ Risk identification and assessment: workshop facilitation, for important and critical projects
■ Mitigation and monitoring plans: assurance that plans exist to address the risk identified, in function of their materiality
Project life: monitoring and risk update
■ Regular project reporting both for operational risks and for project risks
■ Quarterly/six-monthly updates of risk identification and assessment workshop with the risk team and the project team, for important and critical projects
Project closure
■ Debriefing, evaluation of project deliverables, the risks materialized and avoided, lessons learnt, all projects

RISK RATING FOR PROJECTS

Context

In project management, like any other involvement of the risk function in business activities, effective resource allocation requires a risk-based approach. The risk function's level of involvement will depend on the size and criticality of the project.

The approach described below is drawn from experience in financial organizations where it has been necessary to find ways to develop a risk-based approach that defines the level of collaboration between the risk function and project managers. Different stages of involvement, and different levels of information exchange, are defined between the risk team and the project teams according to the complexity and size of the project at stake. Smaller organizations, or those in early stages of operational risk management, will adopt simple project-rating scales and fewer involvement requirements, while more mature or larger organizations might require more detailed project ratings and a closer collaboration between the risk function and the project team for critical projects.

Risk Rating for Projects

In its simple version (Figure 17.1), the project rating would include only a handful of criteria: total budget, process, people and assets impacted. The highest rating of any of the criteria defines the overall rating of the project. The budget of a project is a proxy of its size and of the organization's financial commitment to the project. Figure 17.1 presents ratings relative to EBIT (earnings before interest and tax), scalable to the size

Project rating	Budget (e.g. in % of EBIT)	Impacting a critical process of the organization?	% of organization's people or assets impacted
Critical	>30%	Y	>50%
Important	<30% >10%	N	>20% <50%
Moderate	<10% >2%	N	>5% <20%
Modest	<2%	N	<5%

FIGURE 17.1   Project rating – simple scoring version

of the firm. In practice, however, most employees would be unable to give either the turnover or the EBIT of their firm off the top of their heads and would use absolute budget values, expressed in currency units.

The second rating element relates to impacts on a critical process of the firm (Yes/No) from continuity or a strategic perspective. European banking regulation, for instance, requires all systemically important financial institutions to identify all critical processes and ensure their continuity, even in the event of severe incidents. Therefore, a project is rated critical if it impacts the continuity of one of these processes.

Finally, the percentages of assets or of people impacted by a project reflect the project's complexity and its overall impact and influence – and therefore the potential risks. This is not necessarily captured in the financial budget alone. For instance, consider the digitalization of documents: when a firm decides to go paperless, the change will affect nearly 100% of the staff and a large portion of its assets, even though the cost of the project may not be as large as some physical assets. An office move is another example of a complex project.

Some firms include three additional elements to achieve a slightly more comprehensive approach for risk evaluation:

- Customers: proportion of customers affected by the project.
- Regulatory impact: regulatory components and their criticality.
- Reputation: whether the project is likely to impact the image of the firm externally, through media coverage.

The risk function is involved in projects that are ranked *critical* or *important*. Involvement of the risk function includes participation in the first phases of project scoping and budgeting and at each important step of the project life cycle. In particular, the second line of defense actively supports the project team and the business during the initial identification and assessment of the operational risks generated or amplified by the project execution.

Larger or more mature organizations would use more sophisticated scoring systems to rank the risk level of their projects. Table 17.4 presents a real example of such a scoring system, although adapted to suit both IT and non-IT project types.

PROJECT RISK IDENTIFICATION AND ASSESSMENT

Project risk identification and assessment should closely follow the same RCSA methodology as other operational risk assessment exercises, with the risk assessment unit being the project and its impact on the business as usual operations. The case study illustrates the aggregated results of such risk assessment for several projects in a tier 2 insurance company.

TABLE 17.4 Project rating – sophisticated scoring version

Project risk element	Scoring criteria	Score (1-5)
Level of business lines involvement	1 - Very limited: <5 FTE for a short period of time (<1 year)	
	2 - Limited: 5 – 10 FTE for over a year	
	3 - Moderate: 10 – 50 FTE for less than a year	
	4 - Large : 10 – 50 FTE for over a year	
	5 - Huge: over 50 FTA for one year or more	
Stakeholder complexity	1 - One function solicited to express their views or needs	
	3 - Most functions concerned by the project have been solicited to express opinions or needs	
	5 - Most of the functions of the organization express views and needs on the project	
Dependencies with other projects	1 - No dependencies	
	2 - Project is on critical path of other projects	
	3 - Other projects are on critical path of this project	
	4 - Project requires deliverables of other projects	
	5 - High-risk projects require deliverables from this project	
Project remaining time	1 - Project delivery less than 3 months away	
	2 - Project delivery less than 6 months away	
	3 - Project delivery less than 1 years away	
	4 - Project delivery less than 2 years away	
	5 - Project delivery more than 2 years away	

Internal vs. external skills	1 - Ability to operate and deliver with internal skills only 3 - Need of a mix of internal and external skills to operate and deliver 5 - Project reliant mostly or solely on external skills to operate and deliver	
Regulatory impacts	1 - No or limited regulatory impact 3 - Medium regulatory impact 5 - Heavy regulatory impact	
New technology	1. The company has extensive experience with all technologies deployed by the project 3 - The project deploys some technology unfamiliar to the firm 5. The project deploys unproven or new, unfamiliar technologies	
Data migration needs	1 - No data migration 2 - Partial migration of simple and comprehensive datasets 3 - Large migration of complex data from various sources	
Organization of process changes	1 - No change in organization or process as a result of the project 2 - Some moderate changes in organization or process structure as a result of the project 3 - Major reorganization or process changes as a result of the project	
	Total risk score	

AGGREGATING RCSA RESULTS FOR PROJECTS

Figures 17.2 and 17.3 illustrate a real case of aggregated risk assessments for projects. The number in each area of the matrix indicates the total number of risks assessed in that part of the matrix for all projects. The matrix level 1 and level 2 were presented in Chapter 6.

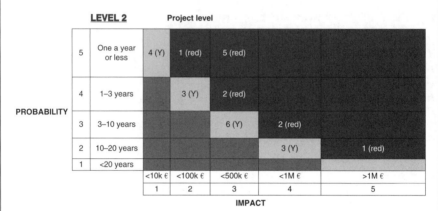

FIGURE 17.2 Aggregated matrix for all projects – count per risk area

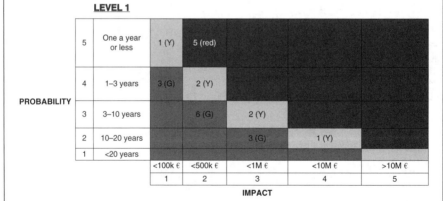

FIGURE 17.3 Executive reporting: matrix shift by one severity column

As it reads, several risks lie above appetite at project level and five remain above appetite at firm level, calling for action plans at firm level as well as at project level.

PROJECT MONITORING AND REPORTING

Common Project Reporting

Besides the RCSA examples above, project monitoring and reporting will address the three key project dimensions of time, budget and quality of deliverables. Tables 17.5 and 17.6 illustrate some common formats of project reporting.

TABLE 17.5   Project timeliness reporting

Monthly dashboard	Date
Major Projects (Risk level xx)	*Status*
New projects for FY xx	
Project 1	
Project 2	
...Project n	
Projects completed	
Project a	
Project b	
...	

Status	
▶	On target
▶	At risk
▶	Late

(to be detailed per project deliverable)

TABLE 17.6   Project budget reporting

Budget estimates (as of date MM/YYYY)				
Project ID no.	Working budget	Actual spend	Forecast spending	Outturn (working budget – forecast spend)
Project 1	$	$	$	$
Project 2	$	$	$	$
Project 3	$	$	$	$
Project 4	$	$	$	$
Project 5	$	$	$	$
Project 6	$	$	$	$

KRIs for Projects

From an operational risk perspective, KRIs for project management should include four categories:

- Information about the project itself: risk rating and its components – complexity, process or time criticality, regulatory component, etc.
- Incomplete business case or missing mitigating components: insufficient cost-benefit analysis, missing or weak project management resources, etc.
- High residual risk identification: missing or late action plans, critical dependencies.
- Project management elements at risk: late deliverables, budget overrun, scope change, low stakeholder satisfaction.

Essentially, any missing or weak elements of project governance, mitigation and resources are possible KRIs for project management. For IT project and change, the testing phase is an essential control to ensure smooth roll-out and quality delivery; therefore, all reductions in time or resource allocated to testing are relevant KRIs for IT projects. Table 17.7 gives an example of a KRIs dashboard in project management.

TABLE 17.7   KRIs for project management

KRIs for projects	Green	Amber	Red
Expected synergies and benefits	Material, even in stress scenarios	Positive if all goes to plan	No clear business plan
Program manager	Yes, with relevant experience	Part-time or new to the role	No dedicated resources to project management
Project criticality	Low	Medium	High
Project complexity	Low	Medium	High
Mitigating action plans	Completed	On track, but not yet in place	Missing or not started
Dependencies/single point of failure (e.g., key people)	None	One	More than one
Deliverables	All on time	1–3, non critical	One or more key deliverables overdue
Testing phase (IT deliverables)	As planned	Expected to be reduced	Reduced by >15%

## CHAPTER 18

Information Security Risks

CONTEXT

Information security risks (ISR) and cyber risks have probably been the greatest concerns for operational risk in recent years. The community of operational risk practitioners, through the yearly risk.net survey, designated cyber risk as the number one risk for three years in a row (2015–2017). In 2018, cyber risk was separated into IT disruption (voted number one), data compromise (voted number two) and fraud and theft (voted number four).

Today's information and data are yesterday's gold bullions. Value has changed and so has the means of transfer and the associated opportunities for crime. Unlike gold or physical values that can be spent only once, information can be used and traded multiple times even when its usage remains invisible to some parties, including its owner. And when it becomes visible, the damage to reputation can be significant, and sometimes fatal.

Contrary to what some people claim, cybersecurity is not all about behavior and people risk. However, cyber risk cannot be minimized through technical solutions alone; cyber criminals will always find ways to profit from the mistakes and carelessness that are part of human behavior. Moreover, information can be lost, disclosed or corrupted by many other means apart from cybercrime.

This chapter explores different types of information security risk and some of the key controls that resulted from a thematic review of information security risks I conducted in a European organization in 2017.

DATA BREACHES AND HEADLINE NEWS

The box presents four public case studies of data breaches: two resulting from cyberattacks and two from internal leaks, including through a third party. They illustrate the types of reputational damage that can follow large data breaches; all the firms mentioned here made the news, but with different intensity, reflecting their brand recognition. Unsurprisingly, the Facebook scandal generated the most attention, even though it wasn't a cyberattack. Paradise Papers made the headlines for a few weeks, due to the high profile of the personalities involved, who included royalty. Interestingly, the company at the center of the hack survived. Equifax was laughed at in many circles, replaced all its senior management and is facing a class action lawsuit, but the company's future doesn't seem in jeopardy. Very few noticed the hack of the U.K.-based insurance company in our fourth case study, apart from the regulator and some of the company's clients, therefore I do not mention the company's name here. The company suffered internally and with its regulator, but there were few news reports. Cambridge Analytica is the only company to have filed for bankruptcy in this sample. Crises, resilience and reputation will be addressed in the last chapter of this book.

CASE STUDIES: INFORMATION BREACHES AND THEIR IMPACT

1. The Paradise Papers
    In the second largest data hack in history, 1.4 terabytes of private information from an offshore law firm tax advisor was leaked to the media (International Consortium of Investigative Journalists).
    Appleby, an offshore legal firm, was the victim of a major data leak regarding offshore structures and the wealth of thousands of A-list personalities and firms. Three hundred and eighty journalists dedicated a year to the investigation of documents spanning 70 years. Top personalities, members of government, corporations and even countries were exposed to reputation damage and public outcry. At the time (November 2017), it was the largest leak since Wikileaks. Appleby's clients include all major banks. The company is still in operation in 2018.

2. Equifax
    The credit-scoring firm was the victim of a hack that exposed the data of 145.5 million customers, the equivalent of half of the U.S. population. The cause was an external intrusion on Equifax servers following an unpatched (known) vulnerability. The vulnerability should have been patched in 48 hours according to company policy, but was unresolved two months later when the intrusion started (May 2017). The company noticed the breach in July 2017 but did not make it public until September 7 of that year. The concealment attracted heavy criticism. The chief information

officer and chief security officer "retired" with immediate effect, followed shortly by the chief executive of Equifax.

An additional and unrelated breach, revealed by the BBC six days later, added insult to injury when it became apparent that a separate cyberattack, this time affecting Equifax's Argentine operations, had been facilitated by weak (to say the least) security credentials: "Admin" was both the login and the password to access the records of thousands of Equifax customers in Argentina.

The Equifax share price dropped 37%, from $141 to $92, in the week following the announcement. By January 2018, the share price had partially recovered, hovering around $120, but the drop still represented a market capitalization loss of about $2.5 billion out of a total capitalization of $15.5 billion in H1 2018. Class action lawsuits against Equifax were in the making at the time of writing.

3. Facebook and Cambridge Analytica

Facebook data from up to 87 million people were improperly shared with the political consultancy Cambridge Analytica and allegedly used to manipulate public opinion in the run-up to important political decisions such as the U.S. election and the Brexit referendum in the U.K.

The revelation triggered a European Parliament testimony from Facebook CEO Mark Zuckerberg, profound reorganization of Facebook's security processes and controls, and widespread commentary about Facebook's role and influence. It underlined the issue of social media regulation and highlighted, once again, the need to extend information security standards to third-party providers. Zuckerberg said: "Today, given what we know . . . I think we understand that we need to take a broader view of our responsibility. That we're not just building tools, but that we need to take full responsibility for the outcomes of how people use those tools as well." Facebook came in for heavy criticism when it became apparent that it had known for years that Cambridge Analytica had collected the data of over 50 million Facebook users and simply relied on the firm self-certifying that it had deleted those records.[1]

Cambridge Analytica filed for bankruptcy in the U.S. on May 17, 2018, just weeks after the start of the scandal.

4. UK insurance company: employee data leak

A UK insurance company suffered a data breach in July 2017 affecting 500,000 customers. An employee fraudulently copied and removed

(Continued)

---

[1]Source: BBC News, April 4, 2018; "Facebook scandal hit 87 million users."

information including names, dates of birth and some contact information, and then posted them for sale on the dark web. The U.K. regulator was informed and a full investigation took place. The employee responsible was dismissed and the firm took appropriate legal action. Besides some ripples within the company and scrutiny from the regulator, the case didn't attract much coverage outside of the specialized press.

INFORMATION SECURITY STANDARDS AND FURTHER REFERENCES

The international standard ISO/IEC 27001: 2013 is the best-known information security standard, providing general guidance to firms to establish the context of information security, governance, policies, support, communication and awareness about information security in organizations. It provides guidance on operational planning and control, information security risk assessment and risk treatment. These three topics are covered in less than one page, so readers should consult other sources for more detailed advice. In its final sections, the standard explains the role of audit and of the management review in the context of information security.

ISO standards in general, and this one in particular, do not provide detailed, implementable guidance to firms, but rather act as evaluation grids for those that want to achieve certification in ISO standards. Many services companies offer more practical implementation guides based on ISO 27001, usually in the form of books, tools, consultancy kits and step-by-step approaches.

Many risk management publications focus on general aspects of governance, communication and awareness with regards to information security. Another type of publication focuses on the technical aspects of cybersecurity, appropriate for IT specialists and IT risk managers with backgrounds in computer science. For these specialists, I recommend *New Solutions for Cyber Security* (MIT Press, 2017).[2]

Most operational risk managers have neither a computer science background nor cutting-edge technical expertise in any particular field. Non-financial risk managers are generalists in content but should be specialists in how to address risks. They rely on subject matter experts for the specific risk type they are helping to assess and manage. To paraphrase Steve Jobs: they play the orchestra.[3] Risk managers work with and

---

[2]Edited by Howard Shrobe, David Shrier and Alex Pentland. The book is the collective work of 28 cyber experts, who collated their views in 16 chapters focusing on, amongst other things, management, organization, strategy, architecture and systems.
[3]A fascinating scene in the movie "Steve Jobs" https://www.youtube.com/watch?v=-9ZQVlg fEAc

depend on many specialists and business people. They must coordinate all the parties and activities and ensure everything makes sense from a risk management perspective.

The case study explained in the next sections is just one of several ways to design and execute a thematic review of information risk assessment at firm level. The aim is to present a practical, generalist and business-based risk assessment of information control and integrity, and to show readers how to develop their own reviews, in keeping with the needs of their respective organizations.

To conduct the review below, I used the generic framework of risk identification, assessment, mitigation and monitoring. The risk identification step would result in a meaningful taxonomy for the organization.

IDENTIFICATION: RISK TAXONOMY FOR INFORMATION SECURITY

Types of Information Security Incidents

Information security is not limited to cyber risks. Information can be stolen, lost or unintentionally disclosed. A laptop can be lost or it can be stolen for its information, but neither the likelihood nor the impact would be the same. An email can be hacked, or an employee can misuse the autofill function on an email address and inadvertently send private information to external parties; neither the drivers nor the preventive measures for those risks are the same. Also, the perpetrators of these losses or thefts are internal or external to the firm and sometimes in collusion, or hybrid, like third parties and suppliers. A study from McAfee in 2017 states that 43% of data leaks are initiated by insiders, half of them unintentionally.[4] Contractors and consultants on site are usually considered as internal parties and the same rules apply to them as to other employees. Finally, paper documentation and other physical data must also be within the scope of information risk management – for example, to avoid the risk of an audit report being left on a train or the physical security assessment report being left on a printer.

Table 18.1 presents the taxonomy of information security risks developed for the review. We used a four-quadrant approach: internal causes (including contracts and consultants on site) versus external causes (including suppliers) and data theft (including voluntary data corruption) versus data loss (including involuntary corruption and accidental disclosure).

Information Asset Inventory

An information asset inventory is a necessary step to prepare for the assessment of risks. It also drives the mitigation plan, as more valuable assets will naturally require the

---

[4]Data exfiltration study: Actors, tactics, and detection. 2017. Available at: https://www.mcafee .com/us/resources/reports/rp-data-exfiltration.pdf.

TABLE 18.1 A typology of information security risks

Data incidents	Theft or corruption	Loss or unvoluntary disclosure
External Causes or Third Parties	1. Digital: Hacking, Virus infection, phishing and other Cyber attacks 2. Physical: Theft, social engineering	3. Disaster, systems disruptions, third-party failure
Internal Causes	4. Theft and transfer of digital or physical information by infiltrated employee or contractor 5. Employees leaving; exiting with information and IP (mishandled exits)	**Digital** 6. Database loss, backup loss 7. Loss of devices by staff members 8. Errors and slips when sending documents (email recipients or attachments) **Physical** 9. Loss of printed documents (e.g., bins/documents disposal) 10. Error or slips when communicating to outsiders 11. Loss of archives

most protection. To establish this inventory, firms typically categorize their documents according to their level of confidentiality, such as:

- highly confidential
- confidential
- internal
- public.

However, in practice the categories are fairly broad and the classification process not always systematic and rigorous, so that documents with the same rating can have very different levels of sensitivity and/or market value. Moreover, the categorization makes sense only if it relates to a clear difference in the level of handling, storage and protection. The market is increasingly moving toward a risk-based protection of information assets, since it is broadly accepted that fully protecting all information at all times is often too demanding and costly for a business.

The Centre for Cyber Security in Belgium recommends the following steps to identify and categorize vulnerabilities and cyberthreats:[5]

---

[5]Cyber Security Incident Management Guide, Centre for Cyber Security Belgium & Cyber Security Coalition, 2015. The document is a pragmatic, "how to" guide of incident management, free access.

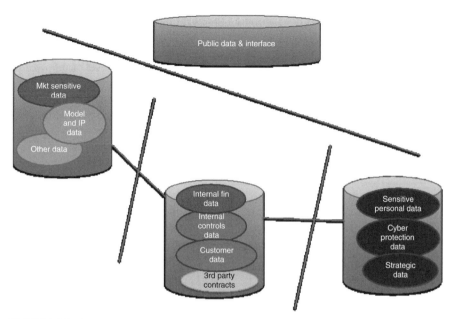

FIGURE 18.1   Theoretical example of data exposure map and risk-based protection and architecture

1. Identify the business and the resources that need to be protected.
2. Determine what your "crown jewels" are.
3. Assign business priorities for recovery.
4. Document how your system works and keep this documentation up to date:
   - network scheme
   - equipment and services inventory
   - account and access lists.

Figure 18.1 presents a theoretical, stylized example of a risk-based architecture, with data locations and levels of protection aligned with sensitivity levels. In practice, however, all types of data can be found throughout the system.

ASSESSMENT: SURVEYS, RCSAS AND SCENARIOS

Risk Assessment Survey

Information is everywhere, part of everything, handled by everyone. It is a diffuse presence not well suited to point-in-time, circumvented risk and control self-assessments. To mitigate this issue, we designed a flash questionnaire that would take a maximum of five minutes to complete. After testing and adjusting the questionnaire with several people, we sent it firm-wide. Two-thirds of the firm responded, which was a representative and successful outcome.

The results gave the risk function a fairly good insight on the level of information security experienced day to day, both collectively and individually – something that is impossible to achieve through RCSAs. The responses to whether people had personally lost or disclosed information, or if they had witnessed data incidents, were particularly useful. Figure 18.2 presents the questionnaire.

Risk and Control Self-assessments

Based on the questionnaire results and a number of interviews across different departments and business lines – including IT, naturally – members of the risk function and I plotted the assessment of the various information security risk types in the RCSA matrix. Figure 18.3 presents an anonymized version of this exercise. Both the matrix and the position of the dots have been modified to protect the firm's confidentiality, but the interpretations are accurate, if fictitious.

Since the firm at the time was rolling out some additional control measures, it felt sensible to also present the expected impact of these controls on the new risk assessment. Figure 18.4 displays a modified example of this representation.

Cyber Scenario Assessment

Tail risk events, like data breaches or cyberattacks, are well suited for scenario analysis. For the assessment of rare events and cyberscenarios in particular, market practice is evolving toward scenario modelling using fault trees, Bayesian networks and other methods, as presented in Chapter 7. Figure 18.5 displays a stylized example of a structured scenario, where three preventive controls are layered between attackers and the data server. Those three controls will be, for instance, two firewalls and human suspicion regarding unknown links or attachments sent through emails. All three controls need to fail simultaneously for the attack to be successful.

The joint probability of failure of these three controls is the scenario probability. If controls are independent and expected to fail in a range of L(ow) to H(igh), the joint probability of failure ranges between the product of three L(ow) cases of failure L×L×L, and the three H(igh) cases of failures H×H×H. Simple models can be manually calculated for discrete probabilities. Slightly more complex models generate probability distributions from Monte Carlo simulations, possible to create only with spreadsheets and add-on features.

Drivers of impacts are also decomposed and quantified, and simulations are made on the range of value. In the case illustrated: impact of data leak = time to detection × data corrupted (or stolen) per unit of time × data value. There again, Monte Carlo simulations lead to continuous distributions of losses per scenario type. Additional

Flash Questionnaire

Information Security Risk Assessment

Name / Dpt	

Exposure	1	Approximately, what proportion of information handled in your division would be considered as strictly confidential?	Comment box (optional)
	11	More than 50%	
	12	More than 20%	
	13	Less than 20%	
Past incidents	2	Have you ever experienced a loss or theft of information (any other than public information)	Comment box - Please use
	21	Yes, we lost some information	
	22	Yes, we had some information stolen	
	23	No, but we had near misses (incident avoided by luck)	
	24	No never	
Impact	3	What would be the damage if you or someone in your department looses or inadvertently disclose some of your most confidential information:	Comment box (optional)
	31	Catastrophic: the future of the firm is put at stake	
	32	Major: legal and / or market impacts and massive embarrassment regarding stakeholder	
	33	Moderate: embarrassing and with some tangible effects	
	34	Nothing very significant	
Awareness	4	Are the people of your division aware of what to do to protect sensitive information in the division?	Comment box (optional)
	41	Yes, they apply our internal rules of prudence and access restrictions	
	42	Yes, we apply the information security policy	
	43	Not really	
	44	Other (please comment)	
Risk types	5	What are the biggest risks to your division, regarding the security of confidential information (more than one answer possible)	Comment box - Please use
	51	Accidental disclosure of confidential information by a member of the team	
	52	Fraudulent disclosure of confidential information by a member of the team	
	53	Theft or hacking of digital confidential information by an external fraudster	
	54	Loss of physical information	
	55	other (please comment)	
Planning	6	Is there an incident management procedure in place for your division (pre-plan in case of incident, procedures to limit the damage)?	Comment box (optional)
	61	Yes	
	62	No	
Likelihood	7	How likely do you judge that would happen?	Comment box - Please use
	71	About once a year	
	72	About 10% to 50% of happening each year	
	73	Very unlikely (less than 10% chance in a year)	
	74	Why? (please comment)	
Risk appetite	9	Are you comfortable with the level of risk faced by your department regarding information security?	Comment box (optional)
	91	Yes	
	92	No	
	93	Other (please comment)	
Other	10	Would you like to tell us anything else?	Comment box (optional)
	101	Yes (see comment box)	
	102	No	
Feedback	11	Did you find this questionnaire useful?	Comment box (optional)
	111	Yes	
	112	No	

FIGURE 18.2 Flash questionnaire for information security assessment

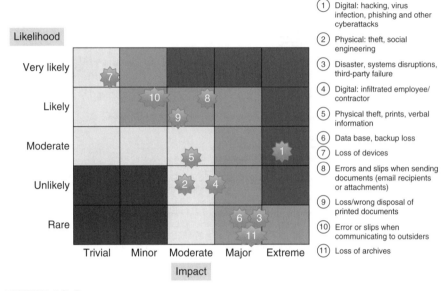

FIGURE 18.3   Information security risk assessment matrix (fictitious)

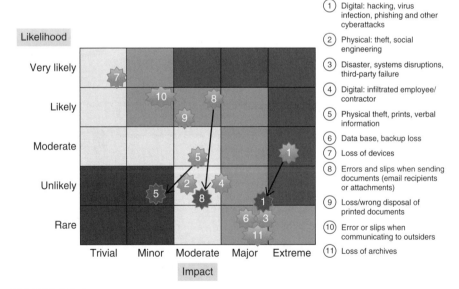

FIGURE 18.4   Revised assessment with additional controls

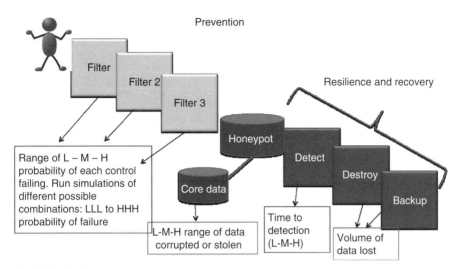

FIGURE 18.5   Scenario structuring in cybersecurity

elements to the scenario can include detective controls, incident management and technical recovery or communication management. Including post-event mitigation will deliver more realistic estimates and highlight the importance of crisis management as a damage control mechanism.

MITIGATION: BEHAVIORAL AND TECHNICAL MEASURES

It would require a book in its own right to fully explore the extensive variety of information controls. Here, we highlight just some of the main steps that organizations take to mitigate information risks.

The protection of information has three dimensions that are often referred to as CIA: confidentiality, integrity, availability. The first two concern information security while the third relates to business continuity and systems uptime.

There are two broad categories for information controls:

- Behavioral controls: these address human behaviors and fallibility when it comes to handling and protecting information. The controls include awareness campaigns, rules of conduct and prudence for employees and contractors, online training, password management, supervision and sanctions. They apply to all types of information security risks, not just cyberattacks.
- Technical controls: these relate to all technical aspects of systems, either for prevention or for detection. Preventive controls relate to system architecture, access, firewalls, encryption, passwords or patching and are essentially directed at

external threats. Detective controls provide early warnings of data leaks, whether initiated internally or externally, like DLPD (data leak prevention and detection) techniques.[6] Finally, mitigating controls focus on keeping redundancies and backups offline.[7]

Table 18.2 presents a non-exhaustive list of key controls for information security. The number and intensity of the controls are also a matter of risk appetite and consistency of choices. Although every firm will claim zero tolerance for information security breaches, they do not necessarily have the same level of commitment to

TABLE 18.2   Some key controls in information security

Behavioral controls	
Awareness and prudence	Awareness campaign
	Training
	Fake phishing test
Conduct rules	Rules of confidentiality
	Code of conduct
	Sanctions rules
Data governance	Data transfer rules
Technical controls	
Architecture	Network partitioning
	Access management
	Firewalls
Encryption	Password rules
	Encryption levels and rules
	Vulnerability management (patching)
Detection	DLPD
	Log-in monitoring
	Honeypot
	X-ray device screening
Testing	Penetration testing
	Password cracking attempt (from IT department)

---

[6]For an excellent discussion on data breaches and DLPD techniques, please read Cheng, L., Liu, F. and Yao, D. (2017) *Enterprise Data Breach: Causes, Challenges, Prevention, and Future Directions*, Wiley.
[7]Centre for Cyber Security, op. cit.

governance, discipline and the technical controls required to guarantee a high level of security. Information security measures cost time, money and effort, so the benefits of risk reduction need to be balanced against the cost of controls.

MONITORING: KRIS

In highly controlled activities such as information security and cyberprotection, risk monitoring will focus on the effectiveness of the controls and on any unexpected deviations from normality, whether in exposure, traffic or staff behavior.

TABLE 18.3   Examples of KRIs for information security risk

Exposure KRIs	
	Spread of sensitive information
	Number of users/administrators in excess of the norm
	Number of third parties with data access
	Number of temporary workers and contractors with confidential data access
Control failures KRIs	
	Overdue vulnerability patching
	Overdue penetration tests/overdue resolution of penetration tests recommendations
	Software obsolescence
	Results of phishing tests, of password cracking attempts
	# inadequate access and overdue revisions of access
Stress KRIs	
	% change in # workload/change request/issues per IT managers
	% vacancies in IT/cybersecurity teams
	Overcapacity usage of systems
Causal KRIs	
	Conduct metrics on employee compliance
	Breach of conduct and information rules on social media "Repeat offenders" (staff failing more than one phishing test) in sensitive data areas Devices or access cards lost/stolen

At a technical level and for cyberattacks and access breaches, most – if not all – monitoring will take place in the IT department. However, in many firms the information security department is separate from IT, reflecting the fact that information security involves more than just securing the business against cyberattacks. The information security department should design, maintain and monitor a blend of behavioral and technical controls, where deviations and failings constitute KRIs. Table 18.3 lists possible KRIs for information security, using the KRI typology presented in Chapter 14.

CHAPTER **19**

Operational Risks in Cryptocurrencies

CONTEXT AND ACADEMIC RESEARCH

The cryptocurrency Bitcoin experienced a bubble at the end of 2017 that was comparable to the tulip mania of the 17th century, when heady speculation pushed the price of tulip bulbs to ridiculous levels before the price crashed abruptly. The sudden widespread interest in the cryptocurrency and associated speculation brought Bitcoins to the evening news. Its future is uncertain, but blockchain, the distributed ledger technology that underpins Bitcoin, is viewed by many as one of the most promising developments for monetary transfer and, more generally, for secure transactions in a peer-to-peer network.

In 2014, when Bitcoin and blockchain began to be discussed keenly in universities and by some payment providers but had yet to capture the public imagination, I had the pleasure of working with UCL colleagues on an academic paper on the risks and implications of virtual currencies from a banking regulation perspective. The paper, pioneering at the time of its publication, looked at some of the main operational risks that banks would face if they decided to trade cryptocurrencies; its section on operational risk is summarized in this chapter. For further detail, please refer to the full publication and its references.[1]

SUMMARY

The paper presented the first basic operational risk perspective for key risk management issues associated with the emergence of new forms of electronic currency in the real

---

[1]Peters, G., Chapelle, A. and Panayi, E. (2015) "Opening discussion on banking sector risk exposures and vulnerabilities from virtual currencies: an operational risk perspective," *Journal of Banking Regulation*, September, 1–34). The working paper is available at: https://ssrn.com/abstract=2491991

economy. In particular, we focused on understanding the development of new risk types and the evolution of current risk types as new components of financial institutions arise to cater for an increasing demand for electronic money, micro-payment systems, virtual money and cryptocurrencies.

We proposed a risk identification and assessment framework for virtual and cryptocurrencies from a banking regulation perspective. The framework addressed the need to understand key operational risk vulnerabilities and exposure risk drivers within the Basel II/III banking regulation, and specifically those associated with virtual and cryptocurrencies.

We highlighted how some of the features of virtual and cryptocurrencies are important drivers of operational risk, posing both management and regulatory challenges that must be addressed by regulators, central banks and security exchanges.

We proposed a structure of risk analysis starting with the vulnerabilities and exposures of virtual and cryptocurrencies as the drivers of operational risk for these new means of exchange. Then, by using risk drivers, our approach allowed us to highlight the sources of possible adverse consequences when using or generating virtual and cryptocurrencies. These were then mapped into the risks associated with the Basel categories, providing an easier view of the regulatory response and better mitigation techniques. In addition, this helps to identify and address the root causes of the operational risks associated with virtual and cryptocurrencies, rather than just presenting their symptoms.

BITCOIN

Bitcoin is the most famous cryptocurrency but it is by no means the only one. Cryptocurrencies are a type of digital token that use cryptography to form chains of digital signatures that create token transfers, with processing via a decentralized peer-to-peer networking system architecture.

Bitcoin relies on public-key cryptography, an asymmetric key encryption scheme used for encrypting messages and verifying the originator of a message. A user wishing to communicate with a public-key cryptography scheme would have two keys: a public key that is available for everybody to access and a private key that must be kept secret. As an example, consider two users, A and B. User A wants to send a message to user B in a public-key cryptography scheme. For that, A would have to obtain B's public key, obtain the "ciphertext" (or the encryption transformation of the message defined by the public key) and send it to B. User B could then decrypt this message using her private key.

In addition, Bitcoin uses the concept of digital signatures to ensure non-repudiation: that is, a third party can easily verify whether a particular signatory has signed a message, using only information that is publicly available (the signatories private key). It is important, then, to keep secret the key belonging to the owner of the

Bitcoin balance. If another individual had access to the private key, they would be able to create a transaction message and sign it as if they were the owner, possibly transferring units of the currency to their own address, and the Bitcoin balance of the owner's address would be compromised.

A time stamp, used through the peer-to-peer network, verifies whether a Bitcoin transaction has been performed, such as the transfer of Bitcoins from one Bitcoin address to another Bitcoin address. This peer-to-peer network is not centrally controlled and anyone may join as a member. There is no central authority responsible for issuance or monetary policy such as money supply controls. In fact, all rules (protocols) regarding the currency design, creation and transaction are publicly available.

Cryptocurrencies are introduced into the economy gradually – for some of the major cryptocurrencies (including Bitcoin and Litecoin), the total number of the currency units to be introduced is fixed at approximately 21 million coins for Bitcoin and approximately 84 million coins for Litecoin, of which an estimated 53 million Litecoin are in circulation (mid-2017). Cryptocurrencies are introduced through a process called mining, which involves solving an increasingly computationally challenging set of cryptographic mathematical problems. It is essentially a race between network nodes, as the node that solves the problem first is rewarded with a certain number of coins. Any member of the network can become a miner of new coins by mining what are known as blocks.

There were 16.7 million Bitcoins available in January 2018 and 4.3 million left to mine. Out of the 16.7 million, it's estimated that 30% may be lost forever as a result of things like hard drive crashes and misplaced private keys.[2]

BLOCKCHAIN

Once a transaction occurs, it is broadcast to the network and is verified by the network nodes. It is then inserted into the blockchain, a shared public ledger of transactions. This means it is straightforward to identify the last owner of a particular unit of currency.

Blockchain is created and maintained by all members of the network. The ledger contains an electronic record of all transactions undertaken by each Bitcoin (in case of Bitcoin exchanges). The public ledger is formed from mined blocks, which provide the solution to either mine new coins or to verify a Bitcoin transaction in the network. The ledger is known as a blockchain, a sequence of transaction blocks where you can find the history of every coin from the day it was mined or created. This blockchain is periodically updated with the latest transaction block when it is created.

---

[2]Source: Steven Buchko, "How many bitcoins are left?", CoinCentral, Jan 2018.

TABLE 19.1 Summary of operational risk vulnerabilities and exposures for cryptocurrencies

Vulnerabilities	Exposures
1. Decentralized governance	1. Multiplicity of jurisdictions
2. Peer-to-peer verification	2. Multiplicity of micropayments
3. Transaction irreversibility	3. Hardware reliance
4. Anonymity	4. Software reliance
5. Handling of sensitive information (private keys and virtual wallets)	
6. Price or value instability	
7. International regulatory risk	

RISK IDENTIFICATION: CRYPTOCURRENCY VULNERABILITIES AND EXPOSURES

This section presents the risk identification method of decomposition for cryptocurrencies according to their specific vulnerabilities, which include decentralized governance, peer-to-peer verifications of transactions, transaction irreversibility and handling of sensitive information. We also address the operational risk profile of cryptocurrencies due to their exposure to multiple jurisdictions; multiplicity of micropayments; and reliance on hardware and software.

Table 19.1 provides a summary of what we consider are core operational risk vulnerabilities and exposures for virtual currencies and cryptocurrencies within a banking environment. In the following subsections we discuss these vulnerabilities and exposures in more detail.

OPERATIONAL RISKS AND POTENTIAL EVENT TYPES FOR CRYPTOCURRENCIES

The risks associated with vulnerabilities and exposures drive the specific operational risk profiles of cryptocurrencies. These risks can be mapped to the Basel taxonomy, documented in Table 19.2.

MITIGATION ACTIONS FOR OPERATIONAL RISKS IN CRYPTOCURRENCIES

From a systemic angle, the regulator may be concerned by the possible anonymity of cryptocurrency operators, as the identifier of transactions is limited to public addresses

TABLE 19.2   Operational risks of cryptocurrencies mapped to the Basel categories

Risk category level 1	Risk category level 2
1. Internal fraud	**1.1** Unauthorized activity **1.2** Theft and fraud
Examples include: ■ misappropriation of assets (i.e. cryptocurrencies through, for instance, theft of private and public keys) ■ tax evasion (this issue has already raised concerns with several regulatory authorities).	
2. External fraud	**2.1** Theft and fraud **2.2** Systems abuse
Examples include: ■ theft of information (this may include virtual wallet addresses, public and private keys as well as other personal identifications such as transactions made between members of the virtual currency and cryptocurrency networks) ■ hacking damage (permanent corruption or destruction that is irreversible for portions of the currency or members' accounts) ■ third-party theft and forgery (theft of virtual currency from exchanges, virtual wallets and storage facilities, and eventually banks and depository-taking institutions should they accept virtual currencies and cryptocurrencies in the future).	
3. Employment practices and workplace safety	**3.1** Employee relations **3.2** Health and safety **3.3** Diversity and discrimination
Not considered at this stage to be particularly relevant.	
4. Clients, products and business practices	**4.1** Conduct **4.2** Advisory activities and mis-selling **4.3** Product flaws **4.4** Improper business or market practices **4.5** Customer or client selection and exposure
Examples include: ■ market manipulation (currently most electronic exchanges for virtual currencies and cryptocurrencies are underregulated, if regulated at all) ■ antitrust (there is potential moral hazard associated with private or consortium-based virtual currencies) ■ improper trade ■ product defects (there may be yet unknown design problems with security, coin generation, verification, etc. in cryptocurrency protocols that could be exploited by malicious users)	

(Continued)

TABLE 19.2 (*Continued*)

Risk category level 1	Risk category level 2
■ fiduciary breaches (since fiduciary relationships are by their very nature relationships of good faith, they may involve a variety of obligations depending on the exact circumstances. Because there is no central authority monitoring virtual currencies and cryptocurrencies, they are open to manipulation. This will complicate the fiduciary responsibilities that are typically required of corporate directors, officers and risk management functions of financial institutions. In addition, the secrecy surrounding cryptocurrencies and their attribution to particular individuals, and the lack of a proper legal framework, may create conflicts of interest and unfair practices) ■ account churning (special forms of account churning may arise in virtual currencies and cryptocurrencies which are related to the incentive commissions paid for proof-of-work as well as incentives paid by transaction fees verification. For instance, in some cryptocurrencies when the output value of a transaction is less than its input value, the difference is a transaction fee that is added to the incentive value of the block containing the transaction).	

5. Damage to physical assets	**5.1** Disasters and other events

Examples include:
■ terrorism (cyberterrorism and attacks on networks and storage facilities may be initiated to benefit certain members or to destroy cryptocurrency account details and digital records)
■ vandalism (cyber vandalism from hackers).

6. Business disruption and systems failures	**6.1** Systems failures

Examples include:
■ software failures (software specific to a particular virtual currency or cryptocurrency may get upgraded or modified, resulting in failures in mining, transaction verification or even encryption)
■ hardware failures (core nodes on the mining network required to process blockchains and perform network verifications may fail, resulting in extensive delays in transaction processing).

7. Execution, delivery and process management	**7.1** Documentation; transaction; account management; reporting; distributor; supplier

Examples include:
■ data entry errors; accounting errors; failed mandatory reporting; and negligent loss of client assets (all may affect different aspects of cryptocurrencies – for instance, the storage of virtual wallets and private and public encryption keys).

and IP, without a clear means of knowing who operates from these addresses. Conversely, the peer-to-peer review systems require fully traceable operations so that anyone can see the balance and the detail of every transaction operated by any address (testable on biteasy.com). This extensive transparency may not be convenient for every operator and is dramatically different from the principle of secrecy in banking operations. Bitcoin users who do not want full disclosure of their operations can install a transaction system that generates a different address every time a payment is executed. This makes tracking more difficult for dishonest parties, but would also be a challenge for the regulator.

Table 19.3 lists some of the mitigating actions for operational risks posed by cryptocurrencies and categorized by risk drivers.

DISCUSSIONS ON OPERATIONAL RISK DRIVERS OF CRYPTOCURRENCIES

This section provides more detail on the vulnerabilities and exposures of cryptocurrencies.

Decentralized Governance and Risk of Coordinated Attacks

Because cryptocurrencies operate via a peer-to-peer network, independent of a central authority or central banks, there is an inherent operational risk linked to decentralization. Although being independent is an appealing feature for many advocates of cryptocurrencies, decentralization means that functions such as issue, transaction processing and verification are managed collectively by the network. This creates a vulnerability to coordinated attacks, which was highlighted already in 2008 by Satoshi Nakamoto, the putative founder of Bitcoin: "The system is secure as long as honest nodes collectively control more CPU power than any cooperating group of attackers' nodes."[3]

This is due to the peer-to-peer review system of transaction validations, where validating power comes with CPU power, in a system similar to "one-CPU-one-vote." Indeed, the confirmation (of not double spending) of transaction requires the knowledge of all previous transactions and their times in order to decide what comes first. Nakamoto argues: "As long as a majority of CPU power is controlled by nodes that are not cooperating to attack the network, they will generate the longest chain and outpace attackers."

The weakness of this argument is, in our view, the assumption that financial criminals or other committed agencies would not attempt to outpace genuine

---

[3]Nakamoto, S. (2008) "Bitcoin: a peer-to-peer electronic cash system." *Consulted*, 1, 2012, 28.

TABLE 19.3   Risk drivers of cryptocurrencies such as Bitcoins mapped to
Basel II/III categories

Risk drivers	Operational risks	Mitigating actions (non-exhaustive list)
Decentralized governance/absence of legal tender	Governance risk Abuse of power Price manipulation Fraud Price volatility Changes in protocols	If in virtual currency and cryptocurrency deposit-taking banks: codify network and governance powers
Peer-to-peer verification of transactions	Double-spending attacks	High computational power
Transaction irreversibility	Aggravated losses in case of errors or theft of private keys	Cybersecurity – type of protection (cold storage, multiple devices, encryption, strong passwords)
Anonymity	Money laundering Fraud Legal risk Compliance	Forcing identification, at minimum via a registered IP address; tax file identification when registering e-wallet
Private key as unique means of access	Loss of value due to: external fraud internal fraud processing errors damage to physical assets attacks	Similar risk mitigation techniques applicable to sensitive information in traditional banking
Publication time gap (transaction malleability)	Fraud in double spending Fake transactions Attacks Transaction malleability	
Multiple jurisdictions	Regulatory breach Tax avoidance Tax law compliance	
Micropayments	Internal fraud External fraud Systems failure Process errors Reporting	
Hardware reliance	Exposure to hardware failures	
Software reliance	Exposure to software failure Drivers of impact of data theft	

network controllers. There is, arguably, a non-null possibility of systemic failure of a cryptocurrency network such as Bitcoin in the case of a coordinated attack. One approach to address systemic risks would be for national and international regulators to ensure that extreme CPU power is allocated only to recognized network controllers such as national agencies and agreed private parties.

More likely than coordinated attacks are failures that may arise from altering the protocols that dictate the processing and creation of cryptocurrencies such as Bitcoin. In Bitcoin, any aspect of the protocol can be altered by consensus. Currencies that employ the proof-of-work system are vulnerable to miners (or groups of miners) that accumulate large computational resources for mining and verification. In such a currency, a pool that controls more than the majority of the computational power can impose conditions on the rest of the network and engage in malicious activities.

Besides the absence of a legal tendering authority, the decentralized, network-based management of virtual currencies, and particularly of cryptocurrencies, acts both as a risk driver and as risk mitigation. On the risk side: the fight for network control, politics and power struggles, and the possible instability of protocols. On the mitigation side: there is no single point of failure. In contrast to traditional payment systems, because there is no central intermediary, any node may drop out of the network and new nodes can enter at any time and are compensated according to the computational power that they contribute. In theory, this should lead to a more resilient network, while also protecting against bad actors trying to change the Bitcoin protocol, as changes have to be approved by the majority of the computing power in the network.

Peer-to-peer Verifications of Transactions and Risk of Double Spending

The peer-to-peer and proof-of-work aspects of cryptocurrencies such as Bitcoin can also create several vulnerabilities, which, if exploited, have the potential to generate substantial losses.

As a consequence of peer-to-peer verification, there is a delay in processing a transaction which can amount to tens of minutes between the execution of a transaction and its publication to the network and registration on the Bitcoin ledger blockchain. This applies even to faster cryptocurrency protocols such as Bitcoin. These delays, though seemingly innocuous, present a significant opportunity for fraud, system attacks, double spending and fake transactions. During these waiting periods, an adversary could attempt to use the same Bitcoins in multiple transactions, and if the goods are released instantaneously, this may easily lead to losses for a vendor.

Also, fraudulent transactions in the Bitcoin cryptocurrency network can be generated in a double-spending attack and may cause losses, even when they have been confirmed by network nodes. If an adversary creates two payment messages (containing a genuine and a fraudulent transaction) using the same Bitcoins but to be sent to two different parties and broadcasts them to the network simultaneously, it is likely that different network nodes will receive the two messages in different order. They will verify the earliest message as being the valid one and reject the second, and attempt to publish them in a transaction block. Two nodes may then publish transaction blocks with different transactions (a "fork" of the network); depending on how this is resolved, either the genuine or the fraudulent transaction may be confirmed. The probability of a successful attack depends on the computational power of the attacker compared with that of the network.

Another vulnerability that arises from the proof-of-work feature is the idea of "selfish" mining strategies. This vulnerability is where a group or consortium of miners, who are critical to the verification of transactions and creation of new currency and who control at least one-third of the mining power of the network, can mine a disproportionately high number of Bitcoins. The consequence of this is that they may fashion a mechanism in which they then selectively publish transaction blocks they have discovered (mined), causing the "honest" majority to needlessly spend computational power in mining the same blocks with little reward or outcome. In addition, this vulnerability may be turned into a form of preferential transaction verification that may open the way to criminal behaviors, resulting in risks of bribery for transaction processing preferences, moral hazard in processing one's own transactions with priority and account churning for transaction fees.

Transaction Irreversibility and Risk of Uncoverable Losses and Mistakes

Transaction irreversibility is another form of vulnerability for cryptocurrencies. In other words, a data entry error cannot easily be corrected. For example, when a bank transfers a large number of Bitcoins, if the amount to be transferred is mistakenly switched with the transaction fee, then the miner verifying the transaction can keep the fee and the bank will be unable to reverse or modify the transaction. This is because of the specification of the currency, where the publication of a transaction block depends on all previous blocks, and because there is no central authority that could generate a new transaction to offset the original one.

A second type of vulnerability relates to the monitoring and maintenance of customer account virtual wallets. A bank would require continuous access to the blockchain to ensure that it can keep track of the ownership and status of its customers' account balances, i.e., number of Bitcoins. Any IT disruption would affect the bank's ability to carry out its operations. If transactions are processed during the disruption without the bank knowing or controlling the transaction, losses would be irreversible due to the nature of Bitcoin transactions and verifications, which would be processed by the network but remain unknown to the bank until its own network or communication problem is resolved.

Finally, transaction irreversibility exposes banks and cryptocurrency holders to the risk of cybercrime and hacker attacks on banking networks, customer virtual wallets or cryptocurrency bank accounts.

Anonymity and Risk of Financial Crime

Anonymity is one of cryptocurrencies' most widely cited vulnerabilities, both for operational risk and particularly for financial crime. There are several aspects of this vulnerability that must be explored from the perspective of financial risk, including the privacy of transaction processing for customers, money laundering and taxation on accounts. Some of these may result in operational risk losses.

A Bitcoin address, with its pair of public and private keys, is currently the only requirement to undertake Bitcoin transactions. The Bitcoin address is not registered to a named individual; only the possession of the private key gives control over the balance associated with the address. While the complete address history of every Bitcoin is traceable, the controllers of those addresses are not necessarily easy to identify, making the transactions anonymous.

However, total anonymity is guaranteed only under certain circumstances, i.e., when employing anonymizing software and transacting directly with individuals who are similarly careful in protecting their identity. In practice, transacting through a website will mean that an individual would, at the very least, leave a digital footprint in the form of an IP address, which could then be tied to a physical address. The use of Bitcoin web "wallets" is an example.

You would expect that in the future, when setting up an e-wallet in a financial institution or when a bank accepts deposits in cryptocurrencies, clients would provide a tax file number or similar form of identification so that any interest credited to their accounts in a virtual currency denomination or in fiat currency could be appropriately considered for taxation purposes. This alone has interesting economic and legal implications for the so-called anonymity offered when transacting in virtual currencies in the real economy. The anonymity would exist up to the point the transactions are processed from accounts registered to a particular client of the bank. Once an account is opened, it would have to be linked to the taxation details of the client, thus providing an identity to transactions in the blockchain, at least related to this portion of a transaction sequence. This can also be valuable for regulators and cybersecurity agencies tracking criminal activity and money laundering in virtual currency international exchanges.

There is another risk associated with cryptocurrencies such as Bitcoin that admit a public blockchain ledger of all transactions and account details in the transactions. The risk is when banks accidentally or willfully accept Bitcoin deposits that are the proceeds of crime or have been involved in some criminal activity. The question is then how to manage the risk that a particular subset of the Bitcoins, held in a bank, may previously have been used (some transactions ago) in a criminal transaction and can thus be confiscated under the U.K.'s Proceeds of Crime Act, or the equivalent law in other countries.

Possible mitigating actions include the adoption and maintenance of a blacklist of Bitcoin addresses. The bank taking a Bitcoin deposit would be obligated to search through the history of the deposited Bitcoins and then reject (and possibly report) any suspicious deposits.

Handling of Sensitive Information and Risk of Fraud

The unique reliance on private keys, coupled with the irreversibility of payments in cryptocurrencies, means that Bitcoins are potentially susceptible to large operational risk losses from the following:

- Fraud and misappropriation of assets: if anyone gains access to a private key, they can create a transaction message and sign it as if they were the genuine owner, possibly transferring units of the currency to their own address.
- Loss due to processing errors: data for addresses may be entered inaccurately.
- Loss of electronic wallet due to the failure of technical support: in the case of Bitcoins, the most common storage account is an electronic wallet. The wallet stores the private/public key pairs for each of the user's Bitcoin addresses, and either one may hold a Bitcoin balance. The wallets may be stored on a user's computer or a mobile device, but may also be hosted online by a web service. Any one of these storage solutions may fail.

Risk mitigation techniques for users are similar to some of the classic methods of cybersecurity and data protection, including cold storage (offline) of digital wallets, storage on multiple devices, both physical and digital, as well as solid encryption of private keys, strong passwords and limited online transactions. Signing transactions offline and using hardware wallets are now increasingly popular solutions to strengthen cryptocurrency security.

Because there is a finite money supply for currencies such as Bitcoins, losses are irreversible. Money cannot be accessed once keys are lost, nor can it be regenerated. When Bitcoins are removed from circulation, the loss is permanent. If there is a large loss, or many smaller losses, whether from negligence, accidental damage or malicious or criminal activity, it can permanently affect the Bitcoin money supply.

Risk Exposures Associated with Cryptocurrencies

Banks accepting cryptocurrencies also face risks related to four significant exposures:

- Multiple jurisdictions: legal complexity, tax avoidance, compliance issues and clarity of interpretations are part of the risks associated with trading internationally.

■ Multiplicity of micropayments: the mainstream use of cryptocurrencies necessitates processing massive volumes of many small transactions corresponding to fractions of cents, which may be undertaken by micropayment systems. This may place stress on processing systems, and with such high volumes potentially being processed, any lack of accuracy or control could lead to substantial losses. There is a risk of internal fraud perpetrated by employees with sufficient knowledge of the micropayment systems. This type of attack allegedly occurred against Mt. Gox, the virtual currencies exchange in Tokyo, ultimately contributing to its closure in February 2014.

■ External hardware reliance: while banks can control their IT infrastructure by resourcing IT departments adequately, this is not the case for Bitcoin and other cryptocurrency networks. The processing functions for blockchain verification and currency creation are external to any individual bank. This means that an external group of entities, in different geographies, is critical to the reliable functioning of the cryptocurrency network, including transaction processing and verification. The reliance on external hardware creates large operational risk exposure for any bank processing cryptocurrencies and deposits.

■ Software reliance: a cryptocurrency protocol is open to amendments or adjustments by different groups within the cryptocurrency network. A bank could be forced to limit its operations following changes in the cryptocurrency specification, or simply because of cryptocurrency software updates, making old transaction protocols either void, open or susceptible to attack, or making it significantly slower to process transactions. Finally, software rollout issues could also be more damaging when dealing with cryptocurrency wallets. In particular, if coding is not carried out by a trusted party, malicious code could be incorporated in a release. Inadequate testing of production software may cause loss of access to wallet files when the software is released and thus a permanent monetary loss due to transaction irreversibility. In addition, software architecture is a major consideration, as a system that is not scalable may fail from a sudden influx of customers or a large increase in the number of transactions.

In conclusion, cryptocurrencies supported by blockchain technology carry significant exposures to operational risk, despite the mitigation measures available today. Any bank or financial institution that embraces these emerging currencies and technologies must ensure that it has the right knowledge, expertise and focus to mitigate the associated risks.

## CHAPTER 20

Resilience and Reputation

INTRODUCTION

Reputation risk, alongside cyber risk, is a top risk in organizations. However, reputation is not so much a risk as an outcome, and firms can manage and control their reputation by the way they conduct their business and how they interact with their stakeholders. This chapter describes how to build and nurture a reputation and what to do when a crisis hits. It explores incident management and resilience, to help preserve a reputation. Resilience and reputation are intertwined and dependent: a lack of resilience during a crisis will significantly damage a firm's reputation, just as significant reputation damage during crisis will surely jeopardize the firm's resilience. Reputation is a "license to operate" – when reputation remains good (enough), the firm will remain in operation.

REPUTATION MANAGEMENT

Reputation Definition

Reputation is "the beliefs or opinions that are generally held about someone or something" (*Oxford Dictionary*) or "the opinion that people in general have about someone or something, or how much respect or admiration someone or something receives, based on past behavior or character" (*Cambridge Dictionary*).

For a firm's reputation management, "people in general" is preferably segmented into different stakeholder groups, while "based on past behavior or character" is the essential foundation of reputation management.

Characteristics of Reputation Risk

A firm's reputation is a consequence of what stakeholders believe, based on past behavior and character. It can be defined as a risk because what people think of someone or something may be uncertain. Reputation can also be a risk because firms and individuals are susceptible to random events that will affect reputation. People commonly combine these two different elements when referring to reputation risk. However, decomposing them provides insights for better management:

- Reputation as an outcome of past behaviors: to manage through reputation building, through stakeholders' satisfaction and good relationships.
- Reputation impact as an outcome of operational risk incidents and other accidental events: to address through incident management and crisis response.

Building a Good Reputation

Since reputation risk is the potential damage to stakeholders' perception, or, to put it another way, the difference between expectations and delivery, you must build healthy, resilient relationships with all stakeholders. There are many levels to a firm's reputation, reflecting the variety of stakeholders and the different types of relationship the firm has with each of them.

There are two elements to consider when building a reputation:

- *Reputation for whom*: leading to stakeholder identification and mapping.
- *Reputation about what*: leading to the identification of what matters to the different stakeholders.

In the heavily regulated financial industry, the main drivers of a firm's reputation with the regulators are:

- the quality of regulatory compliance[1]
- the level of transparency and engagement with the regulator
- the frequency and material consequences of regulatory breaches (if any).

Product quality and level of service are obvious drivers of customer satisfaction. When products and services are high quality, they will enhance a firm's reputation and lead to positive referrals, repeat business and a growing client base.

Investors and shareholders are also key stakeholders. They expect good financial performance and healthy prospects. Many will shy away if they feel that an incident may tarnish a firm's reputation and damage market prospects and future profits. One North American bank I know suffered heavily when hedge funds withdrew abruptly

---

[1]Compliance is not a binary all-or-nothing outcome; there are degrees of compliance, ranging from respect for both the letter and the spirit of regulation (high quality) to barely addressing basic requirements (low quality).

TABLE 20.1   Components of reputation

Reputation to: stakeholders	Reputation about: drivers
Customers and consumers	Product quality
Regulators	Customer service
Staff and job market	Value for money
Suppliers/third-party contractors	Financial stability
Shareholders and investors	Performance
Parent company	Growth prospect
Board and non-executive directors	Transparency and honesty
Media and commentators	Innovation
General public	Workplace
Activists	Governance
Competitors	Citizenship and corporate social responsibility
Governments	Resilience

following an incident involving corrections on financial accounts. For charities and non-governmental agencies, reputation and funding risk are top of the risk register. The scandal surrounding Oxfam harassment in Haiti, revealed in February 2018, led to the almost immediate loss of 7,000 donors.[2] Table 20.1 provides a list of the common stakeholders for financial companies, alongside the drivers of reputation and image.

Stakeholders themselves will influence a firm's reputation because the choices that a firm makes about shareholders, clients, staff and indeed third parties such as suppliers will all impact reputation. Onboarding the wrong type of client is a top operational risk for many firms. This goes beyond questions of anti-money laundering and know--your-customer issues, as some firms do not want to be associated with certain types of client, and they may also be careful about who they do business with on the supply side. Reputation damage cannot be "outsourced" – if a third party damages a firm's image in a client-facing activity, it is difficult to deflect the responsibility onto the third party.

Maintaining a Good Reputation

Maintaining a good reputation is a constant challenge. To be sustainable, a firm's reputation must be embedded in its day-to-day activities. It is good practice to reward staff actions and behavior that protect and improve the firm's reputation. For example, gift

---

[2] *The Guardian*, February 20, 2018.

vouchers could be awarded to teams with the best satisfaction rating from customers, or to communications teams who achieve a positive media profile, or to back-office teams who ensure that transactions run smoothly. There are many possibilities for the financial industry to be more creative and to celebrate success in operational areas.

Indeed, from what I observe, reputation risk management and stakeholder management are still mostly reactive in the financial industry. The focus of senior management and boards seems to be more about protecting reputation in case of an adverse event rather than building a resilient reputation proactively.[3] Engagement with stakeholders is often weak, with reputation management limited to crisis communication plans. This is important, of course, but it is not enough. Management needs to have a clear picture of who interacts with stakeholders and how, so that all interactions are consistent with the firm's vision, values and policies. Everything that shapes the firm's identity and reputation must be clearly and comprehensively communicated to all staff.

Benefits of a Good Reputation

A firm that has a better reputation than its competitors can expect higher sales and more referrals and will attract the best talent.[4] Having talented people is a huge benefit and a major driver of a firm's value, but it is insufficiently measured and accounted for in the industry. In contrast, universities and private education bodies understand the value of talent: they carefully cultivate their reputation for excellence so they can compete every year to attract the best students, who will then make the best alumni and in turn reinforce the institution's reputation. In other words, it's a virtuous circle.

CRISIS MANAGEMENT AND RESILIENCE

Definition of Resilience

Resilience is "the capacity to recover quickly from difficulties; toughness" (*Oxford Dictionary*) or "the quality of being able to return quickly to a previous good condition after problems" (*Cambridge Dictionary*).

To be resilient, to recover swiftly from damage, requires good crisis management.[5]

---

[3]Some large banks in the U.K. have launched marketing campaigns to build a positive and more humane image following the financial crisis. There again, one can see it as a reaction to the crisis, or a proactive action for the future.

[4]Up to 15 times compared with less reputable firms, according to the Reputation Institute.

[5]We define it as recovery from a shock, not the capacity to adapt to gradual change and market evolution (i.e., adaptability). For further discussions on resilience and adaptability, see Seville, E. (2016) *Resilient Organizations – How to Survive, Thrive and Create Opportunities Through Crisis and Change*, Kogan Page.

Essentials of Crisis Management

Crises can arise from any type of event, at any time, so companies need to be ready for all eventualities and know how to react. Events can disrupt the business, requiring the activation of business continuity plans. Even if service delivery is not interrupted, a crisis can still shake a firm, its processes and its people. To be prepared, firms must identify all possible threats to their business and assess their likely impact. This is the task of scenario analysis, described in Chapters 2 and 7. The case study shows some examples of crisis management mistakes.

CASES STUDIES: CAUGHT IN A CRISIS – WHAT NOT TO DO

- Natural disaster: when Hurricane Sandy hit New York City in 2012, it disrupted a business in England for four days. The business's risk map failed to show that the server for its Bangalore (India) call centers was in NYC. Without proper risk identification and third- and fourth-party dependencies, the business disruption lasted ten times longer than it should have.

- Disruption at a third party: people laughed when Kentucky Fried Chicken ran out of chicken, but not KFC. The company had recently changed its delivery partner and admitted to "a couple of teething problems."[6] It meant that chicken had not been shipped to most of its stores, forcing half of them to remain closed. The disruption lasted for days. KFC had neglected third-party vetting and redundancies for third parties who were critical to the supply chain.

- Successful hacking: it took Equifax two months to reveal a massive hack, while Uber concealed the hack of 57 million U.S. customers' data for a year and then paid a ransom in the hope that the hacker would destroy the data. Furthermore, in December 2017, a former Uber employee accused the company of corporate espionage.[7] Both Equifax and Uber changed their top management. Concealment is never a good corporate strategy.

- IT migration meltdown: TSB and its CEO Paul Pester made front-page news in the U.K. from April to June 2018, following the meltdown of an IT migration that left about 100,000 customers without bank access for weeks. Despite continuing problems, the CEO tweeted that the system was "up and

(Continued)

---

[6]*Evening Standard*, February 20, 2018.
[7]*The Guardian*, December 16, 2017.

running." Overall crisis communication was poorly managed, exacerbating customer distress and drawing heavy criticism from the U.K. regulatory authorities.

- System outage: British Airways suffered a lengthy outage of its (outsourced) online reservation and check-in system in 2017, forcing the company to cancel flights in and out of the U.K. for 24 hours and even keep passengers from disembarking from planes. Fury peaked when passengers were asked to pay for their food and drink while stranded on planes, in keeping with recent cost-cutting initiatives. Applying rigid rules in such exceptional circumstances was hardly smart and did nothing for BA's reputation.

- Internal fraud (rogue trading): Jérôme Kerviel generated the largest trading losses on record (€4.9 billion), for Société Générale, in January 2008. Daniel Bouton, CEO at the time, failed to warn Fed chairman Ben Bernanke and had publicly stated that the trader was an "isolated genius," which no specialist believed, with good reason.[8] Concealment and denial are the biggest pitfalls in crisis communication.

To manage a crisis effectively, firms need to demonstrate at least three qualities:

- Speed: crises spread like fire – you must respond quickly, decisively and appropriately.
- Competence: always use the right specialist for each job. If the relevant skills cannot be found in-house, use the services of external experts to handle the communication or the technicalities of the recovery, depending on the nature of the accident.
- Transparency: the worst thing is to lose the trust of your stakeholders (customers, shareholders, board, regulators, etc.). Remember that the media are also key stakeholders – trust is engendered by telling the truth, by being open and honest at all times. Concealment and back-peddling only fuel negative headlines.

Thorough planning is the basis for speedy reaction. In crisis mode, firms have at least two types of incident response team:

- A technical team, or recovery team, composed of specialists who assess the problem and focus on restoring normal processes as quickly as possible. IT and

---

[8]I was part of the remediation training program at Société Générale and studied these questions in some detail. For more on preventing rogue trading, see Chapelle, A. (2017) *Reflections on Operational Risk Management*, Risk Books, Part 5.

security specialists will attend to IT disruptions, including hacking, while business continuity specialists concentrate on supply chain issues and business disruption.

■ A communication team (external and internal), which deals with the media and the different stakeholder groups, including employees. In many large firms, communication teams have specialist media training and crisis communication strategies. As the case studies in this chapter show, plans vary from company to company.

In an emergency, following a script will help to control emotions that cloud judgment and can lead to bad decisions. Composure is essential: a response team must be calm and collected. One of my peers summarized it best: "Have a cold book for hot times."

Continuity testing is commonplace and even mandatory, but it is often limited to the technical aspects of operational recovery, without including sufficient stakeholder management and communication – which of course are key drivers of a firm's reputation. War room simulations, facilitated by business continuity consultants or specialists in organizational resilience, provide useful mitigation practice. The case study presents an exercise that I ran at the World Bank, during the pilot program of the PRMIA[9] Certificate of Learning and Practice in Advanced Operational Risk Management.

CASE STUDY: WAR ROOM TRAINING SESSION AT THE WORLD BANK

In June 2018, a group of 33 risk champions at the World Bank were the first to pass the PRMIA Certificate of Learning and Practice in Advanced Operational Risk Management. During the program, one session involved a war room simulation that participants discussed in small groups. Ironically, our training room that day was in one of the World Bank's crisis rooms. The five topics proposed were:

■ Topic 1: Cyberattack on financial transfers.
■ Topic 2: IT disruption caused by a third party.
■ Topic 3: Epidemic affecting the World Bank's personnel.
■ Topic 4: Terror attack in Washington, D.C.
■ Topic 5: Scandal involving a member of staff.

(Continued)

---

[9]Professional Risk Management International Association. www.prmia.org

Teams were asked to address the following questions:

- What priority actions do you recommend in the following crises?
- Who are your first and second respondents?
- What are the knock-on effects to address?
- Once the crisis is passed, how do you restore confidence in your ability to operate?

Reputation and Resilience

This chapter discussed the relationship between resilience and reputation management, underlining that positive stakeholder engagement and dialogue builds a favorable reputation that improves resilience. Recent Australian empirical research reinforces the point. A study analyzed the content from 10,582 Australian firms' annual reports, spanning 17 years, to identify what senior executives communicate to their stakeholders.[10] The results reveal the interactions between resilience, reputation and financial performance. The authors state:

"We highlight that reputation acts as a source of resilience which provides firms with an enhanced ability to adapt when faced with external difficulties as well as allowing the firm to rebound following a performance decline."

Table 20.2. presents the essential steps for reputation risk management, combining stakeholder management, crisis management and communication, to achieve a favorable reputation and enhanced resilience.

Coming Out on Top

There is an upside to crises when they are managed well: they are opportunities to learn and opportunities to shine. People reveal themselves in adversity – they show their true colors. Like people, firms are judged by the way they handle adversity.

During a training session in 2018, a business manager at UBS told the room: "Adoboli[11] is the best thing that happened to us." He meant that in reacting to the heavy losses sustained by a rogue trader, UBS rediscovered its true self. The ancient Swiss bank refocused on traditional private banking activities, with rigorous controls, and distanced itself from the reckless investment banking activities of recent years.

---

[10]Tracey, N. and French, E. (2017) "Influence your firm's resilience through its reputation: results won't happen overnight but they will happen!", *Corporate Reputation Review*, February, 20, 1, 57–75.
[11]Kweku Adoboli generated $2.3 billon in trading losses for UBS in London in 2011.

TABLE 20.2 Essential steps in reputation risk management

Elements of reputation management
Prevention
■ Image building: positive narrative, value and ethos
■ Stakeholder mapping and relationship building
■ Scenario identification and regular updates
■ Communication strategy and contingency planning in case of event
Mitigation
■ Communication: three Rs: Regret – Reason – Remedy
■ Rapid response
■ Transparency
■ Stakeholder differentiation

Reputations must be built through continuous care and attention – not just in times of crisis. How you respond to client complaints, deal with small operational incidents and interact daily with all your stakeholders will affect satisfaction and loyalty. The result is either negative or positive for your reputation. A bad experience can mean the end of a customer relationship, whereas a good experience will strengthen customer loyalty. It's a lesson that many in the financial industry have yet to learn.

For incidents of all types as much as for crises, the true measure of character is how an organization or individual responds. A U.K. firm, mentioned anonymously by the Financial Conduct Authority, has this wonderful motto to enhance culture and conduct within its teams:[12]

"What defines you is not the mistake you make but how you deal with it."

---

[12] Source: FCA, "5 Conduct Questions" Industry Feedback for 2017 Wholesale Banking Supervision, April 2018.

Conclusion

RISING OPERATIONAL RISKS

Operational risks are generated by business activities and by operating environments. With the evolution of the financial services industry, operational risks have changed and intensified over several areas. This requires a new taxonomy of risks and for specialists in some technical or regulatory areas to manage new risks. In recent years, technological development has had a profound effect on operational risks. With the growth of digital business, and particularly online and mobile communication, data are vulnerable to many forms of cybercrime, which is now the top operational risk for the financial industry.[1] Firms are facing a huge rise in the volume of data as well as changes in the way the data are handled and transmitted. Combined with stringent regulatory demands, and the consequences of non-compliance, this poses a huge challenge for operational risk management. Regulators themselves, especially in the U.S., have started to cooperate with the private sector to understand best practice and design more appropriate legislation. They should be commended for that initiative, and I wish every country would do the same.

Technology, of course, also brings many benefits from a risk perspective. The development of data analytics, big data, artificial intelligence and machine learning enables us to better understand behaviors and provides powerful insights into the nature of risk and cause and effect. It is therefore somewhat ironic that the SMA regulation for operational risk comes back to simple arithmetic to estimate capital, but history will tell how wrong this has been.

Operational risks have been profoundly affected by the transformation of the banking model and changes in the way other financial services are delivered. Third-party management and vendor risks are now strongly apparent, with consequences for business quality and continuity, knowledge retention, reputation, legal exposure, costs and process complexity. There are also implications for the security of information handled by third, fourth, even fifth parties. In addition, after ten years of cost-cutting following the financial crisis, we might see (or are already seeing?) unintended and unwelcome consequences for the quality of services and resources. This may lead to expensive operational incidents that dwarf any cost savings.

---

[1] Risk.net survey 2015 to 2018 inclusive.

Furthermore, technology developments and alternative service providers such as e-commerce giants are challenging traditional business models and encouraging new partnerships.[2]

Finally, geopolitics and physical environment are no small influencers of risks, with international politics, tensions on trade agreements, travel bans and other demonstrations of nationalism threatening international trade and world prosperity. Failure on international cooperation on the ecological front worsens extreme weather events now increasingly impacting industrialized nations alongside Pacific atolls.

Although ever changing in nature, intensity and manifestations, risks can be addressed and managed using a similar framework and set of tools. Identification, assessment, mitigation and monitoring are fundamental risk management actions that apply to all risks, whether financial or non-financial. Most tools are common to all non-financial risks, only the content of information collected and the types of risk responses vary.

THE FUTURE OF OPERATIONAL RISK MANAGEMENT

"Intelligence is adaptation."

Jean Piaget

In an increasingly volatile and unpredictable world, risk identification, assessment and prevention have shown their limitations. Yet, I would not go as far as Nassim Taleb, claiming that risk assessment is a fallacy.[3] The financial sector has made significant progress in post-incident management, robust mitigation, early monitoring and detection, crisis management and corporate resilience. Cybersecurity specialists and business continuity managers rightly take the view that accidents are not a question of "if" but "when," meaning we should be prepared for anything, anytime. In the face of rising risks, the current trend for corporate resilience and crisis management is unlikely to diminish.

"The world is one big data problem."

Andrew McAfee

In 2002, Kahneman and Trevsky won the Nobel Prize for their work in behavioral economics. Now, more than 15 years later, the behavioral approach has made

---

[2] Amazon and JPMC announced talks at the time of writing.

[3] Any of Taleb's books will criticize risk assessment; they are now gathered in a box set, *Incerto*: "an investigation of luck, uncertainty, probability, opacity, human error, risk, disorder, and decision-making in a world we don't understand" (quote from Google Books).

its way from behavioral finance to behavioral regulation, and regulators are focusing on what drives human behavior and how research findings can be applied to regulated financial entities to promote good conduct. The pioneering work of psychologists since the 1970s is benefiting from the massive growth in big data, opening the field of social physics: the quantitative study of peer-to-peer behaviors and social interactions from individual data collected from phones or other types of internet-based activities.[4] Data science is still in its infancy but is developing rapidly, and it will have far-reaching effects. I hope that the financial industry, and particularly the legislators, will commit the time and effort to understand how it can benefit prudential and financial regulation and produce better regulatory design.

"They did not know it was impossible, so they did it."

Mark Twain

In concluding this book, my hope is that operational risk management will become more widely accepted as an enabler of performance, of better management and of higher achievements. Some compare risk management to car brakes: it allows you to drive faster because you can trust your brakes to stop the car when needed. The new COSO framework for enterprise risk management has adopted this angle of better risk management enabling better performance. This positive view of risk management is easily accepted for financial risks but not quite yet for operational risks. In many organizations, operational risk management has still to prove its value beyond regulatory compliance.

Positive risk management will be about capturing information on success stories as well as losses, about discovering why some people, departments or firms are positive outliers and exceptionally good at what they do.[5] Positioning risk management as a quest for upside rather than the avoidance of downside is far more inspiring and energizing for firms and individuals alike.

Operational risk management not only avoids disasters and crises, it also recognizes the importance of opportunity costs. Inefficiency is the largest operational cost for firms, and there is always a hefty price to pay for not being better, faster and cheaper, or for failing to reflect, educate, innovate and evolve. A new generation of risk managers, I believe, will stop worrying so much about regulatory compliance or unreported minor incidents; instead, they will help businesses to seize safely untapped opportunities, achieve their full potential and celebrate success.

— London, July 21, 2018

---

[4]For seminal literature in this field, please refer to the work Prof. Alex Pentland (MIT) and his recent book *Social Physics: How Good Ideas Spread – The Lessons from a New Science*, Scribe (2016).
[5]Gladwell, M. (2007) *Outliers – The Story Behind Success*, Little Brown and Company. This is not about risk management but an enlightening book I warmly recommend.

Index